Understanding Radio
Second edition

D0062848

Studies in Culture and Comunication

General Editor: John Fiske

Understanding Radio

Second edition

Andrew Crisell

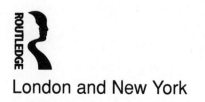

London and New York

First published in 1986 by
Methuen & Co. Ltd

Second edition published 1994
by Routledge
11 New Fetter Lane, London EC4P 4EE

Simultaneously published in the USA and Canada
by Routledge
29 West 35th Street, New York, NY 10001

The author and publishers would like to thank the
following for permission to quote from Garrison Keillor, *A
Radio Romance* (US title *WLT: A Radio Romance*) in the
preliminary pages of the book: Faber & Faber Ltd, Penguin
Books Canada and Viking Penguin, a division of Penguin
Books USA Inc., © 1991 Garrison Keillor.

Typeset in Palatino by
Ponting–Green Publishing Services, Chesham, Bucks
Printed in Great Britain by
Redwood Books, Trowbridge, Wiltshire

Printed on acid-free paper

British Library Cataloguing in Publication Data
A catalogue record for this book is available from the
British Library

Library of Congress Cataloging in Publication Data
Crisell, Andrew.
    Understanding Radio/Andrew Crisell. – 2nd ed.
        p.   cm. – (Studies in culture and communication)
    1. Radio broadcasting–Great Britain.   I. Title.   II. Series.
    PN1991.3.G7C75   1994
    384.54'0941–dc20   93–43580

ISBN 0–415–10315–0

Contents

'I'm hoping to move to Minneapolis someday,' said Francis, matter-of-factly. 'I'm planning to attend the University of Minnesota.'

'You do that, Franny. What'll you study?'

'I want to study to go into radio.'

Art laughed. 'Nobody studies radio, kid. They don't teach it in school because it's too much fun. People go to school to be a teacher or a dentist. Radio is just a bunch of guys having a ball.'

(Garrison Keillor, *Radio Romance*)

General editor's preface

This series of books on different aspects of communication is designed to meet the needs of the growing number of students coming to study this subject for the first time. The authors are experienced teachers or lecturers who are committed to bridging the gap between the huge body of research available to the more advanced student, and what the new student actually needs to get him started on his studies.

Probably the most characteristic feature of communication is its diversity: it ranges from the mass media and popular culture, through language to individual and social behaviour. But it identifies links and a coherence within this diversity. The series will reflect the structure of its subject. Some books will be general, basic works that seek to establish theories and methods of study applicable to a wide range of material; others will apply these theories and methods to the study of one particular topic. But even these topic-centred books will relate to each other, as well as to the more general ones. One particular topic, such as advertising or news or language, can only be understood as an example of communication when it is related to, and differentiated from, all the other topics that go to make up this diverse subject.

The series, then, has two main aims, both closely connected. The first is to introduce readers to the most important results of contemporary research into communication together with the theories that seek to explain it. The second is to equip them with appropriate methods of study and investigation which they will be able to apply directly to their everyday experience of communication.

If readers can write better essays, produce better projects and pass more exams as a result of reading these books I shall be very satisfied; but if they gain a new insight into how communication shapes and informs our social life, how it articulates and creates our experience of industrial society, then I shall be delighted. Communication is too often taken for granted when it should be taken to pieces.

John Fiske

Preface to the second edition

For this edition of *Understanding Radio* I have made one or two major changes and many minor ones. Since 1986, when its predecessor appeared, more and more stations have come on air, virtually all of them dedicated to continuous music of one kind or another. The most glittering arrivals were, of course, Classic FM, which declares its musical allegiance in its name, and Virgin 1215, catering to those with conservative tastes in rock. Many students never listen to anything other than music radio and have only an inkling that stations still exist which broadcast a variety of 'programmes' analogous to those they can watch on television.

It therefore seemed important to write a new chapter on music radio, even though other kinds of output might seem to afford clearer and more interesting insights into the characteristics and possibilities of the medium. Though known as 'music radio' it invariably includes some degree of personal presentation, and so since the presenters' approaches to the music and to the listener also needed to be examined I have actually named the new chapter '*Talk* and Music Radio'.

But while the book as a whole focuses on the sound medium itself rather than attempting any wider cultural perspective, I took this chapter as a good opportunity, dealing as it does with the most popular form of radio, to suggest something of the medium's position within contemporary culture – to show how it has stimulated powerful trends in popular music and advertising, and in turn been influenced by these in its most recent attempt to package and promote classical music.

The chapter which Talk and Music Radio has in effect replaced is that which dealt with radio as a medium of education. This is simply because, in spite of the BBC's continuing, and impressive, range of schools broadcasts, radio seems to be playing an increasingly peripheral role in education. Even with the help of audio-cassettes it is much more limited than the other electronic media. Television, video and computers can offer visual images and texts which are actually or potentially stable, and an actual or potential interactive facility; and even when it was written eight years ago my chapter on educational radio perforce devoted much space to its inherent difficulties as a teaching and learning medium.

An unsurprising consequence is that education has become an increasingly peripheral part of radio. We might describe as 'educational' the documentaries of BBC Radio 4, or Radio 1's public awareness campaigns about drugs or unemployment; but in comparison with the direct-teaching television programmes offered by the Open University this seems to dilute the term beyond what is useful. Of the many stations which have recently come on air, I know of none, even at community level, which carries any kind of programming that could seriously be regarded as educational.

The other changes I have made are relatively minor. Material has been updated wherever appropriate, most obviously in the chapter dealing with the history of British radio. I have also attempted fresh news analyses in Chapter 5, since the previous bulletins dated from 1985, added some facts to the phone-in chapter, and made revisions and updatings to the chapter on audiences. And all these changes have entailed corresponding additions and deletions in the references and bibliography.

As well as these, I have made many small textual alterations in order to correct factual errors, strengthen an argument, or improve the style of writing – evidently tasks that have no end! And as part of what I hope are the stylistic improvements, I have broken the text into rather smaller paragraphs to make it more appealing in appearance and more digestible in content.

Acknowledgements

ACKNOWLEDGEMENTS TO THE FIRST EDITION

My first and general debt is to the editor of the Studies in Communication series, John Fiske, who has been supportive and enthusiastic throughout the genesis of this book. Among my colleagues I must express my gratitude to Patricia Waugh, who made many useful suggestions and though often subjected to my own half-formed thoughts on radio was still ready to brush aside my occasional misgivings about the book's worth. I must also acknowledge the help of Michael Pickering, who directed me to some valuable sources of information about broadcasting history, and John Christopher, whose knowledge of linguistics gave me much food for thought about the nature of radio language. I am grateful to Sunderland Polytechnic for granting me a term's leave during which much of this book was written.

For such practical knowledge of radio production as I possess I am indebted to Virtue Jones and John Lavis, who made my year with BBC Radio Newcastle such a pleasant and rewarding one. I must also express my warm thanks to both Ken Stephinson of the BBC Network Centre, Manchester, and Marjorie Lofthouse of the BBC Network Centre at Birmingham for all the information they have given me on broadcasting and production techniques, audience behaviour, and media organizations in general. Jock Gallagher of the BBC Network Centre at Birmingham was a mine of information on phone-ins, for which I am grateful.

Certain material which appears in this book has occasioned three important debts. I wish to thank Messrs B.A. Robertson and Alan Tarney and the publishers Bar Music Ltd/ATV Music Ltd for permission to reproduce an extract of the lyrics from 'Wired for

Sound'; the BBC for their generous permission to reproduce part of the news bulletins from *The World at One* and *Newsbeat*; and Mr John Arlott and the BBC for kindly allowing me to quote from some broadcast cricket commentary. To Mr Arlott I owe a further debt for the pains he took to provide corrections to the transcript of the broadcast. Having acknowledged all these debts I must however add that in making any mistakes or omissions which occur in the following pages I have needed help from no one: casting modesty aside, but not regret, I claim them as all my own.

Finally I must express my deep gratitude to my wife and two daughters, who throughout the writing of this book have given help, support and encouragement and borne my absences of mind, person and good humour without one word of complaint. It is for them – Margaret, Ellen Jane and Harriet Daisy – that I wrote it.

ACKNOWLEDGEMENTS TO THE SECOND EDITION

I must again express my warm thanks to the BBC, this time for their permission to reproduce part of the material first broadcast on 28 June 1993 on *The World at One* (Radio 4) and on *Newsbeat* (Radio 1); and to Mrs Patricia Arlott and the BBC for allowing me to reproduce some of the late John Arlott's cricket commentary. Every effort has been made to contact copyright holders; where this has not been possible an apology to those concerned.

I must also convey my deep gratitude to two friends who in the preparation and revision of the text helped me to make the transition from the dark ages of typewriting to the wonderful world of information technology: Peter Grundy of the Department of Linguistics and English Language, Durham University, whose ready patience and generosity I could never seem to exhaust; and Hugh Keegan, who combined a reassuring refusal to be impressed by the technology with great virtuosity therein. Without them my task would have been incalculably harder.

I am also grateful to Helen Mather, Programme Research Manager, Metro Radio Group, Newcastle upon Tyne, for much valuable information about radio audience research.

Finally I must thank my wife and two daughters for once again providing such examples of cheerfulness and fortitude against the negligence, irascibility and deafness which characterized 'the writer at work'.

Introduction

This book is intended for students on media and communications courses in higher and further education and would, it is hoped, be of equal benefit to those with an academic interest in radio and those with a practical interest in programme production.

Its purposes can be stated with deceptive modesty. The first is to determine the distinctive characteristics of the radio medium. This is attempted by locating radio among other modes of communication, individual and collective, literary and visual, by examining the historical development of British radio institutions, and by developing a theory of the signs, codes and conventions by which the medium conveys its messages. But in this latter endeavour I am not so much concerned with particular messages or texts and the deeper cultural meanings or 'dominant ideologies' they may enshrine as with how radio conveys or mediates messages of any kind.

The second purpose is to explore the significance of radio's characteristics for its users – the journalist, the advertiser, the dramatist and, not least, the listener – and to examine the potentialities of radio as a medium of information, culture and entertainment for both broadcasters and audience.

The apparently arbitrary and disparate nature of my chapter headings requires some explanation. 'Phone-ins' could, perhaps should, have been dealt with as an element of the 'talk' in 'Talk and Music Radio', which often consists of more than just a presenter's monologue. Moreover talk and music radio is undoubtedly as much a form of 'Light Entertainment' as are the comedy shows and panel games which are separately treated under that heading. 'Commentary' is clearly not a programme category in the sense that 'News and Current Affairs' is and ought, perhaps, to have been subsumed under it. But as anyone who has worked in broadcasting will concede, programmes are notoriously difficult to categorize, or even to distinguish from individual broadcasting techniques. Drama, for instance, could be regarded as a programme category in its own right, or as a technique in some other programme category such as educational radio or light entertainment. Indeed it could be argued that in a covert way drama often informs many other kinds of output by moulding them into its own format of confrontation, crisis and conclusion (Higgins and Moss 1982).

But given that there are at least titular differences between programme categories, it will be apparent that I have not included them all. Encouraged by the fact that the audience does not so much attend to individual programmes as simply listen to 'the radio' – to a general flow or sequence of programmes (Williams 1974: 86–94) – the approach I have adopted is pragmatic: the omission of certain categories and a switching from one category or technique to another as each seemed to afford some particular insight into radio's character or potentialities. I would hope, therefore, that while the kinds of programmes I discuss may be inadequate as a catalogue of what it is possible to broadcast on the medium, they are at least as illuminating about radio as those I have omitted, and broadly representative of them.

Two final points. First, I have made much more reference to BBC broadcasts than to those of independent radio partly because with their longer history they are better known, and partly because the Corporation still produces a range of separate, 'constructed' programmes rather than the predominantly streamed output that characterizes the commercial stations.

Second, I have been anxious to acknowledge that both sexes are amply represented within such broadcasting roles as 'the presenter', 'listener' or 'producer', yet have wished to avoid such tiresome duplications as 'her/his', 'herself/himself', and so on. Hence while I have tried to be consistent in my attribution of pronouns within a single chapter, I have not hesitated to refer to the listener or broadcaster as 'she' in one chapter and 'he' in another. However, if I describe the listener to cricket commentary as 'he' and the phone-in presenter as 'she', I hope I shall not be understood to suggest that there are no female cricket enthusiasts or that no male broadcaster ever chairs a phone-in: nor should my other partial descriptions be taken only at their face-value.

Part I

The medium

Chapter 1

Characteristics of radio

When you ask some people if they listen to the radio, they say, 'No'. Then you ask them if they drive to work and they say, 'Yes'. Then you ask them if they drive to work with the radio on and they say, 'Yes'. They don't listen to it, they sit in it.

(Tony Schwartz, US advertising executive)

What strikes everyone, broadcasters and listeners alike, as significant about radio is that it is a *blind* medium. We cannot see its messages, they consist only of noise and silence, and it is from the sole fact of its blindness that all radio's other distinctive qualities – the nature of its language, its jokes, the way in which its audiences use it – ultimately derive. We can get a clearer idea of radio's characteristics by comparing it with other modes of communication.

The commonest, most basic mode can be described as *interpersonal*, in which the sender of the message and the receiver of it are physically close to and within sight of each other. The contact between them is oral and visual, perhaps even tactile. The primary code, or system of signs by which they communicate, is linguistic, that of *speech*, but likely to be aided by various 'presentational codes' of a paralinguistic nature – facial expressions, gestures, bodily movements and postures, and so on (Fiske 1990: 66–70). The *context* to which the message refers and which enables it to 'make sense' is likely to be understood by both sender and receiver because of its physical proximity or because of their shared background or experience. But in addition lots of 'phatic' remarks are possible to check that the contact is working ('How are you?', and so on), and lots of 'metalingual' remarks to check that the code is being understood ('Understand?'). And both kinds of remark prompt *feedback* – the (in this mode) easily possible transmission of the receiver's reaction to the sender. Hence the message has every chance of being accurately 'decoded', or made sense of.

The obvious advantages of modes of *mass* communication are that the sender can communicate with multitudes of receivers at the same time and at distances beyond that achievable by interpersonal communication. But the contact becomes impersonal and the risk of ambiguity and misunderstanding much greater. Feedback is an impossibility because thousands or millions of receivers cannot simultaneously transmit their varying reactions back to the sender: and because the sender cannot simultaneously present herself in person to each member of the audience she must send a representative of herself – an independent, often visible message in the form of a *text* (as in books and newspapers) or an *image* (as in film and television).

But since the sender and receivers are remote from each other this message has to carry a heavy freight. In varying degrees it has to create the context to which it refers; the sender herself, who is present only within the message, does not effectively exist outside it; and the receivers for whom the message is intended. On the other hand since, as we have seen, feedback is an impossibility in mass communication, there is no genuine facility of metalingual or phatic communication: the sender cannot check that the code or contact is working. For all these reasons it is of considerable advantage that the message should in some way or other be visual.

The oldest mode of mass communication is that of written characters – *literature* in its widest sense of 'writing, written language'. The code, a printed text, may be supplemented by other codes – numbers, drawings, photographs, diagrams: but the permanence of the contact compensates for its impersonality. Bereft of the presence of the sender, the receivers may read and re-read her message at leisure: decoding does not have to be instantaneous. In film and television, modes of mass communication whose message is in the form of an image, decoding does have to be instantaneous. There is no single, static text which can be perused at leisure. But this is offset by the fact that in film and television the conditions of interpersonal communication are partly re-created. The receivers can see and hear the sender: the primary code in which she communicates – speech – is supplemented by various presentational codes. And/or they can hear her while seeing by means of other images, which may include an image of writing, the context to which her message refers.

How, then, is radio distinguishable from these other modes of mass communication? Very largely in ways which seem to redound to its disadvantage. There is no image and no text. The contact, or *medium* as I will now term it, is utterly non-visual: the receivers, who are *listeners*, or collectively an *audience*, cannot see the sender or broadcaster as they can on television or film; nor are they offered the compensation of a visible and lasting message as they are in literature. Radio's codes are purely auditory, consisting of speech, music, sounds and silence, and since, as we shall see, the ear is not the most 'intelligent' of our sense organs their deployment has to be relatively simple. The risks of ambiguity or complete communication failure are high, and so in all kinds of radio much effort is expended on overcoming the limitations of the medium, on establishing the different kinds of context which we would generally be able to see for ourselves.

First, there is the context to which the message refers – a context which most interpersonal communication can take for granted. Physical objects or processes which are normally self-evident have to be described: 'Tell the listeners what you are doing', 'Can you describe this object to us?' Second and more literally, there is the context of the message itself – the surrounding 'messages' (items or programmes) which also help the listener to make sense of what he hears. The description of the object may reveal that it is a fire-dog, but he will have no idea why a fire-dog is being described to him unless he has gleaned from the other messages he has heard that the programme is about antiques. One way of conveying context on the radio is by what is sometimes known as 'sign-posting': for example, 'Later in the programme we'll be talking about the Budget to the Leader of the Opposition'. By indicating the programme's shape or structure, signposting enables the listener to know whether he wishes to keep listening. In purely visual media such as books and newspapers – media whose messages exist in *space* rather than in time – this kind of context is immediately apparent. In a newspaper we can see at a glance what paragraphs or stories surround the one we are presently reading, and in a book or magazine we can flick through the adjacent pages or turn to the table of contents.

But of course not all visual media exist purely in space: television, film and theatre are partly characterized by movement and (in common with radio) sound, which exist primarily in *time*. In film and theatre, however, the need to establish this kind of context is much less since their messages normally consist of a single plot which the spectators have been following throughout, rather than a number of discrete items which they are at liberty to dip into and out of. Like radio, television often solves the problem of context by signposting, but being a visual medium it has other resources too: images of programmes or items which will be shown later, split-screen techniques, captions superimposed upon images, even images consisting only of printed words. Radio has nothing but different kinds of *sounds*, some of which it uses to establish the beginnings and ends of programmes for us by what are variously described as 'frame' conventions (Goffman 1980: 162–5) or 'boundary rituals' (Fiske and Hartley 1978: 166–7) – ways of telling us that what we are about to hear is a play and not a continuation of the news bulletin we have just been listening to. This is sometimes done by a silence (which in these circumstances is a sort of negative form of sound) or by a signature- or theme-tune and/or an announcement: 'And now *The Archers*. Mike Tucker's milk-round hasn't got off to a very good start' (two contexts are established here: that of the programme itself, a drama serial which is following the 7 o'clock news, and that of the point in the story which the serial has reached).

But messages in radio consist primarily of speech, and speech consists not just of words, as writing does, but always and indissolubly of words expressed in *voices*. Hence a third kind of context which often needs to be established is the reality of the radio station and the broadcasters themselves, even when they are not the subject of the programme. In a discussion programme like *Start the Week* (BBC Radio 4) the presenter might, for example, introduce one of his guests with some such remark as 'Glad you managed to beat that hold-up on the M4 and get here on time!' Remarks of this kind are seldom heard on the television, where we can see the presenter, the guests and the studio that surrounds them; but they are common on the radio where their purpose is to locate the station within the solid, workaday world of motorways and indicate that the broadcasters are not just 'voices in the ether' but people like us who are liable to get stuck in traffic jams and miss their appointments.

Hence the constraints imposed by radio's blindness are severe and were underlined by television, which with its growth in popularity during the 1950s was thought to be about to supersede radio altogether. I shall return shortly to the problems which the blindness of the medium can create, but want first to stress that blindness is also the source of some real advantages which radio possesses over other media.

The most famous of these is its appeal to the imagination. Because radio offers sound-only instead of sound and vision the listener is compelled to 'supply' the visual data for himself. The details are described, or they may suggest themselves through sound, but they are not 'pictured' for him; he must picture them for himself, and he may, indeed, use them as a basis for picturing *further* details which are *not* described. Moreover as we all know, the scope of the imagination is virtually limitless: we may picture not only lifelike objects but the fantastical, impossible scenes of an experimental play.

This appeal to the imagination gives radio an apparent advantage over film and television, but we must beware of exaggerating the differences between the visual and non-visual media: because film and television audiences can see, it is often assumed that they are not obliged to use their imagination. However, the imagination is more than a merely visual faculty. It can re-create abstract qualities and processes, as when the viewer imagines the inner thoughts or feelings of a character in a film merely by observing the expression on her face.

Nevertheless the imagination does seem to be mainly preoccupied with re-creating the physical, material world; yet even here its role is not always visual or pictorial. When watching a film of bacon and eggs cooking in a pan we imagine the *smell* they give off; when we read a description of a fun-fair we imagine among other things the *noise* of the crowds and the blare of the roundabout organ. How, then, does the imagination deal with the physical world?

Its workings are various and obscure, but we might make the preliminary suggestion that it is the faculty by which we re-create for ourselves any impressions that we would experience at first hand through one, some or all of our five senses. Since the greatest number of senses through which any of the mass media can communicate to us is two (sight and hearing), it follows that *all* the media, and not just radio, will invoke the imagination to compensate for their various deficiencies. Nevertheless it would seem that the primary and dominant function of the imagination *is* visual, as its derivation from 'image' suggests; for in replicating the functions of our senses it seems also to replicate the hierarchy into which they appear to arrange themselves, with sight at the top: in our ordinary deployment of our sensory faculties our primary means of understanding or interpreting the world seems to be visual. We may hear, smell or touch an object, but it is not until we have seen it that we feel we really 'know' it.

The faculty of sight, then, seems to be a kind of epistemological yardstick which determines how we make sense of the outside world and what credence we attach to our other sensory faculties. Once we have seen the filmic image of the bacon and eggs we can imagine their smell, and once we have pictured our fun-fair we can imagine the noise of the crowds and the organ. But for most of us at least, it would seem to be extremely hard to imagine even that unique and wonderful aroma without some previous or accompanying image, whether literal or figurative and however momentary, of the bacon and eggs themselves or of the situation (for example, the breakfast table) in which they would be encountered in ordinary life. In other words, the first impulse of the imagination seems to be to visualize, even in the case of non-visual sensations such as sounds or smells: but once we have an actual or figurative picture of what approximates to the source or habitation of these sounds or smells our imagination will be able to move down the sensory hierarchy and replicate the subordinate impressions of sound, smell, taste, and so on.

But we must not assume that when we are watching a play or a film or a television programme we never have the need to picture or visualize physical phenomena. On these occasions, as in ordinary life, not only are we capable of looking and visualizing simultaneously, we do it all the time: it is simply that when we have the power of vision we are less aware that we visualize. This means that our imagination is much more active when we watch the visual media than the champions of radio claim, for not everything they deal with is visible. When, for instance, a comedian tells a funny story we watch him, but even as we do so we picture – or *imagine* – the characters and events of his story. And even at the level of the physical reality that is displayed to us not everything can be seen, for it implies a contextual world which is off-stage or 'outside the picture' and which we will also have to imagine – a fact often exploited by horror films in which the menace lurks just off the screen, so that all we can see is the terrified expression of the character who is being menaced!

Nevertheless it seems undeniable that radio will invoke the audience's imagination much more than film, theatre or television, since *nothing* that it deals with is visible. We must imagine not only a character's thoughts and feelings but also her expression, total appearance, physical situation, and so on.

However, two other important points must be made about the role of the imagination. The first is that radio is not the only medium which makes such extensive use of it. It is every bit as active when we read a book, and indeed reading and listening are rather similar in the sense that within the broad limits set by language both reader and listener can – must – form a mental picture of what is being described. But whereas literature's 'pictures' are entirely an effect of language, radio's are also suggested by the sound of voices and of other phenomena which imply the existence of a material world we cannot find in books but can see in theatre, film and television.

Hence the distinctiveness of radio is not that it involves the imagination while the other media do not, but that it involves it to a different *extent*. In literature *everything* must be imagined since nothing can be seen except printed words, nor can anything be heard. In the visual media many things can be seen and heard and proportionately less is left to the imagination. In radio many things can be heard, and this direct intimation of the material world is perhaps why, in its drama productions at least, its verbal descriptions of a physical setting or of a person's thoughts or appearance are generally much more economical than those of literature and closer to those of theatre, film and television. Moreover the fact that its codes are auditory and therefore exist in time explains the greater sense of 'liveness' that we get from radio (and the visual media) than we do from literature; for when we start to read a book we know that the last page has already been written. But radio, even when its programmes are pre-recorded, seems to be a 'present-tense' medium, offering experiences whose outcome lies in an unknown future. Like theatre, film and television, then, it seems to be an account of what *is* happening rather than a record of what *has* happened. But the fact that *nothing* can be seen on the medium means that the demands which it makes upon the imagination are much greater than those made by the visual media and almost as great as those made by literature.

The second important point which we must keep in mind is that the imagination is not confined to matters of fiction or make-believe. When listening to the radio we are obliged to imagine not only the world of a play or story but the *real* world of news, weather reports and current affairs. Indeed, although it is dangerous to be dogmatic in these matters, it seems likely that codes in any medium which refer to any physical thing which we cannot actually see – whether they be words, sounds, or other kinds of symbols and whether they refer to listeners' requests, hobgoblins or stocks and shares – will automatically create pictures in our minds, that we cannot actually 'make sense' of these codes without at some stage and in some measure forming images of what they refer to.

It is largely upon the listener's ability to imagine matters of fact that radio's distinctive and much-vaunted sense of personal companionship seems to depend, for we hear not only the descriptions and sounds of real or imaginary worlds but also the voice of the person who is describing them and we therefore form a picture of her too. As is the case with readers of books and viewers of films or television, the pleasure the listener gains from the company of those whom he 'meets' on the medium is bound up with the sense of his own anonymity, of freedom from the obligations imposed by 'real life' relationships. He is not obliged to talk back to his radio companion or to continue listening if he is bored.

But the role of the imagination is much more crucial to the listener or the reader than to the viewer, because it is with the person *as imagined* from the words and sounds of radio or from the words of books that he forms his relationship, not with a person who is so largely pre-realized for him. And this role of the imagination transcends the conventional distinction between fact and fiction because in books and radio people and things are 'imaginary' whether they actually exist or not. In the visual media there is a general tendency towards the factual: a character in a play may be 'fictional', but she is still physically and visibly 'real'. In books and radio, though, there is a general tendency towards the fictional. Jimmy Young presenting his morning show on BBC Radio 2 may be an actual person, but since we can know him on the radio only by picturing, *imagining*, him he is in a sense a 'fiction'.

Two further points illustrate this fictional tendency of radio. The first is that within the broad limits set by the language and sounds of the medium any listener who has not seen Jimmy Young on television or elsewhere may imagine him to be quite unlike he is without in any way 'misunderstanding' his broadcast or failing to absorb its full impact. And the second point is that since imagining is an individual act there is unlikely to be any uniformity among the 'pictures' of Jimmy Young which the listeners form – even those listeners who know what he looks like. Indeed it is very probable that there will be as many pictures as there are listeners. Hence there is the paradox that while radio is a long-distance mode of communication it is also an inward, *intimate* medium, and so integral does the imagination seem to be to the way in which we decode virtually all its messages, whether factual or fictional, that when we speak of its 'appeal to the imagination' we mean in effect its basic ability to communicate.

Another advantageous effect of radio's blindness, and one which can reinforce its appeal to the imagination, is its *flexibility* – the fact that it can leave the listener free to perform other activities while he is listening. This characteristic has been enhanced by the technological developments of the last forty years or so. The first radios were crystal sets, and since reception was generally poor and took place via headphones, listening was a solitary activity which allowed the listener little scope to do anything else. But by the mid-1920s the crystal set had been largely replaced by the valve wireless, which incorporated a loudspeaker and remained in general use until the end of the 1950s. By modern standards its reception was of somewhat primitive quality, it was heavy and attached to an outdoor aerial so that it could not easily be moved about, and it was expensive. Even in the 1930s its price ranged from £8 to £30 (S. Briggs 1981b: 33). Not surprisingly, then, very few households could boast more than one set, and since there was no television to provide an alternative attraction it was common practice for the members of the household to sit down and listen as a *group* (McLuhan 1967: 327; Pegg 1983: 197; S. Briggs 1981a: 15).

The replacement of headphones by a loudspeaker also meant that it was now possible to do other things while listening and the wireless was often used as mere 'background'; but these were activities that could only be performed within earshot of the loudspeaker: portable wirelesses existed but it was the replacement of valves by transistors at the beginning of the 1960s which revolutionized radio listening. The development of VHF, FM and stereo had already made vast improvements in the *quality* of reception, but the transistor enabled radio sets to be built which consumed much less power and were much cheaper to buy. When the government abolished the radio licence fee in 1971 the cost of buying and listening to the radio was reduced yet further. So cheap had radio become by the end of the 1970s that there were 2.53 sets to each household (Paulu 1981: 350), or virtually one set for every man, woman and child in the United Kingdom. This means that as in the days of the crystal set, listening has once again become a mostly *solitary* activity, which presents us with another paradox about radio – although its audiences may be counted in millions the medium addresses itself very much to the *individual*.

The change in broadcasting styles which has occurred over the years is illuminating. In the days of wireless, the indifferent quality of the reception and the group nature of the audience tended to encourage a somewhat declamatory style of delivery. Now that the broadcaster may, if she wishes, whisper into the ear of the isolated listener delivery has become much less formal, more intimate. Indeed it may not be too fanciful to see this change of style reflected in a change in terminology. Am I alone in sensing that outside formal contexts or fixed collocations such as 'the British Broadcasting Corporation' the word 'broadcast' sounds faintly archaic – aimed, like broadsides and broadsheets, at a vast, passive audience and with little sense of the individuals who comprise it? Whereas its synonym 'transmit', literally 'to send across', seems rather more concerned for the recipient and hence, when a choice between the words is possible, is more often used.

But the cheapness of radio means not only that listening is once again a mainly solitary pursuit, but that the range of things the listener can do *while* listening has been greatly extended, for he is no longer restricted to what he can do within earshot of a set which he must share with several others. He can now afford his own set in his own location. Moreover it is not a *fixed* location, for quite the most important consequence of the transistor was that it enabled radios to be made which were lighter, more compact, and which were therefore easily portable or at the very least movable.

Thus if the owner wishes to listen to his radio he is not confined to his own room or even his own house; he can take his radio with him and listen in at his place of work or while picnicking, watching a soccer match, or whatever. Sets soon became small enough to be carried around like a book and even slipped into a pocket, and thanks to tiny lightweight headphones the listener can now gain excellent reception while threading his way through noisy crowds and thunderous traffic. Similarly if he wishes to listen while driving, radios are fitted in most cars as standard equipment. By the end of the 1970s nearly 70 per cent of all radio sets in the United Kingdom were either portable or 'mobile' in the sense of being fitted in motor vehicles (Paulu 1981: 350). Hence radio is an 'intimate' mode of communication not simply because its messages can be fully 'realized' only inside the listener's head, but because they frequently reach him in circumstances of solitude and privacy and can accompany him in an unprecedented range of places and activities. This means that it can be, and is, assimilated to his daily existence much more than are the other media, and to a much greater extent than ever before.

This use of radio as what is sometimes termed a 'secondary' medium can never be emulated by television, even though the latter has also become smaller and cheaper in recent years: for while it too may be carried round its message cannot be absorbed in the same way. It makes a larger and more rigid claim on our attention, so that if it is treated as secondary (and such treatment is not unknown) we can say that most of its message is being missed, since the visual codes which make up so much of that message are being ignored. The radio listener, on the other hand, can be driving along a remote Highland glen and without taking his eyes from the road can be instantaneously apprised of an earthquake in the Far East.

Neither newspapers nor television can match radio in terms of this immediacy as a purveyor of news and information. Nor in order to demonstrate such immediacy is it necessary to instance news which originates from the far side of the globe. What is happening in the near neighbourhood may be of much more practical importance to the listener, and on an awareness of this fact rest the greatest achievements of local radio. While driving to work the motorist can be warned about an accident which has blocked the road a few miles ahead of him, and local appeals can also reach people who are unable to stop work and attend to any of the other media – the drama club's appeal for a suit of armour for tonight's play, the soccer club's request for help in clearing a snowbound pitch for tomorrow's match. Such items are too numerous and trivial for network radio to broadcast but they are vital to small communities and, quite apart from the numbers of 'secondary' listeners they reach, can be publicized much more cheaply and quickly than in the local press. Indeed, in the time they would take to appear in the press they would cease to be 'news' at all.

The point has often been made that radio's enduring power as a mass medium derives from its unique combination of suggestiveness and flexibility – from the effect of its messages, whether factual or fictional, upon the listener's imagination together with the fact that it can accompany him in a range of other activities he may wish to perform. But the flexibility may also work *against* its suggestiveness in a way not possible in the visual media: for the freedom that radio affords us to pursue other activities while listening can, and frequently does, detract from our full understanding of what it purveys. Listening is a good deal easier than ever before but by the same token often a good deal less attentive – much of the message can be ignored. Radio communicates through only one of our five senses and beyond the bounds of this communication is a kind of no man's land where it must constantly fight for the listener's attention against the other sense impressions which make up the situation in which he presently finds himself – driving the car, washing the dishes, and so on. This perhaps explains why there is now so much music on the radio; for while music may *allow* us to use our imagination it does not 'refer to' anything in the way that speech does and so does not *require* us to use it: it therefore makes ideal background listening.

Such partly complementary, partly conflicting characteristics of radio – its suggestiveness and imaginative appeal on the one hand and its flexibility on the other – have led some observers to discern two categories of listener. A former head of audience research at the BBC distinguishes between the medium's 'predominant role – as a source of entertainment' and its 'subordinate role – as an accompaniment to other activities' (Silvey 1974: 209); while a former Director General distinguishes between those who regard it 'as an art form on its own merits' and those for whom radio is mere background, a 'service element' (Trethowan 1970: 7).

These variations in the audience pose a considerable problem for the programme producer: for if she wishes to create an 'art form' for the listener as distinct from mere background for 'hearers', how far is she at liberty to do so? Her constant dilemma, acute in education programmes but present in other kinds such as dramas and documentaries, is how far to develop a theme which will become increasingly esoteric and how far to preserve its accessibility for the hearer, who pays less attention to radio's messages but who is always, potentially, a listener.

Of course this distinction between listener and hearer, or between the predominant and 'background' functions of radio, is useful provided that we do not exaggerate it; for while there is no doubt that the opportunities to treat radio as a 'service element' have increased greatly in recent years, it is highly likely, even before the advent of television, that a great many people have *always* done something else while listening to the radio – even if only knitting or eating. This does not mean that the greater part of their attention may not be focused on the radio, and in my own use of the term 'secondary medium' I do not wish to suggest that of the probable 98 per cent or so of the audience who treat it in this way hardly anyone is paying much attention to its messages.

Indeed such terms as 'predominant' and 'secondary' tend to obscure the fact that much more than in any other medium a whole *range* of attention is possible, from hearing through 'over-hearing' to listening, from those who want unobtrusive background noise – 'acoustic wallpaper' – to those who seek an object of concentration. But this poses as big a problem for the audience researcher as for the programme producer because the former is always in some doubt as to who the radio audience actually is and whether there is any correlation between the amount of attention which is paid to radio's messages and the extent of its effects or influences, a subject we shall return to in Chapter 10.

My purpose in the following chapters is first to give some historical account of the technological and institutional development of radio and then to explore the characteristics of the medium from the varying perspectives afforded by different kinds of output. I shall begin with talk and music radio, not because it is the most illuminating in this respect but because it is now the only form of programming which the great majority of stations provide. Hence as well as exploring what it tells us about the medium, I shall attempt to explain why talk and music radio occupies so much air-time, and how its contents and conventions have helped to shape modern popular culture. An implicit effect of this discussion will be to show how an investigation of the medium can yield insights into the broader cultural context, but the subsequent chapters will focus more closely on the inherent characteristics of radio, exploring them in the light of its more traditional kinds of programming.

Nevertheless in discussing those characteristics which certain kinds of programme seem to me to illuminate I do not wish to suggest that they are not present in other kinds. In treating the multi-levelled, ambivalent relationship between broadcaster and listener under 'Commentary', for instance, I do not wish to imply that this relationship does not exist in varying degrees in *all* radio involving personal presentation; nor do I wish to suggest by discussing the distinctive nature of radio language under 'News and Current Affairs' that this language is of any less fundamental a significance in other kinds of programmes. As I have already remarked, the distinctions between programme categories are in any case uncertain: it was many years before the BBC was able to disentangle radio drama from its Features Department; drama is often used in educational broadcasts, many of which are closely akin to documentaries; and documentary can often shade into news and current affairs.

The difficulty of maintaining the distinctions between categories must serve to excuse the omission of a separate chapter on adverts – an omission which may seem surprising in the light of the recent development of British commercial radio at national level. But since the impact of adverts depends so much upon their ability to impersonate *other* forms of radio output, notably drama, comedy and news presentation, a chapter which attempted a comprehensive analysis of them would have become a monster that ingested every other chapter in the book. My aim has simply been to select from within a fairly broad range of output so as to gain a composite picture of radio's nature and possibilities.

Chapter 2

The history and development of radio in Britain

the isle is full of noises,
Sounds and sweet airs, that give delight, and hurt not.
(Shakespeare, *The Tempest*, III, ii)

Many histories of British broadcasting have been written, ranging from the detailed and scholarly (A. Briggs 1961–79; Paulu 1956, 1961, 1981; Pegg 1983; Scannell and Cardiff 1991) through the potted (Golding 1974; Parker 1977; A. Briggs 1985; Lewis and Pearlman 1986; Curran and Seaton 1991; Seymour-Ure 1991) to the subjective and anecdotal (Black 1972; Snagge and Barsley 1972). This historical sketch, and it can be no more, takes as its focus the major developments in broadcasting technology – not merely those within radio, but the arrival and subsequent evolution of its great rival, television. It considers how these developments have changed the audience's perception and use of radio over the years, and the effect this in turn has had on its programming structures, on the nature of broadcasting institutions, and on the various political arrangements that have had to be devised for them.

Throughout the nineteenth and early twentieth centuries scientists of many nationalities, most notably the Italian Guglielmo Marconi, were attempting to transmit messages over distances, first by means of wireless telegraphy and then by wireless telephony. But it is important to realize that these were primarily envisaged as means of *point-to-point* communication (for example, ship to shore), and that when radio (or 'wireless' as it was known in the early days) was developed it was largely thought of in these terms.

In Britain the Postmaster General had been empowered to control wireless telegraphy by an Act of Parliament in 1904, and he regarded wireless telephony, whether directed at individuals or at all and sundry, as a natural extension thereof, and therefore as also subject to his control. In fact, for most members of the political establishment it was not only the case that radio was a mere by-product of point-to-point modes of communication; there was even a suggestion of primitiveness, of a lack of refinement, about a medium which *broad*cast – addressed the world at large rather than maintained confidentiality by addressing private individuals (A. Briggs 1961: 34). In February 1920, when the Post Office gave permission to the Marconi Company to begin broadcasts to wireless enthusiasts from a transmitter in Chelmsford, it did so with a sense of unease that they would interfere with point-to-point services (Paulu 1956: 8). This unease was fuelled by the armed forces, who for a long time resisted the encroachment of broadcasting on their wavelengths on the ground that their secret messages would be overheard (Williams 1974: 32). Thus, apart from the wireless manufacturers and the few home enthusiasts with receivers, there was little appreciation of the medium's *social* possibilities. Not until 1922 did the Post Office draw a distinction between technology which addressed individuals and that which addressed all and sundry (A. Briggs 1961: 96). In that year the Marconi Company was allowed to make regular broadcasts from Writtle and shortly afterwards its London station, 2LO, was opened.

Nevertheless the Post Office still feared chaos and congestion on the wavelengths and declined to license other wireless manufacturers who wished, like Marconi, to conduct broadcasts as a way of stimulating the sale of their receivers. On the other hand it was equally reluctant to allow one manufacturer to hold a broadcasting monopoly. It therefore proposed that the leading manufacturers form a broadcasting syndicate or consortium, and as a result the British Broadcasting Company was licensed by the Post Office as a *de facto* (though not *de jure*) monopoly and began transmissions in November 1922. Its funds came from three sources: the original stock, royalties on the receivers which its member companies sold, and a portion of the revenue from broadcast receiving licences. In return for the financial risk of setting up the service the manufacturers were guaranteed protection against foreign competition.

The first general manager, later managing director, of the British Broadcasting Company was J.C.W. (later Lord) Reith, whose

Scottish Calvinist upbringing led him to see broadcasting as a high moral responsibility. Through its programmes he therefore sought to provide a comprehensive public service and quickly turned the company from a commercial enterprise into a respected national institution. Its output embraced a wide range of music, drama and comedy, a children's hour, and with the help of external advisory committees, religious and schools broadcasts. Within three years a national network had been established, and with the opening of the long-wave transmitter at Daventry in 1925 reception was available to 85 per cent of the population, many with a choice of national or regional programmes.

The population reacted to the new medium with prodigious enthusiasm. In 1923 the Post Office issued 80,000 licences, but probably four or five times as many sets were in use: in 1924 1 million licences were issued, but up to 5 million sets were in use (Black 1972: 23). In three more years the number of licences doubled, and by 1939 9 million sets existed under licence (A. Briggs 1965: 6). By 1928 radio audiences were never less than 1 million and often as high as 15 million (Black 1972: 26).

The first radio receivers were crystal sets, which were easy and cheap to make but could also be bought from the BBC, complete with two pairs of headphones, for between £2 and £4 (ibid.: 20–1). They soon gave way to valve receivers with loudspeakers which enabled people to listen in groups and were virtually universal by the early 1930s. It has been calculated that the average price of the cheaper radio sets – £1 to £2 in the 1920s and £5 to £6 in the 1930s – was still quite expensive for the working classes, who were slightly under-represented in the national audience until the arrival of cheap 'utility' sets in 1944 (Pegg 1983: 47–9). But open to them were the relay exchanges, basically central radio receivers which in return for a rental could be wired to loudspeakers in individual homes. It is also significant that as the new technology improved and the demand for sets grew, their prices fell. Two-valve sets which cost £17 10s. in 1923 were retailing for 5 guineas in 1925 (A. Briggs 1961: 231) – though this was still a price which was well beyond anything the working classes could afford.

Despite its range and popularity the programme diet suffered from an important deficiency imposed by a body which was a good deal more prescient about radio's potential than many others of the time: the Newspaper Proprietors' Association. As a result of the NPA's influence with the government, the BBC was forbidden to broadcast any news bulletins before 7 pm and any commentary on public events. Nor could it broadcast news other than that which was bought from the main agencies. These restrictions were not finally thrown off until the European crisis of 1938 (Paulu 1956: 156).

Nevertheless there were some isolated portents of radio's possibilities as a news medium. In 1926 the General Strike occurred. There were virtually no newspapers and so the NPA lifted its restrictions on the way in which the BBC gathered and broadcast the news. But the BBC's reportage of the strike was compromised by the delicacy of its own position. Its Charter had not yet been granted and the government had the authority to turn it into a mouthpiece and even to requisition it altogether. Not surprisingly, then, the BBC's perspective on the events was broadly pro-government. It did not report everything, but nor did it distort, and it was never wholly associated with the government (A. Briggs 1961: 360–73). Some strikers denounced it, but many came to rely on it, and what the strike did in terms of radio was to establish the medium in the nation's life as a vital channel for the rapid dissemination of news and information.

A second event, much less important in itself yet an even more dramatic portent of radio's news potential, was the Crystal Palace fire of 1936. It occurred after the evening papers had shut down and before the morning papers appeared, and was the BBC's first 'scoop'. From the scene of the fire a young reporter named Richard Dimbleby broadcast a live telephone report against a background of shouts, firebells and the crackle of flames (Black 1972: 73; Herbert 1976: 14–15), and demonstrated that as a news medium radio is not only quicker than newspapers but more 'concrete' in the sense that it can convey the sound of what it reports.

But to return to the problems which faced the British Broadcasting Company: not only did it suffer from restrictions on its news output, but the evident popularity of its other programmes did not protect it from financial difficulties. Anomalies and loopholes in its royalty and licensing arrangements left it seriously short of revenue, and so in 1925 the government set up the Crawford Committee to consider the whole future of broadcasting. In fact the situation suited Reith, who wanted the BBC to become a public institution free from commercial pressures on the one side and political interference on the other. The Committee was of like mind and as a result of its recommendations the British

Broadcasting Corporation was set up by Royal Charter on 1 January 1927, with Reith as its first Director General.

Since then its constitution and statutory obligations as a publicly funded yet quasi-autonomous institution have remained largely unchanged. It is obliged to inform, educate and entertain; to report the proceedings of Parliament; to preserve a balance between political points of view; and in a national emergency to broadcast government messages, the source of which it is at liberty to name. It is also happy to accept two prohibitions: it may neither advertise nor editorialize. Under the terms of its Charter (conferred by the Crown) and its Licence and Agreement (its title to broadcast conferred by the government), it has a guaranteed income from receiving licences and maintains full editorial independence. Of course, as Scannell and Cardiff point out (1982: 162), it is subject to state pressures in a number of indirect ways. The Charter is renewable, and only the state can increase the licence fee. It also appoints the Board of Governors.

Soon after its foundation the Corporation underwent a rapid expansion, enhancing its output and its reputation. In 1932 it moved its headquarters into the purpose-built Broadcasting House, an act which symbolized its coming-of-age as a national institution, and in the same year began its Empire Service, the first of an interlocking range of external services whose illustrious history is recounted elsewhere (Mansell 1982). Meanwhile it had also recognized the need for a choice of domestic networks and established the National Programme, which mainly originated from London, and the Regional Programme, which drew its material primarily from six regional services and was also fed by a London key service. Both were 'mixed programme' networks and not markedly different in tone or content:

> Mixed programming offered a wide and diverse range of programme materials over the course of each day and week. Typically it included news, drama, sport, religion, music (light to classical), variety or light entertainment. Not only did it cater for different social needs (education, information, entertainment), but for different sectional interests within the listening public (children, women, businessmen, farmers, fishermen, etc.).
> (Scannell and Cardiff 1982: 167–8)

Reith's aim was to vary the output in such a way that the listener might be 'surprised into' an interest in a subject which she had not previously enjoyed or even known about: the intention was always to give her 'something a little better than she thought she wanted'. Such paternalism may seem somewhat objectionable today and it did not go unchallenged even in the 1930s.

One manifestation of the BBC's broadcasting philosophy was the 'Reith Sunday', the one day when a large majority of people had the leisure to listen to the radio and craved relaxing fare. What they got, however, was a transmission which did not begin until 12.30pm and consisted only of religious services, talks and classical music. But two continental-based commercial radio stations were set up in order to take advantage of the situation. The first was Radio Normandie (founded by someone with the wonderfully apposite name of Captain Plugge), which began broadcasting from the north coast of France in 1931 and offered southern areas of Britain a diet of American-style programmes including soap operas. The second was Radio Luxembourg which opened on an un-authorized wavelength in 1933 and whose programme of mainly light music could be heard all over Britain. On Sundays the number of listeners to these stations exceeded those who stayed tuned to the BBC: it was the first sign of discontentment with the latter's domestic monopoly.

The second challenge to Reith's broadcasting philosophy came mainly from within the BBC itself, although it was doubtless strengthened by the threat from commercial radio – the demand for regular and systematic research into audience behaviour and tastes, about which virtually nothing was known other than through casual letters from listeners. Reith feared that such research would inevitably influence and even dictate broadcasting policy, that worthwhile minority programmes would be sacrificed to the popularity ratings. Nevertheless its advocates won the day and an Audience Research Department was set up in 1936. By 1938, the year of Reith's resignation, it had gathered much information about the British radio audience, including reassuring evidence of its very broad social composition.

With the outbreak of war in 1939 the BBC combined its National and Regional Programmes into a single Home Service, but in order to maintain the morale of the troops forming the British Expeditionary Force in France it introduced in 1940 the Forces Programme, predominantly an entertainment service of dance music, sport and variety which foreshadowed the Light Programme. The Forces Programme was seen merely as a temporary expedient (Scannell and Cardiff 1982: 187): what was not appreciated at the time was that its uniformly 'light' output was the beginning of the end of Reith's mixed programming policy, which would finally disappear with the formation of Radios 1 to 4 in 1967 (Pegg 1983: 207–8). Within two years the Forces Programme was being listened to by more civilians than servicemen and attracting an audience 50 per cent larger than that of the Home Service (A. Briggs 1970: 47).

It is widely agreed that the BBC's performance during the Second World War was impressive. At home it was a means of social cohesion, and abroad it was generally regarded as an island of truthfulness amid a sea of rumour and propaganda. But to the media student the war is of greater interest as a time when radio at last came into its own as a rapid news medium, a role it has maintained even in an age of television. The BBC's 9pm news bulletin commanded huge and avid audiences and it was under pressure of war that the techniques of news broadcasting evolved from the early days of straight bulletin delivery into something like the blend of reading, correspondents' reports and sound actuality that we are familiar with today. The gathering of news became better organized and from 1944 the BBC began to employ its own foreign correspondents. Bulletins were supplemented by extended news programmes such as *Radio Newsreel*, which began in 1940, and new production techniques were adopted such as the association of comment with fact and the insertion of actuality into news broadcasts. But the catalyst to all this was technology: sound recording was vastly improved during the war. As Asa Briggs points out (1970: 325–6) the recording of news and talks acquired a special importance from about 1941 onwards. It removed the need to bring broadcasters into studios which were at risk from air raids, provided reserve material, allowed more outside reporting, made programme exports easier, served the needs of the monitoring service, and enabled producers to anticipate any problems of censorship which might arise with the War Office.

Ironically it was the Germans who pioneered the developments in recording technology, but they made much less imaginative use of it on the air than did the British. BBC reporters like Richard Dimbleby were given the same battle training as the soldiers and sent back front-line dispatches using portable disc-recorders and skilful editing to bring commentary and actuality closer together. The news programme *War Report*, which began on D-Day, 6 June

1944, made extensive use of recorded actuality and commanded regular audiences of between 10 and 15 million in Britain alone (A. Briggs 1970: 662). Such actuality has remained an integral part of radio news, a way of guaranteeing its immediacy and truth to life. Well before the war ended the popularity of the Forces Programme made it clear that there could be no simple reversion to the peacetime system of two substantially similar mixed programme networks. Consequently in 1945 the Director General of the BBC, William Haley, announced the plan of a new tripartite system which had long been in preparation. The Home Service was to continue as a basic London service which a federation of regional services – Scottish, Northern, Midland, Welsh, West and Northern Irish – could draw upon; the Forces Programme was to be superseded by the very similar Light Programme which replaced it without a break on 29 July 1945; and the Third Programme, an unashamedly 'highbrow' network devoted to the arts, serious discussion and experiment, began broadcasting on 29 September 1946.

Taken as a whole, the three networks represented an ingenious reconciliation of popular demand and the old Reithian seriousness of purpose, a compromise of streamed and mixed programming which was to work fairly well for the next ten or fifteen years. As Haley pointed out, the old mixed programme concept had presented the listener with certain problems:

> Before the war the system was to confront him with the necessity for pendulum-like leaps. The listener was deliberately plunged from one extreme to the other. The devotees of Berlin (Irving) were suddenly confronted with Bach. Many listeners were won for higher things in this way, but many were irretrievably lost. For the weakness of the process was that so many intolerances were set up.
>
> (cit. Smith 1974: 83)

Hence although mixed programming was not to be abandoned (in an age without television many people still found it desirable as well as possible to *listen*), within each network the *range* of programmes was narrowed and a certain uniformity of tone created. Moreover a complementary relationship was established between the Light and the Home and between the Home and the Third which gave the plan an edifying cultural purpose.

It rests on the conception of the community as a broadly based pyramid slowly aspiring upwards. This pyramid is served by three main Programmes, differentiated but broadly overlapping in levels and interest, each Programme leading on to the other, the listener being induced through the years increasingly to discriminate in favour of the things that are more worth-while. Each Programme at any given moment must be ahead of its public, but not so much as to lose their confidence. The listener must be led from good to better by curiosity, liking, and a growth of understanding. As the standards of the education and culture of the community rise so should the programme pyramid rise as a whole.

(cit. ibid.)

It was during the war and for the ten years or so after it that radio enjoyed its heyday, providing programmes of distinction in every genre to audiences of many millions. This was the period of what were regarded as radiogenic 'features' programmes – programmes of a factual, often documentary, nature but partly created through imaginative scripting which blended narration, actuality, dramatic dialogue and sound effects. It was also the period of *Children's Hour* and *Radio Newsreel*; of talks programmes such as *Letter from America*; of discussions and debates such as *The Brains Trust* and *Any Questions?*; of radio magazines like *Woman's Hour*; of drama – not only 'classical' plays but popular serials like *Dick Barton* and *The Archers*; of light entertainment such as *ITMA* and *Workers' Playtime*; and of a vast output of classical and popular music both on record and performed by innumerable orchestras including the BBC's own.

What was to end radio's pre-eminence was, of course, television, which had been pioneered by John Logie Baird and others during the 1920s. The BBC began test transmissions in 1930 and six years later opened a regular service for a few thousand viewers in the London area, using both the Baird and EMI systems. The service was stopped by the war, but even when it resumed in 1946 television was commonly thought of as 'radio with added vision' rather than as a medium which was fundamentally different. Before the war Reith had thought of 'integrating' radio and television (A. Briggs 1965: 608) and in 1949 Haley wrote in the *BBC Quarterly*: 'television is an extension of [radio] broadcasting. That is the crucial point . . . [television and radio] are complementary expressions within the same medium. They are part of one whole' (cit. Paulu 1981: 54). This naive misconception was to have prolonged and negative effects on certain aspects of television production:

> When BBC Television began it was inevitable, if not very appropriate, that one of its departments should be called Television Talks. This department dealt, in effect, with anything that was not drama, light entertainment, sport or news. The name continued in use for a long time and is an indication of how difficult the BBC found it to come to terms with the fundamental difference between radio and television, how many of the concepts of radio were taken over and imposed on television and how little the top echelons of the television service understood the new medium.
>
> (Hood 1975: 40)

This insistence on seeing television in terms of radio not only provoked sensational resignations among the more perceptive members of the television service, it dominated the presentation of television news until 1955, when the BBC was finally forced to make changes by the competition from ITN (Smith 1976: 148–9). Nevertheless the post-war rise of television was inexorable and two major events of the 1950s were seen, accurately, as marking its arrival as the major mass medium and less accurately as portending the very extinction of radio, whose blindness was regarded by many as an unequivocal disadvantage.

The first event was the coronation of Elizabeth II in 1953. The way in which it was covered by television would be impressive even today. Over 20 million people (56 per cent of the population) watched the service in Westminster Abbey, far outnumbering listeners in almost every part of the country (A. Briggs 1979: 466–7).

The second major event, which followed a prolonged public debate about the BBC's broadcasting monopoly, was the establishment in 1955 of a second, commercial television network under the regulation of the Independent Television Authority. The debate centred on television but was ultimately of relevance to radio too. Those who favoured the continuance of the BBC's monopoly argued that competition would force down standards and indeed threaten its very existence as a public service. When ITV came on the air the BBC's Director General, Ian Jacob, complained:

It may be argued that the BBC is in a position to ignore the relative size of its audience and that it is not obliged to compete with Independent Television. But, to some extent, it must compete for its audiences, or its audiences will diminish beyond that level at which the Corporation could continue to claim that it is the national broadcasting authority. This is the situation into which the Corporation has been placed by competition.

(cit. Paulu 1981: 42)

In being forced to compete for large audiences the BBC might neglect its duty to provide programmes for minorities. But the arguments against monopoly were also powerful and most tellingly summarized by Sir Frederick Ogilvie, a former Director General of the BBC: 'Freedom is choice. And monopoly of broadcasting is inevitably the negation of freedom, no matter how efficiently it is run' (cit. Smith 1974: 85).

Still, faced with competition from first one and then two television networks, radio went into a long decline that some thought would prove terminal. Between 1949 and 1958 the BBC's average evening radio audience dropped from nearly 9 million to less than 3.5 million, three-quarters of whom were people without television sets (Paulu 1961: 155). Though television was clearly the major cause, there were problems within radio's tripartite programme network. First the element of overlap was too broad, especially between the Home and the Light. *ITMA*, for instance, was broadcast on the Home (A. Briggs 1979: 58). This meant that in so far as each network lacked a separate identity its hold on listener loyalty was weakened. In search of a particular kind of programme, a listener might find herself scanning the schedules of at least two of the three networks.

One consequence of the overlap was that the Light was too serious for some listeners, for whom Radio Luxembourg was again becoming a more attractive alternative. At the other extreme, the Third Programme was regarded by many as absurdly recherché, an exclusive club for highbrows and intellectuals. During the first fifteen years of its existence it averaged only 2 per cent of the total radio audience (Paulu 1961: 156). But from time to time attempts were made to mend matters. In 1957 its output was cut from five and a half hours per day to three and a half hours, the two-hour space it cleared being given over to an educational concept known as 'Network Three'. In tones at once humorous

and sad one retired features producer remembered Network
Three as merely a part of radio's twilight gimmickry. 'This
emerged as specialist listening for every kind of minority interest
from Buchmanism to bee-keeping: it soon became known as the
Fretwork Network and attracted even fewer listeners than the
Third Programme itself' (Bridson 1971: 232).

The year 1964, when pirate broadcasters came on the air and
television provided yet more competition in the form of BBC 2,
marked BBC radio's lowest ebb. The Third Programme was again
dismembered, becoming the Music Programme during the day-
time, Study Session between 6 and 7.30 pm on weekdays, the
Sports Service on Saturday afternoons, and a truncation of its
former self during the evenings. But more significant was the end
of two radio 'institutions', both made redundant by the visual
appeal of television: the Features Department (Bridson 1971:
288–304; Snagge and Barsley 1972: 177) and *Children's Hour*.

Nevertheless three developments in broadcasting technology
had already taken place and although two of these were to
guarantee radio's future, in the case of the most important one it
was not the BBC which was the first to exploit its potential. Perhaps
the least important, although aesthetically very satisfying, was the
development of stereophonic sound. The first test transmissions in
stereo took place in 1958, the first regular broadcasts in 1966, and
stereo is now a commonplace but vital feature of radio, particularly
in 'simulcasts' during which an orchestra or group is televised
while, for those who lack stereo television sets, its music can be
simultaneously and more richly heard on the radio.

Rather more important was the opening in 1955 of the first two
VHF transmitters at Wrotham in Kent. One of the transmitters also
used frequency modulation (FM), which provided listeners with
freedom from all kinds of interference; 'but the future role of VHF
was to reintroduce low-power programming for very specific
audiences, a return in an age of television to the first broadcasting
patterns of 1922' (A. Briggs 1979: 561–2). In other words, it is VHF
which has made possible the extensive development of local radio
– a fact which underlay one of the first policy decisions taken by
the IBA in 1973 (Baron 1975: 76).

But the most important development in broadcasting technology occurred much earlier – in 1947 – and applied not to radio
transmitters but to receivers: the manufacture of the first transistor
(Goldhamer 1971: 901). By replacing the old wireless valve, which

was large, costly and consumed much primary power, the transistor allowed radios to be constructed which used less power,
were more reliable, and most important of all, were much cheaper
and smaller – small enough to be carried around in a hand or a
pocket. In a word, what the transistor would achieve was a
revolution in the way radio was used, something which was
recognized by Frank Gillard of the BBC:

> The transistor has made the radio into the truly ubiquitous mass
> medium. Radio is no longer something to which you necessarily
> have to go. Radio goes with you. So it becomes a personal
> service. You come to count on it . . . to give you a certain service
> at a certain hour, wherever you might happen to be. Conse-
> quently the usefulness of the medium is enormously en-
> hanced, and those in charge of sound in the years ahead must
> increasingly take this service function into account . . . in
> planning their programme output.

(Gillard 1964: 8)

Not only did the transistor allow the listener to take her radio
anywhere, for it was no longer a fixture of the home or factory but
could go with her to the seaside or out into the country; it greatly
extended the number of things she could do *while* listening, such
as working out in the garden or even driving her car. At the
beginning of the 1960s only 4 per cent of all British cars carried
radios (Paulu 1961: 155), but the 1970s saw an enormous growth in
the number of car radios, which began to be fitted as standard
equipment. By 1978 68 per cent of Britain's radio sets were either
portable or mobile (Paulu 1981: 350), and by 1990 85 per cent of
British cars were fitted with radios, over half of which were used
whenever the car was driven (Seymour-Ure 1991: 4). But it was at
the beginning of the 1960s that the transistor revolution began, so
that at the very time when radio had lost its pre-eminence and
seemed, indeed, to be facing extinction it discovered a new and
apparently irreducible advantage in its very limitation. As a
secondary medium it could be carried around and its messages
absorbed in a way not possible even with portable television.

It is, of course, important to realize that while the transistor
greatly *extended* radio's role as a secondary medium it did not
create it. Listeners had always been able to use radio as an
accompaniment to other activities, but they had come to use it
almost exclusively in this way as a consequence of television, for

television had replaced radio as the main leisure medium. Previously the husband in the factory and the wife back home in the kitchen may well have done their jobs while accompanied by *Music While You Work*, but in the evening they would have sat down to do little or nothing except listen to the radio. Now their evenings would be spent watching television. This meant that in so far as radio continued to be heard it was seldom heard as anything *other* than an accompaniment to other activities; and it is highly likely that among the vast majority who used the radio in this way was a substantial number for whom it became little more than a background noise.

In these circumstances, then, Haley's tripartite cultural pyramid was suspect in theory as well as in practice, for it presupposed *listeners* at a time when the radio audience consisted increasingly of 'hearers'. In an age of television, Radio Luxembourg's diet of continuous light music made much more sense, and the evidence suggests that between 1945 and 1955 radio audiences were moving in the opposite direction from that which Haley had hoped for – from the serious and demanding to the light and entertaining (Paulu 1956: 380; A. Briggs 1979: 558). By 1955 Radio Luxembourg was claiming an average evening audience larger than the Home's (Paulu 1956: 360–1), and it is not surprising that during this period Luxembourg was much more in touch with developments in popular music than was the BBC (A. Briggs 1979: 759).

But Luxembourg was unable to take full advantage of the new lease of life, this time as a mainly secondary medium, which the transistor gave to radio during the 1960s; for Luxembourg was confined to evening transmissions and a weak signal. Instead, the initiative was seized by a number of 'pirate' radio stations which began to broadcast almost round the clock from various ships and forts in British coastal waters. Inspired by Radio Luxembourg and even more by US radio, the pirates were unashamedly commercial operations and informed by a realization almost totally lacking at the BBC – that the transistor, at once radio's salvation and its curse, meant that the listener could take her set almost anywhere and listen to it almost all the time; but that since she would almost certainly be doing something else while she listened she would often treat it as little more than 'background'. Continuous pop music was the ideal form of output.

The first of the pirates, Radio Caroline, began broadcasting from a ship off the Essex coast in March 1964, and by 1967 no fewer than nine ships and forts were on the air. Caroline and a nearby ship broadcasting as Radio London were the slickest and most professional and reached the largest population, and their impact was sensational. A Gallup Poll found that in its first three weeks Caroline gained 7 million listeners from a potential audience of only 20 million (Harris 1970: 8). Though these estimates are not regarded as reliable (Chapman 1992: 44–5), it was claimed that within a year the total daily audience for pirate radio was between 10 and 15 million, and that by early 1966 the audience for this and for Radio Luxembourg was over 24 million (Harris 1970: 31, 53).

The BBC's findings were much more sober but no less eloquent. Within its transmission area Caroline commanded an audience about one-third that of the Light Programme; 70 per cent of its listeners were under 30 years old and treated it largely as background listening. Since there was no appreciable decline in the Light Programme's audience it was clear that Caroline and the other pirates were meeting a youthful need for radio that the BBC had neglected (Silvey 1974: 212–13).

The BBC was not totally to blame for this state of affairs: the amount of recorded music it could play was severely restricted by a long-standing agreement with the Musicians' Union. The pirates, on the other hand, observed no restrictions and paid no royalties on the records they played. But their fundamental act of piracy was their usurpation of frequencies, for which they were finally forced off the air by the government's Marine Broadcasting (Offences) Act in August 1967.

Nevertheless their consequences were considerable. The BBC's response to the demand they had identified was to turn one of the two frequencies which the Light Programme had occupied into a continuous pop music network named Radio 1. It began broadcasting in September 1967. Meanwhile the Light, Third and Home continued as mixed programme networks and were renamed Radios 2, 3 and 4 respectively. Audience size was now as important a criterion in moulding the BBC's radio policy as its duty to cater to a wide range of tastes, and Ian Jacob's fears about the threat to its broadcasting monopoly had proved well founded!

But although the pirates had been sunk, BBC radio's worst enemy remained. In the very same year, 1967, the introduction of colour transmissions on BBC 2 was a reminder, if one were needed, that television was now the major mass medium and that in order to survive radio must seek out, and largely confine itself to, those things it could do best. These were spelt out in the BBC's pamphlet *Broadcasting in the Seventies* (1969), which announced a radical new plan for network radio.

The pamphlet began by acknowledging that radio had yielded to television as the main focus of attention and was now treated by the listener as secondary to her other activities. It therefore echoed Gillard's view of radio's new role as a 'service function', the listener relying upon it to fulfil certain requirements at certain times. Since she may not be listening too closely the old mixed programme pattern, with its sudden changes and pleasant surprises, was inherently unsuited to such a role. What was needed instead was a more uniform and predictable kind of content, an uninterrupted supply of music, perhaps, or of information: 'experience, both in this country and abroad, suggests that many listeners now expect radio to be based on a different principle – that of the specialised network, offering a continuous stream of one particular type of programme, meeting one particular interest' (BBC 1969: 3). Moreover since the programmes would all be of one type the divisions between them would become less important and the programme concept itself give way to more extended sequences.

Broadcasting in the Seventies wrote the epitaph on the Reithian principle of tempting the listener to unexpectedly beneficial or pleasurable types of programme. Henceforth the BBC's duty to provide a comprehensive public service would be fulfilled not in any one network alone but through the networks as a whole – a point conceded in the *BBC Handbook 1978* (BBC 1977: 264). In April 1970 Radio 2 became a network for continuous 'middle-of-the-road' music, while Radio 3 lost many of its speech programmes to Radio 4 and devoted a larger share of its output to classical music. Both networks retained some vestiges of mixed programming, notably sport, but only Radio 4 survived in something like its old form: it continued to carry a number of general entertainment programmes, but also specialized to some extent in informational or 'spoken word' output – news and current affairs.

It is important to recognize that radio's new role was forced upon it not simply by the ascendancy of television but by its own technological sophistication. So numerous and portable had transistor sets become that the Post Office could no longer keep track of them in order to collect the licence fee. Bowing to the millions of radio owners who evaded it, the government abolished radio-only licences in 1971. But as Smith points out (1974: 128) this weakened the position of radio *vis-à-vis* television in the BBC because there was no longer a sum of money raised specifically for it: it was therefore being 'carried' by its more successful and glamorous partner. However, notwithstanding the creation of BBC Radio 5 in 1990 the largely specialized pattern of network radio has remained ever since, and there is no evidence that its audiences wish it otherwise. Between 1980 and 1982 there were some stealthy moves towards mixed programming on Radio 1 (Wade 1983a: 9). They cost the network three-quarters of a million listeners (Wade 1983b: 7).

Another major development of the last thirty years has been in local radio. Though the natural heir to the VHF transmitters which had been opened since the 1950s, local radio seems also to have been inspired by the offshore pirates (Harris 1970: 43, 84). Indeed it may not be too fanciful to suggest that the pirates helped in two ways to awaken the latent demand for a service which had been technically feasible for about ten years. First they were in some sense 'local' themselves. None of them broadcast over an area larger than the Home Counties, many of them publicized local events and aroused local loyalties, and a few, such as Radio London and Radio Essex, took local names. Second, although they afforded no broadcasting access to actual members of the public, they broke the BBC's virtual monopoly of radio to fulfil a demand which it had neglected, and so in that sense assumed a public 'voice'. Perhaps, then, they helped to foster what Anthony Smith describes as

> the growth of a public demand that radio (and indeed broadcasting in general) should become a means of 'two-way' communication, that it should no longer remain the exclusive platform of the BBC and its invited guests. Local radio seemed to be a means by which some kind of 'right to broadcast' could be created, within the general framework of the BBC .... [It] was to become a forum for the whole of the cultural life of a community.
>
> (Smith 1974: 151)

After a successful experiment in 1963–4 the BBC opened its first local radio station at Leicester in 1967 and followed up with many others during the 1970s and 1980s, using them ultimately as a replacement for regional radio, which was discontinued in 1983. In the light of Smith's remarks it is not surprising that the phone-in has been a staple of local radio and it was first heard on BBC Radio Nottingham in 1968. It has been a genuinely new broadcasting technique in giving the radio listener her own voice on the air. Local radio was not a BBC preserve for very long. In 1972 the ITA was renamed the Independent Broadcasting Authority and empowered by the Conservative government to license a national spread of independent local radio (ILR) stations. The IBA was a corporate, government-established body rather like the BBC's Board of Governors. It selected and gave contracts to the programme companies, but owned and operated the transmission facilities – for which the companies paid a rent – and regulated the balance and advertising content of their output. As on ITV the advertisers merely bought time-slots, not programmes, since sponsorship was not allowed. The first stations, Capital Radio and the all-news London Broadcasting Company, opened in London in 1973, and there are presently over fifty spread fairly evenly across Britain.

ILR has had a chequered history. Although some stations have been profitable others have shown losses, and there have been closures and mergers. The causes of its difficulties have been both general and specific. First, the gradual establishment of ILR in the 1970s and 1980s coincided with a number of technological and institutional developments in both the sound and visual media that posed a challenge not just to the commercial stations but to radio as a whole. Since 1974 teletext has enabled us to obtain visual updates on the news from our television screens without having to wait for radio bulletins. Video cassettes, video games and home computers have come to provide domestic alternatives to simply 'listening to the radio', and another threat to radio listening exists *inside* many receivers: the cassette recorder. Radio-cassetting and 'time-shift' listening mean that programmes can be heard and re-heard which would otherwise have been missed; but the cassette facility also means that many who would formerly have been radio listeners are now listeners to commercial tapes.

There has also been a vast increase in the amount of television that can be watched. Restrictions on transmission hours were lifted in 1972, and by 1990 it was possible to watch television round the clock. But Breakfast Television, which began in 1983 on both BBC and ITV, was of particular significance to radio because it struck at what had always been the latter's peak listening time.

In the last quarter of that year it caused a 10 per cent drop in the amount of time per week which the average person spent listening to the radio (BBC 1984: 45).

As well as the extension of transmission hours there has been a proliferation of television channels. ITV's Channel 4 went to air in 1982, and from the mid-1980s cable television franchises were being allocated by a newly formed Cable Authority. To date, business has been slow but cable offers important long-term prospects in interactive media. More spectacular, though hardly more successful, has been the arrival of satellite television. Sky TV began transmissions with four channels in 1989 and was followed a year later by British Satellite Broadcasting. Burdened by the enormous start-up costs the latter collapsed in February 1991 and was absorbed by its rival, which relaunched as BSkyB. It is perhaps testimony to the range of programming offered by the four terrestrial channels that satellite television has not so far tempted the British public in very large numbers; but the inevitable effect of this, as of all the other developments, has been to spread the media audience ever more thinly.

There have also been more specific reasons why ILR has not done as well as was expected. First, recurrent economic recession during the 1970s and 1980s affected advertising revenues. Second, the stations suffered until the mid-1980s from an over-regulation by the IBA which was both editorial and technological. Under the Act of 1973 it imposed certain public service obligations, notably to provide a 'balance of programming' and a full news service (Barnard 1989: 74–5). As we have seen, in a television age programming 'balance', which implies some degree of variety, is more than most people require from radio, and very few who listened to ILR enjoyed the variety as such, merely differing elements of it. This meant that an audience emerged which lacked sufficient identity for many advertisers to target (ibid.: 80–1). The balance of programming was thus doubly expensive – costly to produce in itself, and the more so in that it failed to interest enough advertisers. It also meant that each commercial station was required to honour a public service principle at *local* level which most of its explicitly public service competitors, namely BBC Radios 1, 2 and 3, had individually abandoned at *national* level.

The public service obligations placed on ILR were inappropriate not simply because television was the main medium, but for reasons of technology. The original Reithian case for providing a radio service that offered something to everyone and maintained a political balance was the shortage of wavelengths: sound broadcasting was a scarce national resource, and so the few stations which existed should each cater to the full range of listener needs and tastes. But this case had been weakened by the arrival of FM, which created much more room on the spectrum – room for a multitude of stations, each of which could offer its own specialized output, and (like newspapers) its own political 'line'.

Despite this the IBA put its stations into a technological straitjacket too. It required their studios and equipment to conform to unnecessarily high technical standards and charged big transmitter rents at a time when the real costs of broadcasting were falling and it was becoming a relatively simple matter for almost anyone to set up a radio studio and go to air. For only a few thousand pounds an individual could install a radio station in his bedroom and transmit to the neighbourhood, and it is perhaps not surprising that this fuelled a growing dissatisfaction with the existing BBC/ILR duopoly. Among the complaints were that it was a professionals' closed shop; that it denied the public genuine access to the airwaves; and that it offered a lack of real choice, neglecting ethnic minorities, special interest groups and the smaller communities. Those specific to local radio were that most of the commercial output, notably rock music, was not locally originated and that the BBC stations were grievously underfunded.

During the 1980s the legal consequence of this dissatisfaction was a growth of 'in-house' radio stations – campus radio in colleges and universities, hospital radio serving one or a whole network of sites, even stations serving large housing developments such as Radio Thamesmead in south-east London. The government permitted these because they were piped to closed communities: they did not, in effect, *broad*cast.

However, illegal developments made a bigger impact. For a time, an old-style offshore pirate, Laser 558, lured listeners from Radio 1 by minimizing disc-jockey chatter; but much more significant was the developing concept of 'community radio' (CR). The CR movement was a direct response to the inadequacies of local radio (Lewis and Booth 1989: 105), and by the middle of the decade some fifty community stations, mostly catering for ethnic groups, could be heard across Britain, reinstating themselves almost as quickly as the Home Office could shut them down. In contrast to the legitimate ILR stations they had low set-up costs. In 1984 the

IBA would not allow Viking Radio to transmit to Hull until it had spent £200,000 on bringing its studios and equipment up to a certain standard: meanwhile a pirate station in London was broadcasting successfully on equipment costing one-twentieth of that sum (Webster 1984: 1). Moreover, since the pirates were not bound to provide a balance of programming, they could more easily yield targeted audiences to their advertisers.

In 1985, when the Home Office seemed about to legalize twenty-one of the CR stations on an experimental basis, the IBA at last moved to ease the plight of its licensees. It relaxed restrictions on station ownership, on the sponsorship of programming, and on editorial 'balance' (the output of most ILR stations has now flattened out into a Top 40 and capsule news format). And it also allowed stations to split their frequencies in order to target audiences more closely, a practice sometimes known as 'narrowcasting'. In 1988–9 alone, eighteen ILR stations split their frequencies (Wroe 1989: 23), mostly pounding out rock and contemporary hits on FM and comforting their maturer listeners with golden oldies or soft melodies on the medium wave.

The IBA also responded to pressure, most of it coming from the CR movement, to widen lawful access to the air. In 1989–90 it licensed a wave of twenty-one 'incremental' stations within existing ILR areas in order to serve niche markets of various kinds – ethnic groups (for example, Spectrum Radio in London); special interest groups (for example, Jazz FM, also in London); and small geographical areas (for example, Wear FM in Sunderland) (Donovan 1992: 134).

However, by the end of the decade the rate of technological change in both television and radio was such that the government needed to devise a whole new broadcasting framework. Television had also become much more flexible: in technical terms production was cheaper and easier than ever before, and thanks to cable and satellite there were many more channels to be watched. The government's overall task for both radio and television was therefore to facilitate that greater access to the airwaves which technology had made possible, yet also to regulate output that partly transcended national frontiers. And within this overall task there were particular issues to be addressed: the future of the BBC's licence fee; the destruction of two monopolies – the BBC's of national radio and ITV's of television advertising; the preservation of programme standards (this, apparently, something of an afterthought!); and the need to ensure diversity of broadcasting output and to cater for specialized and minority tastes.

Although the 1990 Broadcasting Act dealt at length with television it also made major changes to radio. The BBC was left pretty much alone, though still held to its increasingly tenuous 'public service' obligations. (In 1986 the government had appointed the Peacock Committee to consider such options as allowing the BBC to take advertising and the privatization of Radio 1, but had been dissuaded from both.) The IBA, however, was split into the Independent Television Commission and the Radio Authority, which was intended to be a much looser regulator than its predecessor. ILR was relieved of its vestigial public service obligations, notably the need to provide 'balance', and the individual stations were allowed to operate their own transmission facilities instead of leasing them from the Authority. Many more stations are likely to be launched within the next few years.

However, the real change was at national level: three new stations were to be licensed here, one on FM, the other two on medium-wave frequencies the BBC had been forced to vacate. Accordingly Classic FM, Britain's first home-based national commercial station, came on air in September 1992, to be followed eight months later by Virgin 1215 with a diet of 1960s to 1980s rock music. Another independent national station, whose output must be speech-based, is expected to join them in about 1995, and each licence will run for eight years. The Radio Authority also intends to license five new regional stations which should go to air by the end of 1994 (Wroe 1992: 15).

Despite all this, the outlook for independent radio remains uncertain. For the listener the logic of greater competition is to encourage diversity, but will the increase in stations merely have that baffling but all-too-frequent effect of producing more of the same? National commercial radio may thrive, but is just as likely to do so by taking audiences – and advertising – from the local stations (whose output is in any case hardly 'local') as by generating new listeners. The incrementals have never seen anything other than hard times, although valiant Wear FM took the Sony 'Radio Station of the Year' Award in 1992 for its community spirit and innovative programming.

A more sombre sign of the times was the death of Radio Luxembourg in 1991, crowded out of the pop scene first by Radio 1 and then by the superior FM signal of ILR. There are other signs that radio listening may be near saturation-point. Between 1985 and 1990 total radio output in Britain increased by 65 per cent, yet average weekly listening during the same period increased by only 17 per cent (Nicholson-Lord 1991: 4). Nevertheless since 1989 the Ireland-based Atlantic 252 has attracted large British audiences to the long wave, perhaps confounding the experts' prediction that the medium-wave Virgin 1215 will not thrive unless it can move to FM.

As many media analysts have pointed out (for example, MacCabe and Stewart 1986; Smith 1990), the really intriguing question is what will become of the BBC. Its recent activities in radio suggest an organization both vigorous and optimistic. By 1990 it had switched its four major networks to FM and created another, Radio 5, on medium wave.

Not only has the BBC retained a mixed programming network, Radio 4, for its loyal and by no means tiny band of adherents who wish to listen to the radio and not simply hear it; for a short time it attempted to provide another in Radio 5, which offered such things as sports commentary, magazines and schools broadcasts. Radio 5 could be seen either as a brave attempt to reinstate old listening practices or as a foolish anachronism. Radio 4, partly drawing on its glorious past, eats its cake and has it: it offers mixed programming, yet manages to project a coherent identity as a spoken word/news and current affairs network. Radio 5, how- ever, had no glorious past: it was known as a child of base pragmatism, 'conceived in response to the Government's radio policy . . . which required the BBC to end simulcasting . . . and give listeners more choice' (Donovan 1992: 218). Consequently it was – or was seen to be – little more than a dumping ground for a number of programmes that did not fit into any of the other networks and was relaunched as a popular news and sports channel in March 1994.

If they are to be judged by their popularity, Radios 1 and 2 are easily the BBC's biggest assets, yet there is a plan to distinguish them from the many other pop music stations by increasing their spoken word output in the realms of the arts, religion, consumer issues and social action (Dugdale 1993: 13). Similarly BBC Local Radio aims to become more speech-based and minorities-focused in order to complement music-based ILR. Implicit in these plans is a partial and interesting redefinition of the old public service concept, for what is being mooted is not simply a greater variety of content that faintly echoes the mixed programming of the past, but the 'public service' of giving out information on matters of social importance, such as how to find a job or where to get treatment for drug addiction.

Nevertheless the strategy looks risky, for a likely consequence of reducing the music content of these networks is a drop in the numbers of listeners, perhaps below a point where the imposition of a universal licence fee can be justified. If a radio listener (or even more pertinently, a television viewer) spends all or most of her time tuned to the commercial stations, why should she be expected to pay licence money to support the BBC?

Which brings us neatly to the momentous year of 1996, when the BBC's Charter is due for renewal and the whole question of its funding arrangements to be reviewed. If by that time the BBC's decreasing share of the market – a decrease which is inevitable given the proliferation of radio and television channels – has indeed reached a point at which the licence fee can no longer be defended, how else can the Corporation be funded as a public service institution? If it were allowed to take commercials, the need to maximize audiences for advertisers would soon overshadow the need to offer a range of programming. If it were to be funded by subscription, would enough subscribers be found in a nation used to 'free' radio and 'free' ITV to pay for a range of public service output which is bound to be expensive?

But if the uncertain outlook for broadcasting institutions is largely a result of technological advances, it is at least certain that these will make the actual business of listening to the radio yet more pleasurable – and easier – than ever before. The development of digital audio broadcasting (DAB), a process in which the signal is digitally encoded at the station and then decoded by the radio set so that transmission noise is eliminated, promises a vast improvement in the quality of reception, to the point where radio music will sound as good as the music of a domestic CD player (Croft 1991: 13).

More important, however, is the recent development of the radio data system (RDS), since it is likely to modify the way in which the listener uses the medium. RDS exploits the large bandwidth of FM broadcasts to transmit data as an inaudible signal along with the output. It is an automatic tuning system which without pre-programming selects the strongest signal carrying the broadcast the listener wants, irrespective of the frequency. Thus if a motorist were driving the 237 miles from Exeter to Sheffield and wished to listen to BBC Radio 2 throughout her journey, she would have to do no more than select that station at the outset, even though the radio would automatically tune to seven frequencies in the course of the journey. A display panel on the receiver will give her the name of the station she is listening to, and if she wishes it and pre-sets the radio accordingly, announcements will interrupt the Radio 2 broadcast with local travel information.

By removing any need to re-tune, RDS would appear, then, to strengthen yet further that station loyalty which has always been much more characteristic of radio listeners than of television viewers. Whereas the latter will frequently change channels in search of programmes they like, the typical listener keeps her radio fixed to one particular channel, reaching only for the on-off button. There seem to be two main reasons for this. The first is that because she is only half-listening to it she is much more tolerant of those parts of the output she does not particularly like: the radio is just a background to some other activity. The second reason is that re-tuning a radio set, normally a matter of carefully turning a knob, has always daunted audiences to a much greater extent than merely jabbing the channel-select button on their television sets (Brown 1990: 15).

However, RDS also offers another facility – a choice not simply of stations but of *output*: the listener can push a button for news, current affairs, rock, classical music, drama or whatever, and the radio will search among the stations for her choice. Thus a much more likely consequence of this technology is that it will *weaken* station loyalty by allowing the listener to shop around even more than push-button tuning would. It could replace loyalty to one particular station by an even stronger loyalty to one particular kind of output.

Though RDS has been on the market for some years – it was first incorporated into car radios by Volvo in 1988 (Donovan 1992: 218) – it has made slow progress, partly because it can more than double the cost of a cheap radio set. But the long-term likelihood is that it will become a standard feature; and if it stimulates a greater autonomy in the listener, or encourages the stations to compete even harder for her attention, that can only be a good thing.

Chapter 3

Radio signs and codes

Radio is the art of communicating meaning at first hearing.
(Laurence Gilliam, former Head of Features, BBC Radio)

We must now look more closely at the raw material of radio, at the signs which its codes make use of in order to convey messages, and for this purpose I shall borrow some rudimentary distinctions from what is in fact a highly sophisticated classification of signs devised by the American philosopher, C.S. Peirce (1839–1914).

Peirce, who is commonly regarded as a founding father of semiotics or semiology, the study of signs, distinguishes between the *icon* – a sign which resembles the object which it represents, such as a photograph; the *index* – a sign which is directly linked to its object, usually in a causal or sequential way: smoke, for instance, is an index of fire; and the *symbol* – a sign which bears no resemblance or connection to its object: for example, the Union Jack as a symbol of Great Britain (Peirce 1960: I, 196; II, 143, 161, 165, 168–9; Hawkes 1977: 127–30; Fiske 1990: 47–8). In radio all the signs are auditory: they consist simply of noises and silence, and therefore use *time*, not space, as their major structuring agent (Hawkes 1977: 135). The noises of radio can be subdivided into words, sounds and music, and we will look at each of these in turn and also at the nature and functions of silence before attempting some general observations about the codes of radio.

WORDS

Since words are signs which do not resemble what they represent (we may represent a canine quadruped by the word 'dog' but we may equally refer to it as *'chien'*, *'hund'* or *'cur'* or even invent a private word of our own), they are symbolic in character. Their symbolism is the basis of radio's imaginative appeal which I mentioned in Chapter 1, for if the word-sign does not resemble its object the listener must visualize, picture or *imagine* that object. But there is an important difference between words which are written or printed on a page and words on the radio, and that is that words on the radio are always and unavoidably *spoken*. They therefore constitute a binary code in which the words themselves are symbols of what they represent, while the voice in which they are heard is an index of the person or 'character' who is speaking – a fact which was perceived and researched fairly early in the medium's history (Pear 1931).

In other words, such factors as accent and stress have semiotic functions, or at least effects (O'Donnell and Todd 1980: 95). Almost irrespective of what is said in a French accent, for example, the listener may automatically ascribe a romantic personality to its speaker. In fact, voice can be so powerful an expression of personality that merely by virtue of some well-delivered links a presenter or disc-jockey can impose a unifying and congenial presence on the most miscellaneous of magazine or record pro-grammes. Moreover the voice of a continuity announcer is an index not only of herself, whom she may identify by name from time to time, but of the whole station or network. As a matter of deliberate policy she will give a kind of composite unity to its various programmes, set the tone or style of the whole network (Kumar 1977: 240–1). Indeed an announcement such as 'You're listening to Radio 4' is ambivalent, for it means not only 'The programmes you're presently hearing are the output of Radio 4' but 'Since the network has no other self-conscious means of expression, *I* am Radio 4'. The ambivalence can be seen rather more clearly, and is taken even further, in the name of the USA's world service, where at intervals we can hear 'You're listening to the Voice of America' – the 'voice' being an index not only of the continuity announcer and the radio station, but of the entire nation.

By now it will be clear that signification is not static or rigid, but a highly fluid or elastic process which varies according to context and the preconceptions we bring to it – a fact which is not sufficiently acknowledged by some semioticians. A voice may be interpreted merely as the index of a human presence; or on another level as the index of a personality (a country bumpkin, seductive French woman, and so on); or on yet a third level as the index of a programme, broadcasting institution or entire nation. It might be useful to see the latter two levels as examples of *extended* signification.

SOUNDS

Unlike words, which are a human invention, sound is 'natural' – a form of signification which exists 'out there' in the real world. It seems never to exist as an isolated phenomenon, always to manifest the presence of something else. Consequently we can say that sounds, whether in the world or on the radio, are generally indexical. We could of course say that recorded sound on the radio is iconic in the elementary sense that it is an icon or image of the original sound or that a sound in a radio play is an icon of a sound in the real world, but if we do we are still faced with the question of what the sound *signifies*, what it is that is *making* the sound. Thus sounds such as the ringing of a door-bell or the grating of a key in a lock are indexical in signifying someone's presence.

Shut your eyes for a moment and listen. The chances are that you will become aware of sounds which you have been hearing for some time but which you have not been aware of before. You have not been aware of them because you are reading such a fascinating book that you have ignored the messages coming from your ears. Suppose, however, that your desire for a cup of coffee is almost equal to your absorption in this book and that a friend has agreed to bring one to you about now. You will be quite capable of picking out from the welter of unimportant noises which surround you the keenly awaited sounds of rattling cup and turning door-handle. But the radio medium is such that the listener cannot select his own area of attention in this way: the broadcasters must prioritize sounds for him, foregrounding the most important ones and eliminating the irrelevant ones, or if this is not possible reducing them to the level of the less important ones. This has been illustrated in respect of radio drama by Erving Goffman (1980: 162–5).

Taking as his scenario a conversation at a party Goffman points out that whereas in real life we would be able to distinguish the important from the less important strand of sound, this has to be done for us on the radio by certain conventions. Among the possibilities he instances:

1 Fading in party chatter then fading it down and holding it under the conversation, or even fading it out altogether.
2 Allowing one or two low sounds to stand for what would actually be a stream of background noise.

What Goffman is concerned to stress about these conventions is their artificiality, which is aptly conveyed in the stock phrase 'sound *effects*':

> the audience is not upset by listening in on a world in which many sounds are not sounded and a few are made to stand out momentarily; yet if these conditions suddenly appeared in the off-stage world, consternation would abound.
>
> (ibid.: 163)

But it is important to realize that such conventions are indispensable even in radio which deals with real life. In a location interview, for instance, the interviewer will set the recording-level on her portable tape-machine so that the sound of her voice and that of the person she is interviewing will be foregrounded against all the other noises of the location.

Let us imagine an interview which takes place against a background of traffic noise. If the interview is with a superintendent of highways about noise pollution the traffic noise, while of less importance – and therefore less loud – than the interview, will still be of relevance to it. If, however, the interview is with the Chancellor of the Exchequer about his Budget proposals the noise of traffic will be quite irrelevant, an unavoidable evil, and the listener will be fully capable of distinguishing between these positive and negative functions of background noise.

This second type of location interview is, of course, a *faute de mieux*: it brings a broadcasting facility to an interviewee who cannot be brought into the studio, for an important function of the studio with its sound-proofing is that it eliminates irrelevant noise altogether. My point, then, is that radio does not seek to reproduce the chaotic, complex and continuous sounds of actual life: it may tolerate them to a degree, but seeks to convey only those sounds which are relevant to its messages and to arrange them in a hierarchy of relevance. Nevertheless the ultimate test of relevance is the verbal context: it is the subject under discussion in the interview which will tell us whether we should be paying any attention to the traffic noise.

Sounds on the radio may also carry what I have termed an extended signification. An owl-hoot, for instance, may open a documentary about feathered predators or it may evoke not merely an owl but an entire setting – an eerie, nocturnal atmosphere, as it would in a melodrama or a programme about the occult. A crowing sound frequently signifies not only 'a cock' but 'daybreak', while the sound of strumming may suggest not simply a guitar but a Spanish setting. Because radio broadcasters seldom walk while broadcasting, the sound of footsteps, often heard – and ignored – in real life, acquires a peculiar suggestiveness on the radio. Drama producers will use it sparingly, and to convey not only that a person is moving but that an atmosphere of tension or solitude is developing. Though in these cases partly indexical, extended signification seems to embody a tendency towards the symbolic. The guitar sound is certainly an index of an instrument which is commonly found in Spain, but when used to evoke a Spanish setting it will 'stand for' many other Hispanic things, abstract as well as concrete, which have nothing to do with guitars.

It is precisely this aspect of extended signification – a form of stereotyping – which can annoy those to whom it is applied because it sometimes causes in the rest of us a naive confusion of signifiers and signifieds. Spaniards grow understandably irritated if we expect them all to strum guitars and stamp their feet, Scotsmen with people who believe they always wear kilts and eat nothing but porridge.

It can be interesting to speculate on the origins of certain kinds of extended signification, but they seem to become firmly established by a process of custom and habit. On the radio it is likely that such sounds as the owl-hoot and the footsteps were originally chosen as an effective way of reinforcing particular pieces of dialogue or narration. But since they *are* effective and part of what is a rather limited range of resources open to the radio producer they were chosen again and again and came to acquire the status of a convention, an acoustic shorthand, in that they could replace or *absorb* much of the adjacent language. In hearing the hoot of the owl the listener might begin to brace himself for darkness and mystery before a word had been uttered. But while such conventions may be useful in replacing *much* of the adjacent language they cannot *wholly* replace it, for ultimately it is only the words which follow upon our owl-hoot that will tell us whether what we are listening to is *The Natural History Programme* or *Thirty Minute Theatre*.

But it is not simply the case that radio broadcasters must indicate to the listener whether and in what way the sounds he hears are relevant: in some instances they must clarify the very *nature* of those sounds. Why?

Shut your eyes and listen again to the sounds around you. You may be surprised at how few of them you can identify with any precision. The frequency range of most sounds is narrow and what we often overlook about the way in which we normally recognize them are the clues our other senses afford, notably the visual sense. When we do not actually see what is causing them they often mean nothing at all. Moreover studio simulations of sounds can often sound more 'real' on the radio than the actual sounds themselves would. Among the better known and genuine examples of these studio simulations are the clapping together of coconut shells to convey horses' hooves and the rustle of a bunch of recording-tape to convey someone walking through under-growth (McLeish 1978: 252). These are not straightforwardly indexical, since the sounds made by coconut shells and recording-tape have no *direct* connections with horses and people in under-growth. They are 'images' of the sounds made by horses and people and are therefore best described as iconic indexes. They might also be described as 'non-literal signifiers' analogous to an actor in the theatre who represents a table by kneeling on all fours (Elam 1980: 8); but in radio such signifiers must approximate rather more closely to that which they signify than signifiers in the visual media.

Yet however carefully selected and 'realistic' the sounds may be, the listener may still be unclear as to what aspect of reality they are meant to signify. The rustle of recording-tape may sound like someone walking through undergrowth, but it also sounds like the swish of a lady's gown and remarkably like the rustle of recording-tape. In a radio play which of these things would it signify?

Accompanied by 'Damn! I don't often hit it off the fairway': a golfer searching for his ball in the rough.

Accompanied by 'Darling, you'll be the belle of the ball tonight': a lady in an evening gown.

Accompanied by 'This studio's a pig-sty. Throw this old tape out': a bunch of recording-tape.

In other words, sounds require textual pointing – support from the dialogue or narrative. The ear will believe what it is led to believe. This pointing might be termed 'anchorage', which is how Roland Barthes describes the function of words used as captions for photographs. Visual images, he argues, are polysemous. But so are sounds. Hence words help to 'fix the floating chain of signifieds in such a way as to counter the terror of uncertain signs' (Barthes 1977: 39).

MUSIC

Music on the radio, as on television, seems to perform two main functions. It is an object of aesthetic pleasure in its own right, in record shows, concerts, recitals, and so on; and either by itself or in combination with words and/or sounds it performs an ancillary function in signifying something outside itself.

As an object of pleasure in its own right, music is quite simply the mainstay of radio's output. Some stations offer little or nothing else. Even on the five BBC networks, two of which – Radios 4 and 5 – devote over 90 per cent of their time to spoken word, music accounted for 51 per cent of total output in 1992 (BBC 1992: 28).

The difficulty is to define such music in semiotic terms since there is some doubt as to the sense in which music can be said to signify. Broadly speaking, words and images refer to something outside themselves but the assertion cannot be quite so confidently made about music. Music with lyrics seems to present less of a difficulty since we could say that the significance or meaning of the music is expressed in the words; but it might equally be argued that the music means one thing and the lyrics mean another and that they are quite capable of counterpointing as well as complementing each other.

Quite apart from this, the question of what meaning (if any) attaches to wordless music is a formidable one. It can of course be seen as an index of the instruments and musicians that are playing it. When we hear a record on the radio but miss the presenter's introduction to it, we may still be able to identify which band is playing by the characteristic sound it has evolved. But to leave the matter there is a bit like saying that spoken words are signs of nothing but the identity of their speaker.

Dictionary definitions of music generally ascribe an emotional significance to it, and some compositions (for example,

Tchaikovsky's *1812 Overture*) evoke historical events: but while acknowledging this we would have to point out that music does not convey these emotions or events with anything like the precision that words do. Indeed there is room for disagreement about the emotional significance of certain compositions with unrevealing titles like *Opus No. 3* or *Study in E Flat* – and who could tell merely from hearing it that Chopin's *Minute Waltz* is about a dog chasing its tail?

This means that written commentaries which point to particular features of a piece of music as referring to particular emotional or historical conditions tend to rely consciously or unconsciously on circumstantial evidence – the title of the piece and/or the famous legend which it 'narrates', the situation in which it was composed, the biographical and psychological details of the composer, and so on. Hence our very difficulty in discerning what music refers to means that if it does signify, then apart from its local imitations of 'natural' sounds its mode of signification will be almost entirely symbolic.

The virtual absence, or at any rate imprecision, of meaning in music makes it at once highly suited to the radio medium and somewhat unilluminating as to its nature. It is highly suited because in being largely free of signification it allows us to listen without making strenuous efforts to imagine what is being referred to, but to assimilate it, if we wish, to our own thoughts and moods – a fact that helps to explain why music has become even more popular since radio's rebirth as a secondary medium. But it is unilluminating in the sense that in its fully realized form (that is, not as a written score) it consists almost purely of sound, refers scarcely at all to anything outside itself, and is therefore one code which is not distinctively shaped by radio since radio is itself a purely acoustic medium.

This was recognized fairly early in broadcasting history by a features producer who wished to dismiss the idea that there was anything especially 'radiogenic' about music:

> There is no such thing as radio music. Composers go on composing music just as if wireless had never been invented, and the music of all periods is played before microphones in exactly the same way as it has always been played. It does not have to be 'adapted'.
>
> (Sieveking 1934: 24)

Apart from the fact that radio allowed the listener to hear music without visual distractions (and even in this was anticipated by the gramophone), the point is that music is rather less revealing about the nature and possibilities of the medium than, say, news, drama or light entertainment: for whereas we can compare radio versions of the latter with their corresponding forms on the stage, screen or in newspapers and see the distinctive way in which the medium has adapted them, music in its essential form is always and everywhere the same. Not modified by radio, it does not particularly illuminate it.

Nevertheless the broad emotive power of music enables it to be combined with words and/or sounds as a way of signifying something outside itself, and some of these forms of signification are worth considering in detail.

Music as a 'framing' or 'boundary' mechanism

Musical jingles (sometimes known as 'IDs') identify or 'frame' radio stations just as signature or theme-music frames an individual programme by announcing its beginning and/or end. Station IDs are similar in function to the voice of the continuity announcer; they set the style or tone of the station and could be seen as both index and symbol.

It is interesting to speculate why musical IDs are more closely associated with 'popular', and verbal IDs with 'quality', stations; but it is certainly the case that the work done by continuity announcers on BBC Radios 3 and 4 is performed largely by jingles on Radios 1 and 2 and on Virgin 1215. As a way of framing individual items theme-music is also common in film and television, but it is of particular significance in radio because of the blindness of the medium.

Silence, a pause, can also be used as a framing mechanism, but unlike that of film and television it is *total*, devoid of images. To give the programmes connotations, an overall style or mood, music is therefore an especially useful resource on radio – less bald, more indefinitely suggestive, than mere announcements.

Let us take a formal but lively piece of eighteenth-century music played on a harpsichord – a gavotte or bourrée composed by Bach, perhaps – and consider its possibilities for the radio producer. It is highly structured and symmetrical in form and therefore common-ly regarded as more cerebral or 'intellectual' than the Romantic compositions of the following century. She might therefore regard it as ideal theme-music for a brains trust or quiz programme. But its characteristics have other possibilities. The 'period' quality of both the harpsichord and the music is unmistakable and might lend itself to a programme about history or antiques. Alternatively the 'tinny' tone of the instrument combined with the rhythmic nature of the piece might introduce a children's programme about toys or music boxes or with a faery or fantasy theme. You can doubtless imagine other possibilities for yourself, and I would simply make two further points.

The first is that depending on the specific contents of the programmes I have suggested, it would be possible to discern all three modes of signification in such theme-music – the symbolic, the indexical and the iconic.

Second, I would stress that these are *extrinsic* meanings of the music: we could not say that it is 'about' cerebration or history or toys. Another way we might describe them is as 'associative' meanings: in a serial, for instance, the theme-music will bring to the listener's mind what he already knows about the story-line: even more than this, it is a 'paradigm' of that *genre* of programme (Fiske and Hartley 1978: 169).

This function of music as a framing mechanism and the two following functions are noticed by Goffman (1980: 164–5).

Music as a link

Snatches of music are often heard between the scenes of a radio play or the items of a programme. They are analogous to curtain drops in the theatre, since they keep certain aspects of the programme apart and may additionally signal advertising breaks. But as well as keeping apart they bridge the changes of scene or subject, thus providing a kind of continuity.

'Mood' music

Such music is sometimes heard during a play. It acts as a background enhancement which is understood not to be heard by the characters, but is heard by the listeners as a clue to the characters' feelings or thoughts. The provision of both 'mood' and 'links' could be seen as symbolic, but there is another which Goffman appears to overlook.

Music as a stylized sound effect

This music is part of the stock-in-trade of radio drama, where it is used to simulate sounds that occur in the real world – storms or battles, for instance. It is understood that the characters also 'hear' this music, but not in its own form, only as the naturalistic sound – the storm, battle or whatever – that it is meant to evoke. Such music has an imitative function and is a sort of iconic index.

Music in an indexical function

This is music as part of the ordinary sounds of the world which radio portrays. These sounds are usually known collectively as 'actuality'. Here is a typical example from a news programme:

FADE IN SOUND OF BAGPIPES AND DRUMS
Presenter: The Band of the Argyll and Sutherland Highlanders, who were today granted the freedom of Aldershot.

The semiotic function of the music would be much the same whether it were live actuality from the freedom ceremony, or a recording of the actuality, or simply taken from a gramophone record (radio producers often 'cheat'). In the first instance the music would be indexical and in the other two instances the recordings would simply be acting as icons of the sounds the band was making at the ceremony – sounds which are an index of its presence. They would therefore be iconic indexes.

SILENCE

Though it is natural for us to speak of radio as a sound medium we should remember that the *absence* of sound can also be heard. It is therefore important to consider silence as a form of signification. It has both negative and positive functions which seem to be indexical.

Its negative function is to signify that for the moment at least, nothing is happening on the medium: there is a void, what broadcasters sometimes refer to as 'dead air'. In this function silence can resemble noise (that is, sounds, words and music) in acting as a framing mechanism, for it can signify the integrity of a programme or item by making a space around it. But if the silence persists for more than a few seconds it signifies the dysfunction or non-functioning of the medium: either transmitter or receiver has broken down or been switched off.

The positive function of silence is to signify that something is happening which for one reason or another cannot be expressed in noise. Because radio silence is total (unlike film and theatrical silences, which are visually filled) it can be a potent stimulus to the listener, providing a gap in the noise for his imagination to work: 'Pass me the bottle. Cheers . . . Ah, that's better!'

But such silences or pauses can suggest not only physical actions but abstract, dramatic qualities; they can generate pathos or irony by confirming or countering the words which surround them. They can also generate humour, as in a famous radio skit which featured Jack Benny, a comedian with a reputation for extreme miserliness:

> The skit consists of a confrontation between Benny and a mugger on the street. Says the mugger: 'Your money or your life'. Prolonged pause: growing laughter; then applause as the audience gradually realises what Benny *must* be thinking, and eventually responds to the information communicated by the silence and to its comic implications.

(Fink 1981: 202)

How, then, does the listener discriminate among these various negative and positive functions of silence? His guide is clearly the context – in the first instance whether any noise frames the silence and in the second, what that noise signifies.

THE PRIMARY CODE OF RADIO

In fact context (as will by now be clear) is the key to the meaning of the sounds, music and silences of radio – and the means by which the context is established is at bottom *verbal*. Sound conventions can indicate the relative importance of the different strands of radio content by means of levels and fades, but they cannot explain the *nature* of that importance. On the other hand we have seen that silence and sounds draw not only their meaning but in some cases their very identity from the words around them.

It is clear too that in its ancillary function music also requires the clarification of words, for music alone will not be able to tell us whether we are about to hear a brains trust or a history programme or a children's fantasy; and even when music is broadcast as a background enhancer it is not clear without the words in the foreground precisely what is being enhanced.

But with respect to music which is broadcast for its own sake our case is harder to argue because the peculiar semantic status of music has somewhat contrasting implications. If it is at least agreed that music does not enshrine the kind of meaning that words do, there is an evident need to set it in a verbal context: it is not 'self-sufficient'. But on the other hand it could be argued from the same premise that music is literally inexplicable and therefore entirely self-sufficient: and it is surely true that music is much less parasitic upon context than sounds are. A series of shuffling or clicking noises divorced from their visual or verbal surroundings will leave us totally baffled as to their nature and significance; but a piece of music is instantly recognizable as music and can be fully appreciated as such, even if we have never heard it before and have no inkling as to what it is or who composed it. Public sound-systems in restaurants, airports and supermarkets pump out continuous 'muzak' with no attempt at verbal contextualization.

Nevertheless there seems to be a deep and abiding impulse to explain or identify music – an impulse that no radio station ignores entirely. If we are interested in any kind of music our first desire is to know what it is, even if the answer is an unrevealing *Symphony in G*. Moreover it is clear that because the inherent meaning of music is elusive the linguistic context can *invest* it with meaning. A particular rock record will seem progressive and 'heavy' when presented by John Peel, yet bland and 'middle-of-the-road' when announced by Simon Mayo. Nor is this peculiar to pop, but common in music traditionally regarded as 'significant' in both senses of the word. We all know about the bright idea of the marketing man confronted with an album containing such solemn pieces as the *Toccata and Fugue in D Minor*: he boosted its sales by calling it *Bach's Greatest Hits*, and we shall see in Chapter 4 how Classic FM apes the behaviour of the pop and rock stations by running its own 'serious music' chart show as the snappily named 'Classic Countdown'.

It seems reasonable to suggest, then, that the primary code of radio is linguistic, since words are required to contextualize all the other codes. Indeed, our consideration of semiotic codes whether on radio or in any other medium may tempt us to the conclusion that the primary signification of things is *always* verbal – not acoustic or even pictorial. At any rate, we need to look a little more closely at this primary code in terms of radio.

Since the medium is blind the words cannot be *seen* by the receiver but only *heard* by him: hence the linguistic code of radio approximates much more closely to that of *speech* than writing. But there is an important measure of difference. Much radio talk is first written down – scripted. Indeed at one time *all* of it was (Rodger 1982: 44–5), and to that extent it has a *literary* nature. This means that much radio talk is premeditated rather than spontaneous. It is also more explicit than spontaneous speech in that it creates its own context or situation to a much greater extent (Gregory and Carroll 1978: 42–3). It is more fluent, precise and orderly, less diffuse and tautological, than ordinary speech, and the adoption of these literary characteristics can, in a subtle way, make it seem more authoritative (Kress 1986: 407). As well as these advantages scripted talk runs to time and ensures that no important information is omitted or presented out of sequence.

Hence words on the radio could be regarded as the application of oral language to a situation which normally calls for writing, that is, where what is referred to is not simultaneously apparent to sender and receiver since they are separated – remote from and invisible to each other. These words do not constitute conventional orality but what has been termed 'secondary orality' (Ong 1982: 3, 136).

But there is a general convention on the radio that scripted speech does not 'admit' to being scripted. Aspiring broadcasters are taught to regard scripts as the 'storage of talk' (McLeish 1978: 65) and encouraged to work into them expressions which occur less frequently in writing than in speech, 'Well now . . .', 'Come to think of it . . .', the latter an implicit denial that anything has been premeditated. The purpose of such colloquialisms is to discourage the flat, expressionless tone of the unskilled broadcaster who concentrates on the *words* of her script rather than on what they refer to – a problem which does not arise in unscripted talk.

The secret of much apparently impromptu delivery was revealed many years ago in Professor John Hilton's broadcast on how to give a radio talk:

For, of course, I read every word. If only I could pull it off every time – but you have to be at the top of your form. Yes, of course,

every word's on paper even now – this – what I'm saying to you
now – it's all here.

(cit. Cardiff 1980: 31)

Even lectures on Radio 3 are usually described as 'talks' to deflect
attention from the fact that they are read.

Why should reading disguise itself as spontaneous talk? The act
of reading implies *absence* – the separation of addresser and
addressee. The addresser has been replaced by a text, so that if a
radio listener is aware that a broadcaster is reading he will assume
that she is either relaying the words of somebody else or erecting
a barrier between herself and her audience. Hence to avoid
creating this impression of absence and impersonality much radio
talk which is actually scripted – programme presentation, weather
forecasts, continuity, cues, trailers and so forth – is delivered as if
it were unscripted and impromptu.

But there are certain kinds of radio talk which are not passed off
as impromptu but announced as being *read*, notably the news
('This is the 6 o'clock news *read* by Brian Perkins') and readings
from novels and stories ('A *Book* at Bedtime'): and while even
within the BBC presentation-styles vary greatly from the rapid
and urgent to the solemn and sedate, I would contend that our
awareness that they are being read derives much more from these
announcements than from any distinctive 'reading tone'. Indeed
in the sense of being a mode of expression analogous to a
'speaking tone' it seems doubtful whether such a thing exists.

I base this contention on the fact that the differences between
orality and literacy seem a good deal less absolute than is
commonly supposed. It has recently been shown that writing
carries a considerable 'oral residue' (Ong 1982: 40–1, 115, 149),
that writers instinctively and inevitably conceive of the word as
primarily a unit of *speech* and their readers as quite literally an
audience. An obvious but not unique example would be a Churchill
or Macaulay, whose oratory was committed to the page but which
always addressed the ear rather than the eye. We revere Shakespeare as a giant of literature, but the major part of his work
consists of plays – plays whose dialogue, however 'literary', was
written to be delivered as if it were spontaneous speech. Such
dialogue is also plentifully enshrined in that genre which is pre-
eminently the child of print, the novel; and even in works which
contain little actual conversation, like *Catcher in the Rye*, there is

often a first-person narrator who addresses the reader throughout in what is highly colloquial language – a fact which is bound to be reflected in any broadcast reading of it.

It could be objected that such an example is atypical, that much literary language is a good deal more formal than Salinger's and that this would be reflected in the tone in which it was read. But formality is not a preserve of literary language: much unscripted *talk* is formal – the off-the-cuff explanations of a teacher, for instance, or the reprimand she might deliver to a pupil. Conversely, the language of radio news, which is self-evidently written down, is formal too: at least it is not colloquial in the sense that Salinger's is. Yet when the newscaster reaches a tragic or humorous item, her voice tone becomes suitably grave or light-hearted, even on Radios 3 and 4. (We might notice in passing that just as words when voiced can evoke a sense of the broadcaster's personality, so the personality of the broadcaster can enhance the words; and of course different personalities may produce subtle differences of expression, which is not to say that their various readings may not be *equally* expressive.)

Formality, then, is not a *lack* of expression, it is not the same thing as a reading tone – and I would argue that what determines the tone of voice is not so much whether a communication has been written down or is spoken extempore as the *purpose* of that communication and the circumstances in which it is delivered. It seems likely that if a reader gives literary language its full expressive value her tone will not be very different from an ordinary speech tone, and that what we are accustomed to describe as a reading tone is really a flat and expressionless preoccupation with the words on the page rather than with what they mean. Since this tone is common among inexperienced broadcasters the measures prescribed by their instructors are understandable: but I would suggest that the tone of the accomplished news or storyreader, whose skill lies in bringing out the full meaning of the words, is virtually indistinguishable from the tone of the ordinary articulate speaker, and is an implicit recognition that writing is merely 'programmed talk' – not separate from speaking but a technological development of it.

But if it is true that a reading tone is not readily detectable among skilled broadcasters, why should news and stories on the radio *declare* themselves to be read? In each case the text must be accorded a primacy (or 'foregrounded', to re-employ this term, this time in its linguistic sense) – though for rather different reasons. In the news the words must carry an air of definitiveness and accuracy; it must seem to be 'authorless' – originated by the events themselves. The impression that the newscaster is extemporizing it would negate its very purpose. She is therefore cued as a news *reader* and is likely to speak with a 'received pronunciation' (RP) so that her reading will maximize the symbolic function – the meaningfulness – of the words while minimizing her voice's function as an index of her personality. By this means it is suggested that she is the mere mouthpiece of the words and not their originator.

In the case of storyreadings the text is also foregrounded but for its beauty, not its truth. It is writing which is in one way or another good enough to act as an object of interest in its own right instead of as a barrier between broadcaster and listener – of more interest than the broadcaster's own words. Its literariness is declared as the main justification for the programme and it is the reader's function to express that literariness, or linguistic beauty, in whatever manner seems appropriate.

Yet even when the listener is aware that the words on the radio are being read to him he must still be able to grasp their meaning through the *ear*, an organ which is a good deal less comprehending than the eye, particularly when deprived of the help which it receives from the other organs in most acts of interpersonal communication. The cause of this lack of comprehension has been eloquently defined:

> Sound exists only when it is going out of existence. It is not simply perishable but essentially evanescent, and it is sensed as evanescent. When I pronounce the word 'permanence', by the time I get to the '-nence', the 'perma-' is gone, and has to be gone.
>
> (Ong 1982: 32)

This is another reason why the scripted nature of radio talk is rarely acknowledged, for it is a general truth that much language is written down precisely because its meaning is too complex to be assimilated by ear, and the listener's awareness that it is read is therefore likely to make him feel that he will be unable to follow it. And it is certainly the case that radio language will not be easily followed unless it is syntactically fairly simple or else fairly concrete in subject-matter. The descriptions of physical phenomena which are characteristic of novels, stories and even news items, their preoccupation with personalities, utterances and events – all this lends itself to radio. So too do ideas, opinions and arguments when expressed in the syntax of spontaneous speech. But when these ideas and arguments become more abstract and their expression is premeditated, or when they require sustained explanation or specialist knowledge, the radio medium is less effective (McWhinnie 1959: 49–50).

The BBC's Audience Research Department once tested a group of people on how much they could understand of a talk intended for the 'average' Light Programme listener: the average listener in the group could correctly answer only 28 per cent of the questions which were asked about the talk after it was broadcast (Silvey 1974: 141). Indeed it has been observed that the importance of the radio interviewer is not only as the poser of questions but as the interpreter of answers, the 'plain man' who in brief paraphrases renders the complex or specialist responses of the expert into language intelligible to the lay public (Cardiff 1980: 38).

It will be helpful to summarize our findings so far. Much radio talk is 'literary' in the sense that it has first been written down, but with certain notable exceptions it suppresses these literary origins and even when it does not its expression must be simple or concrete enough to be comprehended through the ear alone. Its messages will therefore tend to have a high level of *redundancy* (Ong 1982: 39–40; Fiske 1990: 11–13) – that is, material which is predictable or conventional; for speech is notoriously evanescent, as are all signs that exist in time. The listener has no chance of retrieval; he cannot introduce his own redundancy as a reader can by reading something twice.

Radio language is, then, very similar to that of television, which Fiske and Hartley have characterized as an intersection of oral and literary language (1978: 160): but the main differences are that the linguistic code of television has rather less to do in establishing context or situation, since much of this can be done visually, and it is potentially more 'literary' in the sense that it can and frequently does appear on the screen in the form of writing – as captions, tables, and so on.

Yet within the overall conditions created by the medium's blindness – conditions which make themselves felt to varying degrees in different kinds of programmes – the linguistic code of radio is capable of the same variety of function as ordinary speech:

Even by comparison with its sister medium of television, it is chaotically eclectic in the hospitality it affords to different kinds of language. The formal rhetoric of Churchill's wartime speeches would surely have sounded phoney if one had been able to watch him making them on television; radio allowed them their necessary distance and resonance. At the other end of the scale, the introduction of the phone-in programme a few years ago soon made one accustomed to hearing voices on the radio speaking as informally, often as inarticulately, as if one had heard them drifting through one's window from the street. In the course of an hour spent as an idle radio listener, twiddling between stations, one drifts from the most elaborate and carefully scripted language through every shade and tone to the most unofficial and unrehearsed grunts and squawks. On radio there is no median register, no particular way of speaking that could be said to represent the medium in neutral gear, ticking over. . . . Radio is by turns gossipy, authoritative, preachy, natural, artificial, confidential, loudly public, and not infrequently, wordless. Its languages bleed into one another.

(Raban 1981: 86–7)

We can take a more systematic look at this functional variety by using a familiar communication-model – that of Roman Jakobson (1960: 350–7). Many other models exist which could also be used (McQuail and Windahl 1981) but Jakobson's has the merit of simplicity and flexibility. It arranges the six elements which he regards as making up the communication act (and which we have already identified in Chapter 1) in the following fashion:

	context	
sender	message	receiver
	contact	
	code	

If, as Jakobson asserts, one or other of these six elements is always dominant in a single act of communication, not only can we classify the act according to which of the elements is dominant –

	referential	
emotive	aesthetic	conative
	phatic	
	metalingual	

– but where that dominance is sustained over a series of acts of communication we can develop in radio terms an analogous theory of programme types or genres.

For instance, radio language whose dominant function is primarily *referential*, whose orientation is towards the context of the real world, is language which is characteristic of news and documentary programmes or of commentaries on public events. On the other hand, chat-shows or interview programmes such as *Start the Week* and *Desert Island Discs* are dominated by an *emotive* use of language in the sense that the guests are encouraged to talk about themselves, their feelings and their attitudes to life. Radio is also capable of *conative*, persuasive or rhetorical, functions – most conspicuously in commercials or 'public service' notices advising road safety, for example, but also in party political broadcasts. On the other hand, the broadcasting of plays, storytellings and poetry-readings foregrounds the message for its own sake, for its inherent literary merits, and is therefore characterized by language in its *aesthetic* function.

Two further points should be made. First it is important not to push these classifications and the distinctions between them too far. Educational programmes might be generally recognizable by their predominantly referential language, but in making occasional use of drama or poetry-readings can also be characterized by language whose dominant function is aesthetic. And in a comic play it may be hard at times to decide whether the dominant function is conative – to make the audience laugh – or aesthetic – to foreground the 'message' for its own sake. The second point is that there is, of course, nothing exclusively radiogenic about such classifications: the Jakobson model could be used to classify forms of writing or television in much the same way.

I would, however, wish to suggest that there is one kind of programme classifiable in terms of this model which, if not peculiar to radio, was at least originated by it and is of unique significance therein: the phone-in. I shall be arguing in Chapter 9 that the purpose of the phone-in is to attempt the ultimately impossible feat of providing feedback for the listener and that the dominant function of the programme is therefore phatic and metalingual. In other words the phone-in enables radio broadcasters to create the illusion of a two-way medium and to verify both that they have an audience and that the audience is capable of responding to the codes they transmit. But in order to demonstrate this I have to stretch the Jakobson model somewhat, since it does not accommodate the notion of feedback: for once the receiver responds to the sender their roles – and the model – have been reversed, the receiver is now the sender. But if we were to regard the original situation as persisting and the radio phone-caller's remarks as a *response* to the broadcaster's communication rather than a part of it, the function of that response is both *phatic* – a demonstration that the audience is 'present' and can hear the radio message – and *metalingual* – that it is capable of understanding and even contributing to it.

Such a concept of the phone-in does of course imply some divergence between what is actually and what is only apparently the dominant function of its language. The apparent function of a phone-in on the subject of nuclear energy may be to allow the listeners to become broadcasters and air their views in an emotive or conative way, like the speakers on *Any Questions?*; but its actual function will simply be to demonstrate that the radio station has many listeners and that they are responsive to the publicity which it chooses to afford to such an issue.

Yet even if it is the case that phone-ins exist primarily to demonstrate the presence and understanding of an audience rather than to ascertain what any individual member of that audience may think, it might still be doubted whether they are of unique significance to radio. The other mass media are equally bereft of feedback in the real sense, and television has also made use of the phone-in to create a semblance thereof. But I would argue that in none of the other media, with their images or visible texts, are the phatic and metalingual considerations – the need for feedback to the communicator – so pressing or persistent.

In Chapters 4 to 9 I shall be looking at various kinds of radio programmes which seem to use the medium in illuminating ways, and in Chapter 10 at radio audiences and the functions the medium has for them.

SUGGESTIONS FOR FURTHER WORK

Form a small group with your fellow-students – say, five or six of you – and each write a two-minute 'voicepiece' or radio talk (360 words maximum) on any subject which will suit the length and the medium.

Remember that your listeners will not be able to see you or your text and will be 'absent'. Its register should therefore be conversational, rather like that of a letter you might write to a friend, and it should be 'chatted' to the microphone – *performed* rather than merely read out. McLeish (1978) provides invaluable hints on writing for radio.

When you have written your piece rehearse it *aloud* to ensure that it reads easily and effectively. The group members should record their pieces in isolation, then re-group for playback and evaluation. The less experienced and more nervous you are at the microphone, the more likely it is that your remarks will sound 'literary', like those of an essay, your voice tone impersonal and 'read', and your delivery hurried. But you might notice how quickly you can improve with practice. Your eventual aim might be to see if you can make your talk sound so 'warm' and natural that you can convince an uninitiated listener that it was extemporized!

Chapter 4

Talk and music radio

Into the car, go to work and I'm cruisin'
I never think that I'll blow all my fuses
Traffic flows – into the breakfast show. . .
AM – FM, I feel so ecstatic now
It's music I've found
And I'm wired for sound.

('Wired for Sound' sung by Cliff Richard)

We noted in Chapter 2 that because of the rise of television and its relegation to an almost wholly secondary or background medium, radio largely abandoned its pattern of varied, separate, 'constructed' programmes, a pattern known as mixed programming, and adopted instead 'streamed' programming, output of one particular and predictable type organized into strips or sequences, each lasting several hours.

This continuous, specialized output has become known as 'format' radio, and though there are some all-news formats – LBC Newstalk, for instance, soon to become London News Radio – it consists for the most part of different types of *music* format. This will not surprise us. We noted in Chapter 3 how well suited to radio music is because it is purely acoustic: aside from its lyrics it has meaning only in its sound. Decoding is minimal, we do not have to work out what it 'refers to', as we have to with words: hence it is ideal for secondary listening. It is perhaps the only kind of output we can enjoy on the medium without feeling in some degree handicapped by a lack of vision. Nevertheless music on the radio is never continuous: it is always punctuated, however briefly, by talk. Why?

A preliminary answer is that music alone is insufficiently

meaningful, that the listener needs to have it identified for her in what we have seen is the primary code of words. But given that not all presenters consistently identify the music they are playing, some of which will in any case be well known to the listener, we must look further.

If it is accepted that words are the primary code – and on radio they are always human utterances, never printed signs – this implies that radio, unlike muzak systems or even cassette and CD players, is a 'live', predominantly *personal* medium, and unrelieved music with no visible human origination is dauntingly *im*personal. Even when the music requires no identification there is a need for the human presence, the companionship, that the sound of words entails, even though it may only be expressed in meeting the practical needs of the listener for information about traffic jams or concert dates.

For many listeners, then, the alternation of music and talk seems the ideal radio output in a television age, characterizing even those formats which are nominally all-music; but for the student of radio it creates a paradox. However pleasant in itself, it seems in its basic form of a presenter and what are usually recordings – vinyl records, cassettes, tapes, compact discs – to be something of an impoverishment of the medium, a mere fraction of what sound broadcasting is capable of: the plays, comedies, outside broadcasts, quiz shows, features, documentaries and so on, that have largely been ceded to television. It apparently consists of long stretches of the same thing in which the only real variations are the changes of presenter – a kind of acoustic prairie where there are no natural features to mark the boundaries, merely the arbitrary fences of those who are working it.

On the other hand when the pieces of music are short, as on rock stations or classical stations offering only 'bites' or excerpts such output has an infinite ability to incorporate *extra* programming elements such as adverts, jingles proclaiming the station or the presenter, news summaries, weather and travel reports, competitions, studio interviews or discussions, trailers, phone-ins, live music sessions and so on, and thus seems a virtual matrix of those traditional programme genres it has replaced. In miniature all radio is here: the snatch of dialogue in an advert is a tiny play or sitcom; the location report in a news bulletin is a brief commentary or outside broadcast; the on-air telephone caller answering a competition question is one of a series of challengers in an intermittent quiz show.

In later chapters we shall explore some of these traditional genres in their own right. Here I wish to look at the basic talk and music combination – not in detail at the different kinds of music format and the particular audiences they might target, for that has been done elsewhere (Fornatale and Mills 1980: 67–88; Barnard 1989: 158–77; Barnett and Morrison 1989: 30–40), but at its generic features. I shall begin with the monologue that punctuates the music and shall apply to it the usefully vague term 'presentation' – vague because what is being presented might be the music or a studio guest, or many other things including in effect the presenter himself. I shall look at the differing relationships the presenters may make with the music and at how they overcome the limitations of the medium to forge a relationship with the listener; and lastly I shall assess the effectiveness of radio presentation in comparison with that of television.

The discussion will then move from the talk to the music and consider the phenomenally successful partnership that radio has maintained with recorded music over the past forty years or so – a partnership which has been crucial to the formation of modern popular culture. I shall be arguing that this is not simply because recorded music has become a central part of so many people's lives but because records on the radio have been an unusual and striking demonstration of the power of advertising; and in subsequently promoting through a variety of media the many other products of popular culture – fashions, films, computer games and so on – advertising has itself become a thing of prestige and intellectual interest *within* that culture. I shall conclude with a brief look at Britain's first national commercial station, Classic FM, and its attempt to apply to music of a different kind a mode of presentation that has been so successful in respect of rock and pop. And in doing all these things, I hope to show how a close analysis of the sound medium and its conventions can yield useful insights into the broader cultural context.

To return to the presenter. As we might expect the ways in which he frames the music are variable, depending first of all on his listeners' requirements but also on the kind of music he is playing, the time of day he is playing it, and on his own personality. At one extreme there will be listeners who will expect the companionship afforded by the presenter to extend no further than the identification of what he is playing. He will establish only an indirect relationship with them by focusing on the music and on those who are performing it, and perhaps also by reading out any listeners' requests for it. His approach is what we would describe in terms of the Jakobson model as 'referential'. Until the arrival of Classic FM in 1992 this was especially characteristic of classical music presentation, on the assumption that the music is too important, the listeners' interest in it too serious and specific, for it to be mediated through a 'personality' presenter.

At the other extreme there is the presenter who makes a direct relationship with the listener in the sense that he is not circumscribed by the music he plays. He feels free to talk about other things – his own experiences or observations on life, perhaps, or on some story he has read in the papers. This essentially self-expressive approach is what Jakobson terms 'emotive'. Not surprisingly, the emotive presenter tends to play music to which his listeners need no detailed introduction – music which is or has been in the Top Forty. These listeners will prefer pop to other kinds of output, but their interest in it is unlikely to be specific or well informed: they enjoy 'music' rather than particular songs or bands, and with a fairly generous measure of the presenter's company. The emotive presenter is therefore likely to host prime-time shows, whereas presenters with a more referential approach tend to occupy the margins of the broadcasting schedule, playing new releases or less well-known, more specialist music in shows at 'unsocial' hours of the night or weekend.

In practice, of course, almost all presenters combine these approaches in some degree. The most referential and self-effacing presenter will afford a modicum of companionship to the listener simply by being heard, a point we shall return to in Chapter 6; and his most emotive and self-assertive counterpart will probably identify at least some of the records he presents (though in a random hour's listening to Simon Bates on BBC Radio 1 I heard him name only *two* of the twelve records he played!). But in terms of Radio 1, for instance, we might trace a spectrum from the likes of John Peel and Johnny Walker at the referential, music-focused extreme, through Jakki Brambles and Mark Goodier somewhere in the middle, to the likes of Nicky Campbell and Steve Wright at the emotive, self-assertive extreme.

Perhaps the best example of the self-assertive presenter on Radio 1 until his departure in 1993 was Simon Bates. Much of

Bates's talk was of broad relevance to the music in that he relayed a great deal of pop and show-biz gossip: but it seldom related directly to the individual records he played, and in his 'Our Tune' spot he used the music to support the words he read out – a reversal of the norm in which, if they relate to it at all, the words support the music (Montgomery 1991: 154). In *The Steve Wright Show* the talk between records – comic sketches, trails, studio chat on some issue, 'true stories', weather reports and so on – bears no relation to them, thus providing a kind of counterpoint to the music. In a similar example of the independence of talk from the music it frames, Adrian Juste intercuts records with clips from the sound-tracks of comedy shows.

But whatever their relationship to the music, all presenters have to cope with the exigencies of the medium in making their relationship with the listeners. As we saw in Chapter 1, radio is a fusion of mass and personal modes of communication – 'mass' in the sense that its audience is numerous, 'personal' in the sense that the members of that audience mostly listen to it as individuals in their own separate spaces. There has been much interesting discussion of the language that broadcasters use to combine these two modes (Moss and Higgins 1984; Montgomery 1986; Scannell 1991: 1–3).

Montgomery points out that unlike the newsreader's or narrator's characteristic use of the third person, the music presenter establishes a direct relationship with the listener by focusing on the axis of the first and second persons 'I' and 'you'. Nevertheless since his listeners are numerous the field of reference of 'you' is constantly shifting from individuals who are identified by name, region, occupation or whatever, to the whole, indeterminate audience; but no element of the latter is ever really excluded and often two audiences are being simultaneously addressed (1986: 424–7). The listenership is reached as a mass, but through a second-person mode of address which is informal, intimate, ostensibly directed at a single individual. This intimacy is, of course, established in large part by the manner of delivery, the tone and pitch of the presenter's voice; but as Montgomery observes (1986: 429) it can also be created explicitly through such 'response-demanding' utterances as 'How are you today?' – a question which could not obtain separately discoverable answers from a mass audience.

Of course the television presenter must cope with the similar exigencies that his medium imposes, for he too is unable to see his mass audience: but the audience, at least, can see him. On the face of it, then, the companionship that a radio presenter can provide seems, however 'inevitable' it may be, to be fairly limited: yet in this as in much else, what in one respect are radio's deficiencies turn out in another to be its strengths. The radio presenter is at once actual and imaginary – an audible reality directly presented, yet someone who must be created inside the listener's head. In this sense he is much less of a 'companion' than the television presenter because he exists only as a voice – to use our semiotic terms, as an *index* of himself from which the listener must construct a complete person. But in another sense he is much *more* of a companion because the listener can fashion him as she wants him, free from all those blemishes and shortcomings that would be declared in his appearance; and this companionship is nourished not simply by the blindness of the medium but its secondariness – by the fact that he is often able to accompany her in many more areas of her existence and for longer stretches of time than a television presenter could, and to that extent provides a more constant and intimate presence.

This assimilation of radio to the patterns of daily life explains why it is such a 'banal' medium – its output not so much an escape from the passage of time, which television's often is, as a pleasant way of *marking* it. To strengthen their rapport with the audience the presenters often use points of reference within its expected daily routines – the 'Tea at Three' spot or 'Mid Morning Coffee Break' – and devise programme titles such as *The Breakfast Show* and *The Drive Time Show* (Hobson 1980: 106) within which there will be additional markers such as hourly news summaries to help the listeners structure their day. But the medium is not banal pure and simple, for the combination of a constant and somewhat idealized companion with the emotional power of the music serves to tinge the workaday world of the listener with glamour and excitement. Indeed it has been pointed out that in pop music formats at least, the presenter acts not simply as an associate of the music but as a kind of broker between it and the mundane concerns of his listeners, for he

> fuses together the very latest list of 'Top Ten' records through a welter of jokes and chat, creating an atmosphere in which other items (news, weather reports, traffic information, sports results)

can be handled as if they too generated the same immediate excitement.

(Armes 1988: 109)

As part of this purpose Radio 1 presenters usually hold rock music under the travel reports they read out, especially on drive-time shows.

On television too there is a fair amount of personalized music presentation, but it does not seem to make the same impression on the audience – even when, as in its most famous example, *Top of the Pops* (BBC 1), the presenters are already well known to us from radio. Vision seems to diminish and distance them, and they cannot accompany us in our usual range of activities. This perhaps explains why Music Television (MTV) often dispenses with presenters and uses visual forms of presentation instead, screening music videos 'back-to-back' – that is, without spoken links – and identifying them by graphics and captions. Radio, on the other hand, can manage no more than about four records played back-to-back. Even so, the often unmediated and 'visual' music of MTV is not to everybody's taste. Lacking a spoken context it seems to some to be relentlessly impersonal and indifferent to its audience: with all its images it remains remote and automated – not something which the viewer can easily absorb into the mundane patterns of her existence.

The talk and music combination is, then, very effective on the radio, but why is the latter almost entirely *recorded* music? In fact radio made relatively little use of records (which I shall henceforth use as a term to embrace vinyl platters, reel-to-reel tapes, audio-cassettes and compact discs) until it was more than thirty years old. This is because during that period it was the major mass medium and as such obliged to carry a whole range of programming, not just music. But in any case it strove to broadcast *live* music as often as possible, in the belief that it should be offering original performances to its listeners rather than what they could already obtain commercially. In 1945 the gramophone record was still being regarded within the BBC as an 'understudy' to live music (Barnard 1989: 27).

What forced radio to make much greater use of recorded music was, of course, television: music, because as we have seen it is ideal for secondary listening; records, because they are cheap, enabling stations to dispense with their own bands and orchestras.

This trend began in the United States, where the major networks turned their energies to television straight after the Second World War. The proportion of stations unaffiliated to a major network increased from 18 per cent in 1946 to 47 per cent by 1952 (Chapman 1992: 12–13), and even affiliated stations were required to originate more of their own programming (Barnard 1989: 35). Unable to afford live broadcasts or syndicated programmes recorded by famous bands, the smaller stations relied increasingly on gramophone records.

But what was originally conceived as a mere substitute for live music soon came to seem in many ways preferable to it. First of all, records offered a rich variety, an eclecticism, that could not be matched by live music. There were physical as well as financial limits to the assortment of individuals and bands that could be squeezed into a studio, and so live shows consisting of just one or two musical acts appeared pointlessly restricted, however good they might be in themselves. The peculiar appeal of the record show for the listener was, and indeed still is, the sense of the presenter in a pleasant, womb-like void, able to conjure up any kind of musical or non-musical sound from an isolated voice or single instrument to massed orchestras or the roar of a stadium crowd. And a void is in essence what a studio is – an acoustic canvas on which any imaginable sound can be painted and mixed with others. This is where the spirit of radio now seems to reside, especially as television has annexed almost every other space.

The second advantage perceived in records was that their musical quality is often better than that of live music. Mistakes are eliminated and the record usually represents the best performance that the artists are capable of – a performance that can be recaptured any number of times. Third, the listeners were hearing something which unlike an evanescent, live performance they could purchase for themselves and play at any time.

During the 1950s and 1960s a famous and lasting marriage was made between rock and pop records on the one hand and commercial radio (which in Britain meant Radio Luxembourg and the offshore pirates) on the other; and since it has had enormous implications for modern popular culture we need to examine the medium for the reasons it has been so successful.

In any station which derives its income from advertising the paramount consideration is, of course, the commercial breaks. What determines their frequency and length? They must be frequent enough and long enough to please the advertisers, yet not frequent enough or long enough to displease the listeners. In this respect pop songs and rock 'n'roll tracks have been a godsend to commercial radio. First they are all of roughly similar length, or rather brevity. This means that the commercial breaks can be at fairly regular intervals and that (subject of course to statutory controls) these intervals can be relatively short – something which is important in a blind, temporal medium like radio, where messages are easily ignored or forgotten.

Second, the individual pop or rock record is of broadly comparable duration to the commercial break – a duration to which news presentation can also be made to conform as 'capsule' news. Thus commercial radio output typically consists of a string of acoustic beads, a sequence of records interspersed with commercial breaks, presenter's talk, news, weather information and so on – each 'bead' of approximately similar length to the others and lasting no more than a few moments. For this kind of output I shall borrow the term 'segmentation' which has been coined in relation to television programming (Ellis 1982: 116–26). It is true that Ellis sees almost all broadcast output as segmented – ultimately divisible into 'bites' consisting of a scene in a play, an advert, a statement from an interviewee, and so on: but the term seems particularly useful here because the segments which make up talk and music sequences on the radio are much more apparent, more discrete and detachable, than those which co-operate in a 'built' programme such as a play or documentary. To a far greater extent they can be added, subtracted or reordered without discernible damage to the whole.

In Chapter 10 we shall be looking at its practical benefits for the radio listener, but here I want to begin with the fact that the evident aim of this segmentation is to homogenize the output in order to make the commercial breaks and the informational content seem as entertaining as the pop songs and rock 'n' roll tracks. We noticed earlier that one function of the presenter's chat is to invest such items as weather and travel information with the glamour and excitement of the music, and at one level the segmentation achieves much the same thing for these and for the commercials: but I would suggest that the overall effect is more complicated because records themselves have a profoundly ambivalent status on the radio. They are undeniably entertainment, the primary reason we listen, and the largest part of the stations' output, from which the latter derive no income as they do from the adverts in the commercial breaks. Nevertheless the assimilation of the commercials to the music also reminds us that at another level the records are advertisements every bit as much as the conventional commercials which punctuate them; for when we hear a record on the radio we are hearing what is in effect an invitation to buy a product that is available in the shops.

It has often been said that in Britain especially, radio advertising has been slow to develop. In one sense this is true and the reasons are apparent. Whereas commercial television dates from 1955, home-based commercial radio was not heard until 1973, and on a national frequency, not until 1992. But this overlooks the fact that since records became the mainstream of radio's output some thirty or more years ago, most of the editorial content of the medium has been indistinguishable from advertising, even in those ostensibly non-commercial stations like BBC Radio 1: what from one perspective is entertainment for the public is from another a sequence of adverts for the record companies. Indeed so closely is the broadcasting of records bound up with advertising and promotion, and so glamorous and effective have these activities thus become, that Radio 1, although allegedly 'commercial-free', adopts a highly segmented mode of presentation which includes a variety of adverts of another kind – trailers for the station's own programmes (I counted no less than seven of these in a single hour of the *Simon Bates Show*); competitions which are in effect promotions for concerts since they offer tickets as prizes; and public service adverts offering advice to the young jobless, those with sexual or drug problems, and so on. These are all forms of advertising that are conformable with the station's public service obligations, and the BBC would no doubt argue that many of them promote worthier causes than conventional commercials do: but my point is that they quite consciously follow the commercials in style, duration and frequency. It should certainly not be inferred that because BBC Radio 1 is commercial-free it broadcasts more music than its rivals!

It is worth reviewing the reasons why records are such an effective form of advertising on the radio. To begin with, they have to overcome less consumer inertia or resistance than, for instance, adverts for paper tissues or oven cleaner, since they promote a product which is not dully utilitarian but designed for pleasure or gratification. Second, unlike adverts for other pleasurable products such as sweets or foreign holidays, the advertising of a record on the radio does not have to bridge a credibility gap between itself and the product. Radio adverts for sweets or holidays may be entertaining, as indeed those for tissues or oven cleaners may be, but in both instances they cannot provide any of the satisfactions afforded by the products themselves. The adverts are one thing, the products quite another. But in the case of records played on the radio, advert and product are one and the same thing: what you hear is what you get.

This technique of self-advertisement (in which, to use our semiotic terms, the product acts as an *icon* of itself) is relatively rare, but it is by no means unknown: in various media other products can be used to promote themselves. On the radio another self-advertisement we might encounter is for a car-alarm; on the television we might see a film-clip advertising a cinema movie or commercially available video; and on the door-mat we might be regaled by a free sachet of coffee powder or shampoo. But with the possible exception of the latter it seems to be the case that these samples cannot provide the satisfactions contained in the products themselves: indeed they would *fail* as adverts if they did so to any extent, because the whole point of advertising is to arouse desire – to prompt us to buy that which is advertised – not to gratify it. The noise of the car-alarm we hear on the radio cannot be used for this purpose in real life; if effective, the film-clip will make us want to see the whole movie; and the idea of the coffee sachet is to tempt us to buy the full jar (though we might find it pleasant enough in itself without wishing for any more).

We should remind ourselves at this point that the record we hear on the radio is also only a 'sample' of the full purchasable product. Even if it is a best-selling single the station is likely to play only the A side, but the product itself, the record, will consist of two sides (although sometimes the B side is nothing more than a second version of the first). Obviously this is not to deny that people will often buy a record for the A side alone: at the very least they are buying it in order to be able to play the hit song in their own time. With the recent decline in the sale of singles and the commensurate rise in album sales, the isolated tracks that people hear on the radio constitute an even smaller sample of the total product – though again, they are quite likely to buy the latter merely on the strength of enjoying the sample they have heard.

But the real point I wish to make is that unlike certain other self-advertising products such as our car-alarm or film-clip, the record we hear on the radio provides an entirely sufficient and satisfying experience in its own right, however much it may tempt us to go out and buy the single or the entire album. It is a complete aesthetic unit, a song, and that relatively rare thing, an advert that may indeed gratify our desire as well as stimulate it. There can be no doubt that radio (and more recently television) has provided a colossal stimulus to pop-record sales; but many of us are still happy to treat these records on the radio as mere entertainment with no thought of going out to buy them.

For precisely this reason the record companies and the radio stations have never quite been able to determine who should be paying whom for their services, so finely poised are the economic laws of supply and demand. The stations supply air-time and demand recorded entertainment to fill it, the companies supply recorded entertainment and demand air-time to advertise it. The latter claim that their sales are often harmed by excessive air-play and choose to see records as editorial content–entertainment for which they should be paid royalties by the stations. They assert that the broadcasting of records would still cost much less than the hire of live bands, and their case has prevailed in Britain, where the radio stations are obliged to make payment. But the issue remains vexatious. A few years ago, the Association of Independent Radio Contractors (AIRC) complained that the payment was inherently unjust, that it placed a heavy burden on stations going to air for the first time, and that it gave an unfair advantage to an Irish station which could be heard in Britain, but which paid much lower royalties because it was subject to different copyright law (Wroe 1988: 15).

In the United States, on the other hand, the promotional value of radio to the record companies has been so freely acknowledged that the question of whether stations should pay royalties has never seriously arisen (Barnard 1989: 94). The general view is that the stations are providing the record companies with free advertising for their products (Fornatale and Mills 1980: 44). Indeed judging from the activities of 'pluggers', who attempt to secure air-time for particular records, and the sporadic revelations of 'payola', bribes offered to radio presenters to put certain records on their play-lists, it is advertising for which the companies might reasonably be expected to pay. In the mid-1950s the two major British firms, EMI and Decca, were quite willing to do so: they each acquired their own shows on Radio Luxembourg for the exclusive promotion of their products – 'the novelty being that the product advertised was *itself* the entertainment provided' (Barnard 1989: 33–4).

I would suggest that the success of radio (and only latterly television) in making records sell in such vast numbers, yet in the same process affording pleasure and entertainment to its listeners, is as responsible as anything for the glamour and fascination which advertising has acquired in our culture. The specific achievement of music radio is to have helped nourish the idea that as well as its designated function almost everything acts as a unit of advertising or publicity for itself – an idea that has culminated in the vogue for 'designer' clothing; for just as on radio records act as adverts for themselves, in the visible world designer clothes do likewise by virtue of their external labels, logos and stylistic idiosyncrasies, thus achieving an ironic reversal of the traditional arrangement whereby it was the manufacturer and not the consumer who paid for the privilege of advertising the product. At a more serious level the status of advertising seems also to have helped stimulate a philosophical interest in systems of signs and signification generally, one manifestation of which is the modern study of semiotics or semiology which we considered in the last chapter.

Finally we must look at how commercial radio treats classical music – a pertinent task since this is what is being broadcast by the first home-based national commercial station to be licensed in Britain, Classic FM, which went to air in September 1992. We should, however, remember that for many years there has been another national station specializing in classical music, the non-commercial BBC Radio 3, and it is helpful to compare their modes of presentation.

We must begin by reminding ourselves of what advertisers like in radio – regular commercial breaks which occur as frequently as the listeners (and the Radio Authority) will tolerate. The problem is that classical music is a good deal less susceptible to this treatment than pop music is: classical pieces are not of roughly uniform length as pop songs are, but are almost all very much longer and fall into a variety of genres – sonatas, symphonies, operas, concertos, oratorios, and so on. The problem is not insurmountable: even lengthy works have their natural breaks into which commercials can be dropped, and Classic FM broadcasts full concerts as part of its daily output. Nevertheless its prime-time shows are highly segmented, comprising in addition to the music, chat, fairly frequent advertising breaks, news, weather and travel summaries, trailers and so on. But the only kinds of music that can be accommodated within this structure are short pieces or mere excerpts from longer works, and so the music on the prime-time shows is highly miscellaneous, a pot-pourri of genres and composers ranging from bits of Bach concertos and snatches of operas to madrigals, plainsong and Viennese waltzes.

What kind of listener are these shows – and by implication the station itself, since they go out at the times it will build its core audience – seeking to appeal to? Not the connoisseur, for she will know the provenance of the music, including the works from which the excerpts are taken and which, at *any* time in its daily schedule, Radio 3 is prepared to broadcast in full. For her, the musical diet of these Classic FM shows is like the offer of a tray of snacks to someone craving a full meal – or, to take an even closer analogy, like asking the devotee of the serious rock music played by John Peel or Johnny Walker to settle for the bland chart songs of *The Steve Wright Show*. I suggested earlier that the listener to Steve Wright probably has a general liking for pop and rock music but is not greatly informed about it: likewise the putative listener to prime-time Classic FM appreciates classical music in a general and uninformed way and will enjoy hearing the second movement of a concerto without caring, or even knowing, about its relationship to the unplayed first and third movements.

Despite its musical orientation, then, Classic FM is not in competition with Radio 3: the controller of neither station was impressed by the fact that only three months after its launch it had captured twice as many listeners (Wroe 1993a: 13). It is the pop and rock stations that its bitty, segmented mode of presentation is intended to match, for it is *their* listeners that Classic FM is targeting – those on the one hand who find the likes of Radio 1, Virgin 1215 and ILR too raucous, and those on the other who find the easy listening of Radio 2 (probably its closest rival) a trifle *too* easy.

A hearing of Henry Kelly's morning show or Petroc Trelawny in the afternoon will confirm this. The very titles of such shows would dismay the classical purist, for whereas the full concerts of Radio 3 are likely to be described under the composers' names or in terms of a musical genre or instrument ('The Esztergom International Guitar Festival'), the only names which can lend coherence to these musical miscellanies are the presenters' own, thus giving them an almost blasphemous precedence over the music itself! However, on rock and pop stations the length and number of the songs is such that shows have always had to be named after their presenters.

It is true that Henry Kelly, for instance, acknowledges the greater 'seriousness' of classical music by identifying all the tracks he plays, and that some of them, though short by classical standards, are very long by those of pop (the longest track I heard in a random hour's listening – Mozart's *Divertimento in B Flat Major* – ran for almost ten minutes). But unlike a typical Radio 3 presenter, and like Steve Wright on Radio 1, he does not discuss the music in any detail. It is worth noting at this point that one or two presenters on Classic FM such as Adrian Love and Paul Gambaccini have a background in Radio 1 and other pop stations, and they have clearly been recruited as 'personality' presenters rather than for their knowledge of classical music.

It is important to remember that by no means all pop music presenters say little about the music: we noticed earlier that those such as Johnny Walker and John Peel take it very seriously. But a 'freedom' from the music played and a general informality of style are much more characteristic of pop than of other kinds of presentation, probably because almost by definition pop (that is, 'popular') songs are well known to the listener and need relatively little contextualization, thus allowing the presenter to be more 'companionable' in his own right. As I have already hinted in the case of Radio 1, it is usually on the mainstream, chart-based shows that the emotive, personality presenters are to be found. And on Classic FM Henry Kelly's show is certainly characterized by this kind of presentation, which includes a racing tip, 'Henry's horse', and a sponsored daily recipe delivered by Michael Barry, 'the Crafty Cook'. The implicit message of this and much other presentation on the station is that you don't have to be stuffy or highbrow to enjoy classical music. Its distinctive product could, indeed, be defined as classical music transposed to popular culture – at weekends even matching Radio 1's Top Forty with Paul Gambaccini's Classic Countdown.

As we would expect, the packaging of classical music in this way has provoked a fierce division of opinion. Some see it as ludicrously inappropriate – the distortion and trivialization of a serious art form – others as a way of nurturing an interest in that art form among those, especially the young, whom it would otherwise fail to reach. We will confine ourselves to one general observation. Classical music on commercial radio does not *have* to be segmented like this – Classic FM's 'off-peak' output demonstrates that full works can be accommodated within flexible commercial breaks: but the segmented nature of its prime-time shows is testimony to the pulling power of a popular culture which has itself largely been created by radio. This inference, like the earlier inference we were able to draw about the enhanced status of advertising in the modern world, shows how a close look at the medium can throw light on wider cultural issues – or, to put it more academically, how media studies can make a vital if modest contribution to the work of cultural studies.

In the next section we will move out from the hermetic, artificial world of studio chat and recorded sound and explore how radio deals with the vital, public world of political and social events.

SUGGESTIONS FOR FURTHER WORK

Over the span of about a week compare the output of three pop music stations – BBC Radio 1, Virgin 1215 and your nearest ILR station. Allow two or three days to each and make a point of listening at different times of the day, paying careful attention to both the presenters and the music. You might try to place some of the presenters at various points along the 'emotive–referential' spectrum we discerned in this chapter. What kinds of companionship do their differing approaches provide? How far, for example, do they seek to satisfy the listener's need for the familiar and predictable on the one hand and for freshness and novelty on the other? Is there any correlation between the types of presenter and the times of the day or week they can be heard? Can you deduce from both the music and the presenters' talk what kinds of listener they are aiming at? Do these listeners vary much with the particular presenter and the music he plays or can you identify a single, composite audience that each station is trying to reach? If each station does have a particular audience in mind, is it the *same* audience in every case or are they seeking separate niches in the market?

Finally do you consider that the newer stations have brought anything original to talk-and-music radio? And apart from the absence of conventional commercials, is there anything in Radio 1's output which still merits the name 'public service broadcasting'?

Part II

The world outside

Chapter 5

News and current affairs

A man may see how this world goes with no eyes. Look with thine ears.

(Shakespeare, *King Lear*, IV, vi)

Radio news has a long and venerable tradition. One can still listen to the Second World War bulletins read by Alvar Lidell and Frank Phillips and appreciate them both as broadcasting models and historical documents. Indeed radio seems so natural and successful a way of presenting the news that we tend to underestimate the demands which the medium makes and the restrictions it imposes, especially in comparison with the two other main news media, newspapers and television. The absence of a visual dimension means that radio lacks the printed words of the former, nor can it complement its sounds with the images of the latter.

The limitations of radio news are most seriously exposed when it is compared to the newspaper. The newspaper sets out diverse material across several pages. The reader can take an overview of the material, see several items at a glance, decide which she will read and in what order, and re-read anything if she needs to. Radio perforce offers much *less* news. Why?

In semiotic terms we might say that signs which exist in *time* are rather less efficient than those which exist in space; or to put it more simply, it is quicker to read something for oneself than to listen to somebody else reading it. The average newsreader utters 160 to 180 words per minute. A ten-minute radio bulletin is equivalent to a mere one-and-a-half columns of news copy – and a newspaper may carry thirty or forty columns of such copy (McLeish 1978: 19–20). Thus even an hour of radio news and current affairs cannot equal the coverage of a newspaper, and since it has to be much more selective and summary than a newspaper listeners get the impression that radio news is much more highly edited. This has led to the view that radio (and television) really offers a different *kind* of news from the press:

> Radio and television can offer instantaneous coverage of an event – an air disaster, a kidnapping, a freak storm, the falling to earth of a satellite – but the press alone can offer extensive explanation and amplification of such occurrences. Newspapers, by providing comprehensive coverage of complex issues, can thus complement the more immediate reports of radio and television.
>
> (O'Donnell and Todd 1980: 99)

Programme planners have long been sensitive to the limitations of the medium and have attempted to give width and depth to the news through a host of ancillary current affairs and 'background' programmes – programmes which complement the questions of fact which are raised and answered by the news with attempts to explain *why* such facts occur (Paulu 1981: 193). No less than 71 per cent of BBC Radio 4's total output consists of news, current affairs and related programmes (BBC 1992: 28) – for example, *The World at One, Today in Parliament, PM, The Financial World Tonight, Analysis, Today, File on Four, From Our Own Correspondent* and *Special Assignment*. The BBC has also turned Radio 5 into an all news-and-sport channel and on FM one of the independent stations, LBC Newstalk (soon to become London News Radio), is wholly given over to news and current affairs.

Nevertheless on a ratio of quantity to time all this is a less efficient mode of news presentation than is print; nor within any programme can the listener get so detailed an *overview* of the material as the newspaper reader. It is true that many bulletins begin with a general announcement of the items to follow, but it is seldom exhaustive, and unless the item she wishes to hear is broadcast first the selective listener cannot go straight to what she wants, as the reader can. She is presented instead with a sequence or 'thread' of items from which no deviation is possible. Hence the need for 'signposting' not just in the news but in *all* kinds of radio – 'Coming up shortly . . .', 'Later in this bulletin . . .' – a need which was referred to in Chapter 1.

Indeed, in contrast to the newspapers radio news programmes pose problems for the selective and non-selective listener alike –

for those who wish to hear only certain items and those who want an overall perspective on the news. In newspapers a kind of prioritization (albeit one which is determined by the political and social bias of the individual paper) is suggested to the reader by typographical devices, photographs and overall layout. The most important item or items tend to be located under large headlines at the top of the front page, the least important occupy three lines at the foot of the inner pages. It is evident that newspapers pay as much attention to spatial composition as to the individual news items (Hartley 1982: 31). But the reader can, if she chooses, ignore this implied order of priorities by going straight past the 'lead' story on page 1 to read about sport or scan the weather forecast in the inner pages: but she can scarcely fail to notice that a *kind* of order exists.

On radio, order is both a more and a less rigid matter. It is more rigid in the sense that unlike the reader the listener cannot ignore it and adopt her own. She must at least half attend to the items she is not interested in so that she can catch those she is interested in – a situation which may be good for the news editor but is frustrating for the listener. One solution is that adopted by the current affairs magazine, *Today* (BBC Radio 4), which broadcasts such 'fixed' items as the sports news and weather forecast at the same times every day, but this may still mean a wait for the impatient listener.

But order in radio news is less rigid in the sense that the sequence in which the items are broadcast is not necessarily the same as the order of their importance. The non-selective listener, who wants an overall perspective on the news, is likely to assume that the most important items will come first, the less important later. But while this is generally the rule it sometimes gives way to another rule of sound broadcasting, especially in the more ex-pansive 'news background' and current affairs programmes – that that inattentive organ, the ear, must be offered fresh stimulus through variety. The reader can introduce her own variety by turning the pages and turning back again: the listener must have her variety introduced for her, which means that the sequence and indeed the *choice* of items are partly dictated by the nature of the medium (Smith 1976: 173). Serious items are often interlarded with light or humorous ones which might otherwise have been thought unworthy of inclusion, but such a measure avoids mono-tony only to run the risk of dilettantism and lack of perspective. The news editor has no visual means of indicating that certain items are more important than others. Some may last longer than others but longer is not necessarily the same as more important, and in any case our sense of duration is less certain than our awareness of spatial length. There is therefore a risk that everything in radio news will assume an *equal* importance – or lack of it.

Let us summarize what we have asserted so far. As a result of being purveyed purely through sound, radio news suffers from a number of handicaps. In its overall range it is perforce much more *selective* than a newspaper, yet makes selection on the listener's part a much more difficult matter than for the newspaper reader; and it also affords her much less of a sense of the relative importance of the items it includes.

But radio news suffers from a further problem: the *kind* and *compass* of language in which it has to be expressed. The language of newspapers is permanent: the reader sets her own pace and can re-read what she has missed or cannot understand. This means that the press is capable of considerable linguistic variety. It can therefore divide the heterogeneous audience with which every mass medium is confronted into different intellectual levels by providing different kinds of newspapers for different kinds of reader. Their varying treatments of a single event can often be amusing. Where *The Times* might announce in a headline 'Employment Secretary Plans New Trade Union Legislation', the *Daily Mirror* might content itself with the exhortation 'Come off it, Norman!'

But as we saw in the last chapter, the language of radio is evanescent. The radio newsreader sets an arbitrary pace and her words dissolve into thin air. (It is possible for the listener to record and 'retrieve' news bulletins but in practice this is seldom done and is probably illegal.) This means that however complex the material – and complexity is especially likely in news, documentary and educational programmes – it must be expressed in language which is fairly simple and straightforward in style and diction. Since radio lacks the linguistic range of the newspapers we would expect it to be less capable of providing different levels of output for different kinds of listener and to remain confronted with a largely heterogeneous audience.

This certainly seems to be the case with television, whose language code is also evanescent – a point made by Fiske and Hartley (1978). They argue that the heterogeneity of the television audience dominates and even 'originates' the television message, creating a tendency towards cultural centrality. From this they develop their concept of 'bardic' television (1978: 85–6). Most of its output, they suggest, uses a 'broadcast' linguistic code – that is, language which is colloquial, contains much redundancy, is phatic rather than referential (relatively easy where pictures and images can supply much of the referential content) and assumes a background of shared experience to emphasize things its audience has in common rather than apart.

Students of language will recognize a similarity, if not identity, between the notion of a broadcast code and Bernstein's restricted code (Fiske 1990: 73–6; Bernstein 1971: 76–92, 123–37). Hence the function of the television message is very largely one of reassurance and confirmation. Generally it avoids the use of 'narrowcast' language (analogous to Bernstein's elaborated code), which is typically literary, contains little redundancy, is highly referential and assumes a shared educational or intellectual experience to teach what is not known. Its function is to challenge or enrich audiences.

But if the television message is influenced by the heterogeneous nature of the audience I would suggest that it is even more fundamentally determined by the evanescent nature of its language; and indeed that this evanescence is the main reason *why* the audience remains heterogeneous. Moreover I would argue that such language is an even more powerful determinant in radio than in television because in the latter we can at least *see*, however briefly, what some of the words refer to and even, on occasions, the words themselves. But on the radio we can see nothing.

We might sum this up in terms of the Jakobson model: in both television and radio the heterogeneous nature of the receivers imposes constraints and restraints on the referential power of the message, but the nature of the contact makes a prior, even more basic imposition for it requires that the message should be relatively simple: and it must be even simpler in the case of radio since it is unassisted by visual codes and must therefore be apprehensible through the ear alone.

Yet as I mentioned earlier, despite all these difficulties radio has an illustrious history as a news medium and in the last twenty years or so has set out to emulate the press by providing its audience with both quality news (for example, *The World at One*, BBC Radio 4) and popular news (*Newsbeat*, BBC Radio 1).

How do these types of programme set out to offer a choice of news content and mode of presentation comparable with that offered by *The Times* and the popular press such as the *Daily Mirror* or the *Sun*? Can they match the visual differences of language and layout which are immediately obvious to the reader with acoustic differences that are equally obvious to the listener?

What follows is an outline of an edition of *Newsbeat* followed by an outline of *The World at One*. They were broadcast on the same day (Monday, 28 June 1993) and within half an hour of each other. In both I have reproduced the news headlines and the first news items in full, and all the other items I have either summarized or paraphrased in order to give some idea of the sequence and shape of each programme. The points of interest and comparison in the programmes and the points of comparison between both programmes and the corresponding types of newspaper could occupy a book in themselves, but although I sometimes mention certain common features of radio news which do not occur in these particular broadcasts I have kept my findings as brief as possible.

Newsbeat – BBC Radio 1: Monday, 28 June 1993   *approximate*
at 12.30 pm   *duration*
Last record of *Simon Bates Show* plays straight into the
Newsbeat theme-tune which fades out under –
NEWSREADER 1: On today's *Newsbeat* the village vigil-
antes get their sentences cut.

> Woman's voice in street: 'I am disappointed that we're not taking them home with us tonight. But it is good news it is reduced to six months rather than a five-year stretch.'

JINGLE: 'Newsbeat!' Theme-tune fades down and is
held under –   0′ 31″
NEWSREADER 2: Also the Iraqi secret service vow to
avenge the US strike on Baghdad.
NEWSREADER 1: Medical care by satellite?
NEWSREADER 2: And is it Techno RIP?
Newsbeat theme fades up for last three beats punc-
tuated by –
NEWSREADER 1: I'm Maggie Shields –
NEWSREADER 2: – and I'm Tina Ritchie.
Music fades out under –

(1) SHIELDS: Two vigilantes jailed for five years for trying to sort out a suspected thief have had their sentences reduced to six months by the Court of Appeal. Duncan Bond and Mark Chapman were jailed at Norwich Crown Court earlier this month for dragging a youth into the back of a van and threatening him before letting him go unharmed.

RITCHIE: There was outrage at the length of their sentences and a campaign was launched to have them cut. Friends and family were at the court to hear the judge's ruling, and this was their reaction.

Man's voice in street: 'We're disappointed that Duncan and Mark aren't out of prison today, but we appreciate that the legal arguments which Lord Taylor was making didn't allow him to do that. And reducing the sentence to six months maybe was the best he could do. I should think they'll be disappointed as well, but I think we were all prepared for them staying in prison.'

Woman's voice in street: 'Six months is a lot better than five years and we have to ... I realize in the judge's summing up he had to, erm, impose a custodial sentence. We accept they made a mistake and we realize they did wrong and we've never condoned what they did. But we just thought that the sentence was too steep and obviously the judge in there did as well.'

2' 13"

SHIELDS: Joining us live from the Appeal Court is our reporter, Mike Williams. Mike, what reasons did the Lord Chief Justice, Lord Taylor, give for reducing these sentences?

Williams: 'In summary there were three. He said the previous good character of the men was obvious. He was impressed by the remorse that they clearly felt for their actions. And he also said that they had been under extra stress because of the severity of the initial sentence, they'd spent the past eighteen days under some considerable pressure, and he also took that into account when he reduced the sentences.'

SHIELDS: And what was the reaction from the two men when the judge read out his ruling?

Williams: 'There was absolutely nothing from them. Er, their campaigners, the friends and family outside, a very, very mixed reaction from them. They were glad – very, very glad that the five-year sentences had been reduced; but also a little disappointed that the men hadn't been able to leave court today.'

SHIELDS: Did the judge make any comment about the action of vigilante groups like these?

Williams: 'Yes. He said the gravity of this case lay in the threat to public order, he said that no civilized society could allow individuals to take the law into their own hands. He said people can be vigilant and must be vigilant but being a *vigilante* was just not acceptable.'

JINGLE: 'Newsbeat!'

(2) RITCHIE introduces an item on the US bombing of Baghdad.

SHIELDS adds that the British government is supporting the action but other nations have misgivings. Cues defence of the action by the US ambassador to the UN, Madeleine Albright.

Actuality of remarks by US ambassador.

RITCHIE cues response of Iraqi ambassador to the EEC.

Actuality of remarks by Iraqi ambassador.

SHIELDS describes Labour Party reactions and cues MP, Ken Livingstone.

3' 35"

Remarks by Ken Livingstone.

RITCHIE cues remarks by Tory Chairman of the back-bench Foreign Affairs Committee, Michael Colvin.

Telephone actuality of remarks by Michael Colvin.

RITCHIE cues NBC reporter Tom Aspel live from Baghdad.

Brief interview of Aspel on the telephone by Ritchie in the studio.

Newsbeat theme fades down and is held under –

(3) SHIELDS announces other news this lunch-time:

SHIELDS (i) Measures to stop children phoning sex lines.

Actuality of remarks by chairwoman of watch-dog group.

RITCHIE (ii) Arthur Scargill claims the unions may break away from Labour and form their own political party.

SHIELDS (iii) Chairman of the British Medical Association says the government is fooling the public over the NHS.

RITCHIE (iv) In South Africa arrests have been made after last week's attack by white extremists on political talks in Johannesburg.

Music fades up to 'This is *Newsbeat* on 1 FM!'

1′ 12″

(4) RITCHIE introduces an interview with the new British Scrabble Champion, 15-year-old Alan Saldanha, by '*Newsbeat*'s own dictionary king', David Willis.

Location interview of Alan by Willis, during which Alan's father is also heard.

JINGLE: 'The Newsbeat – on 1 FM!'

1′ 52″

(5) RITCHIE announces a new medical development – diagnosis by satellite television.

Actuality of dialogue over satellite link between doctor in Aberdeen and paramedic treating an injured skier in the mountains.

RITCHIE cues Dr Ross McLean.

Interview of Dr McLean by unidentified female interviewer.

JINGLE: 'Newsbeat!' – and straight into 'Techno' music which fades down and is held under –

2′ 25″

(6) SHIELDS announcing final release of Techno band 'Alternate'.

Interview of members of the band by unidentified female interviewer, with the music faded up and down within it.

JINGLE: 'BBC Radio 1 FM: the best sounds around.'

Newsbeat theme fades down and is held under –

2′ 44″

(7) RITCHIE: The headlines again:
RITCHIE: (i) The two Norfolk vigilantes have had their
sentences cut.
SHIELDS: (ii) Labour demands a government statement on
the US missile attack on Baghdad.
RITCHIE trails story in *News 93* at 6 o clock about ITN's
News at Ten.
SHIELDS: And China accused of cruelty to bears in the   0' 44"
name of medical science.

'Tune in for Tina and her new teeth' [sound of Ritchie
laughing] at 1.30, when she'll be back with the news
update.
Theme-music fades up to –
JINGLE: 'Newsbeat! . . . . 1 FM!' – and straight into musical
introduction to the *Jakki Brambles Show*.

Total 15 min 16 sec

The World at One – BBC Radio 4: Monday, 28 June   *approximate*
1993 at 1 pm   *duration*
PRESENTER: *The World at One*. This is James Naughtie
with forty minutes of news and comment. The headlines: two men jailed for five years in the so-called
'village vigilante' case have had their sentences reduced
to six months. The men's supporters say they should
have been freed.
Will the Home Secretary's plans to shake up the police
inspire new confidence in the forces of law and order?
Downing Street says the Prime Minister advised President Clinton that any action against Iraq should be
limited and proportionate. We'll be hearing Tory back-
bench concern at Britain's support for the cruise missile
attack on Baghdad and I'll be talking live to the US
Ambassador here in London.   0' 56"
England's cricket selectors have made sweeping changes
for the Third Test, though there's still no room for David
Gower. One of his firmest supporters tells us it's the last
chance for England's selectors and managers. And we've
got a special report from Northern Cyprus, where
support for the one-time local hero, Asil Nadir, is
showing signs of ebbing away.

First the news from Brian Perkins.

NEWSREADER: (i) Two men from East Anglia who were jailed for kidnapping a suspected thief have had their sentences reduced to six months by the Court of Appeal. Duncan Bond, who's 35, and 29-year-old Mark Chapman, the so-called village vigilantes, admitted kidnapping the teenager whom they believed had been stealing. The sentences provoked outrage in their Norfolk community. The Lord Chief Justice, Lord Taylor, said the sentences were grossly disproportionate. Michael Williams was in court.

Report from Michael Williams.

(ii) Emergency government statement in the Commons this afternoon about the recent American missile attack on Baghdad.

Report from Political Correspondent, Tim Fenton, at Westminster.

Perkins continues with newspaper reports that the head of Iraqi intelligence has vowed to avenge the attack. 5′ 45″

(iii) The Chairman of the British Medical Association has warned the government that its Health Service changes are not working.

Actuality of part of Chairman's speech at a conference in Torquay.

(iv) The pound has been rising sharply on the foreign exchanges this morning.

(v) Two measures have been announced to restrict the use of telephone sex lines.

(vi) The England cricket selectors have made big changes to the team for the Third Test against Australia.

Report from Cricket Correspondent, Jonathan Agnew.

Perkins gives details of full squad.

(vii) One of the greatest operatic basses of the century, Boris Christoff, has died.

(viii) The President of the Board of Trade, Michael Heseltine, is making good progress after his heart attack a week ago.

(1) PRESENTER introduces item on the US missile attack on Baghdad. The Opposition and some Tory back-benchers have expressed unease despite the government's support for the action, and there is strong support for the President in the US.

Actuality of Vice-President Gore defending the attack on CBS television.

PRESENTER – studio link. There is support for the President from the former national security adviser to President Bush, General Brent Scowcroft.

Actuality of remarks by General Scowcroft.

PRESENTER – studio link. Introduces Tory back-bencher Cyril Townsend.

11' 12"

Naughtie interviews Cyril Townsend.

PRESENTER – studio link. Egypt has expressed disquiet. Cues own earlier recorded interview with the Egyptian Chargé d'Affaires.

Naughtie interviews Egyptian Chargé d'Affaires.

PRESENTER – studio link. Introduces the American ambassador in London, Ray Seitz.

Naughtie conducts live interview with US ambassador.

(2) PRESENTER introduces an item on the selection of the England cricket team for the Third Test and cues –

Interview of the England team manager, Keith Fletcher, by Cricket Correspondent, Jonathan Agnew.

PRESENTER – studio link. There is opposition to the selectors among members of the MCC. One of these is former editor of the *Observer*, Donald Trelford. Cues own earlier recorded interview with him.

Naughtie interviews Donald Trelford.

5' 12"

PRESENTER – studio link. Cues a telephone interview with Jonathan Agnew.

Naughtie interviews Jonathan Agnew.

(3) PRESENTER reviews the case of the jail sentences imposed on the two 'village vigilantes', then cues interviews of reporter Carol West with campaigners and relatives of the two men.

Juxtaposed interviews of two people over the telephone by Carol West in a studio.

PRESENTER – studio link. Relates this case to that of Ivan Fergus, a 16-year-old youth wrongfully convicted of assault, and cues reporter Roger Currill.

Currill reports on the Appeal Judges' criticisms of the lawyers and police who dealt with Fergus's case, then cues a statement read out by Ivan's mother after the acquittal.

Actuality of Mrs Fergus outside the court reading out her statement.

Currill – studio link. Cues interview he recorded with Fergus's solicitor.

Remark from solicitor in outside location.

Currill concludes report in the studio.   8' 32"

PRESENTER – studio link. Relates case to future of the criminal justice system and the Home Secretary's forthcoming publication of a White Paper on the future of the police. Cues Roger Harrabin reporting from Liverpool on what the Home Secretary's changes will mean there.

Actuality of police interviewing a crime victim fades under –

Harrabin – studio link. Reports on the proposal to nominate more business people to police authorities.

Cues Ian Berry of Liverpool Chamber of Commerce.

Location interview with Berry.

Harrabin – location link, on a piece of derelict land in Liverpool. Cues interview with Margaret Simey, former Chair of Liverpool Police Authority.

Location interview with Margaret Simey.

(4) PRESENTER refers to the debate about ITV's proposal to re-schedule *News at Ten* and cues own earlier recorded interview with Sir David Nicholas, former Editor-in-Chief of ITN.   3' 10"

Responses of Sir David Nicholas in a telephone acoustic.

PRESENTER – studio link. Cues own earlier recorded interview with David Mellor, the former Heritage Secretary who steered the recent Broadcasting Act through Parliament.

James Naughtie interviews David Mellor.

(5) PRESENTER points out that former Northern Ireland minister Michael Mates is about to make a statement on the events that led to his resignation. It is uncertain whether he will refer to Asil Nadir, who is in Northern Cyprus and continuing to allege unfair treatment at the hands of British justice. However, there are signs that Nadir is no longer so welcome in the island as he once was, since his economic power is fading. Cues report from Charley Lee-Potter.

Actuality of bar opposite Nadir's house fades but is held under –

Lee-Potter link. Introduces item, with an account of Nadir's waning local influence. Cues leader of the main opposition party.   5' 12"

Location remarks from leader of opposition party.
Actuality of noises of newspaper office fades under –
Lee-Potter link. Cues interview with editor of rival newspaper to that owned by Nadir.

Location remarks from editor of newspaper, at the end of which fades up –

Actuality of music in Cypriot bar. Music fades but is held for some time under –

Lee-Potter link. Cues interview with President of Northern Cyprus, Mr Denktash.

Location remarks from Mr Denktash.

Lee-Potter link. Cues leader of the opposition party.

Location remarks from the leader of the opposition party.

(6) PRESENTER delivers closing headlines:

(i) Two men convicted of kidnapping have had their sentences cut.

(ii) The Defence Secretary will answer a question in the Commons about the Baghdad missile attack.

(iii) Sweeping changes made by the England cricket selectors after the test disaster against Australia.   0′ 35″

(iv) Death of the opera singer Boris Christoff.

(v) In the City the 100 Share Index up.

(vi) The weather: dry, warm and sunny.

PRESENTER signs off.

Total 40 min 53 sec

LANGUAGE AND PRESENTATION

On the linguistic differences between popular and quality newspapers we might venture the following generalization: that whereas the language of the latter is relatively complex in structure, 'literary' in vocabulary and objective in tone, that of the former is relatively simple in structure, colloquial in vocabulary and emotive or sensational in tone.

But one's first impression of the news copy of *The World at One* (WO) and *Newsbeat* (NB) is that it is couched in fairly similar language: indeed Brian Perkins' opening sentence in the former about the two vigilantes is almost identical to that of Maggie Shields in the latter. The language of WO is clearly not that of *The Times*. In order to be easily intelligible to the ear its vocabulary is familiar and its syntax uncomplicated. The presenter and newsreader do not scruple to say 'we'll' for 'we will', 'who's' for 'who is', and there is an element of simplification, even personification, in 'Downing Street says . . .' where a quality newspaper would be likely to identify a government spokesperson. Similarly the Home Secretary's plans to 'shake up' the police is not meant, or understood, in its literal sense but as a kind of vivid colloquial shorthand expressing something like 'radically reorganize in order to give them a new perspective on their work'.

The fairly elementary nature of radio news language has often been pointed out, even in quality news where one might hear such colloquialisms as 'a *row* in the House of Commons'; and in analysing a script from Radio 4's *PM* programme O'Donnell and Todd (1980: 92) point out the relative simplicity of sentence structure and the occurrence of verbless sentences, a phenomenon also noted by Quirk (1982: 13). Despite this simplicity radio news also acknowledges the need for 'redundancy', or reinforcement through repetition, which is a characteristic of colloquial language. WO mentions its main stories three times: in the headlines, the bulletin proper and the closing summary.

But if the language of WO does not closely resemble that of *The Times*, neither does the language of NB altogether resemble that of the popular newspapers. Whereas on a particular day some years ago *The Times* led with the collapse of the miners' strike, the *Sun* led with the conviction of a rapist known as 'the Fox'. This item, which was headlined 'Porn lust of the Fox' was included in *The Times* on page 3, under the headline 'The Fox's reign of terror ends in jail for life'. It is highly unlikely that the *Sun*'s baldly sensational headline, which is fairly representative of popular press presentation, would be heard on NB: 'Porn lust of the Fox – details in a moment'. Such language would be used only as a quotation which could be ascribed to its outside source – and in this respect all radio news resembles the quality press in its concern to keep the reportage of the news as free as possible from comment and emotive judgement, a concern which is not greatly shared by the popular newspapers.

In the case of the BBC the obvious reason for this is that the Corporation is forbidden to editorialize, but I would suggest that there is another reason which is to do with the nature of radio itself. Whatever the language it conveys, print is a machine-made medium. It bears no mark of individual authorship but seems impersonally originated, *authoritative*. This gives statements like the *Sun* headline a superficial air of objectivity, of fact or truth. But radio news is always heard in the voice of an individual and such statements would sound idiosyncratic – be attributed to the newsreader, dismissed as propaganda, or even more likely, misunderstood as drama or comedy. Hence I would argue that irrespective of any Charter obligations radio news is recognizable for what it is only when couched in quasi-objective language.

Furthermore the nature of the medium produces a kind of *inversion* of the relationship between news and comment which exists in the press, and in so doing establishes the editor's presence in a quite different way. In the press, comment and opinion are felt to be at the heart of the enterprise, matters of much greater editorial import than the accuracy of the news, which seems to be declared in the medium itself. We are accustomed to describe his leading articles somewhat loosely as 'editorials', as though the editor had no responsibility for other parts of the paper, and to ask first of all what a newspaper's political views are – whether it is Conservative or left-wing, for example – and only then how comprehensive or accurate its news reportage is.

In radio it is the reportage of the news which is felt to be at the heart of the enterprise and where a strong editorial presence is often established in the person of the newsreader or news presenter, while comment, speculation and argument are dependent, peripheral matters from which the broadcasting institution is at some pains to distance itself. Alistair Cooke's *Letter from America* is in many respects similar to a *Times* leading article, but whereas the latter is understood to be the paper's editorial voice there is no corresponding suggestion that Alistair Cooke's views are those of the BBC.

This means that much radio news is at an advantage over the newspapers in that, on the face of it at least, its editorial stance is non-partisan – a position brought about by the unavoidable presence of voices in the medium. This is not, of course, to say that radio news is never distorted or biased, only that to be recognized as news it must at least be objective in *tone*.

This objectivity is reinforced by the fact that the great majority of readers of both popular and quality news speak in RP, whose somewhat paradoxical effects are equally useful. Historically it is the accent of those whom education, professional success or social background has enabled to transcend their regional origins and form a kind of privileged, cosmopolitan community. RP thus evolved as a lingua franca – intelligible not only among the members of this community but to the larger, geographically diverse population over whom they held sway. Not surprisingly, then, it remains widely regarded as the accent of 'those who know best, the most authoritative'.

On the other hand because RP is not a dialect with specific regional roots (its speakers are encountered all over the country) it has also acquired the status of a 'non-accent', and thus minimizes the element of idiosyncrasy and even of 'personality' in the voice.

Thus news which is being read in RP is not something which can easily be associated with a particular origin or viewpoint, but has something of the impersonality of print.

So successful were the pre-war bulletins in minimizing personality that many listeners believed there was only one news-reader (Black 1972: 69). If this was so, how did the BBC readers come to be identified by name when previously they had been anonymous? Naming began in 1940 to prevent the news bulletins from being counterfeited by the Germans and was immediately popular, 'a recognition that the source was more important than the medium or the message' (A. Briggs 1970: 202). By this is meant that the personality of the newsreader became a guarantee of the 'impersonality', or objectivity, of the broadcasting institution – the 'source', strictly speaking, being the organization which compiles the news not the person who reads it. It is an indexical function which the newsreaders have performed ever since.

But all this is only to declare the *similarity* between popular and quality news on the radio and the *difference* between such news and all newspapers of whatever kind; for I have been suggesting that the nature of the medium compresses its range of language and style of presentation and allows it to resemble neither *The Times* nor the *Sun* and *Daily Mirror*. Nevertheless I would argue that there remain certain differences between NB and WO which do evoke the difference between the popular and quality press. Whereas the news delivery of Brian Perkins on WO is slow and sedate, Shields and Ritchie adopt a much brisker, more urgent style – an urgency which is enhanced by the rapid alternations of their remarks, sometimes within a single item or section of the programme.

But a much more marked difference is in pronunciation. RP is still widely heard among readers of both quality and popular news, but in the latter especially, there is a growing incidence of what could be described as *modified* RP – pronunciation which is still universally intelligible but coloured in some measure by a regional accent. One possible reason for this is the expansion over the last fifty years or so of mass education, which has resulted in increasing numbers of well-qualified and successful people who have retained their regional accents, and therefore in a weakening of the association between RP and 'authoritativeness'.

Because speakers of pure RP no longer hold a monopoly of knowledge and authority, the artificiality of their dialect (it is the only one that has its origins in *class* rather than region) has perhaps become more noticeable, especially to the younger listeners who make up so much of the audience of popular stations like Radio 1. To their ears, pure RP may sound not 'impersonal' at all but affectedly posh and stuffy. In order that the newsreader may be widely understood a measure of RP is still necessary; but if she also has a regional accent this helps her to sound unobtrusively natural and authentic.

This would explain why both Tina Ritchie and Maggie Shields speak in modified RP, whereas Brian Perkins, who is newsreading on a station with an older and more conservative listenership, speaks in pure RP. On NB Maggie Shields is the first reader to be heard, and we are immediately aware that she is Scottish; but her accent is not so strong as to interfere with our understanding of, or preoccupation with, what she is saying. Nevertheless the accents of the newsreaders of WO on the one hand and NB on the other do seem in their own way to parallel the differences between the quality and popular papers.

There are also important if sometimes subtle differences in language. One of these relates to the names of the programmes, a difference which is not reflected in the titles of most newspapers. Since many of the latter have long histories during which they have frequently been forced to seek new types of readers, they do not generally reflect their differences of appeal in their titles. The name *Daily Mirror* has different connotations for us from *The Times* because we have long been aware of their different formats and different readerships; but there seems to be nothing intrinsically more populist about one title than the other.

With much shorter histories, WO and NB do seem concerned to establish differing connotations through their titles. That of WO is an alliterative pun meaning 'How the world looks at 1 o'clock' and having the larger, more objective sense of 'The world as a unity, taken in at a single view'. 'Newsbeat' is also a pun, a compound formed by analogy with 'heartbeat' and therefore suggesting a programme with its finger on the pulse, one which keeps abreast of the latest news. 'Beat' also carries the suggestion of a patrol or assignment, but for a programme set into a pop music network its primary association is with rhythm and music. Generally, then, the title has connotations of pace, 'up-to-dateness' and vitality – very different from the judicious detachment implied by 'The World at One'.

But there are also important linguistic differences in the head-lines and news copy of the two programmes. Whereas WO demurely reports in the past tense that the two offenders 'have had their sentences reduced' NB makes use of the vivid present and two similar-sounding colloquial monosyllables, '*get* their sentences *cut*'. Overall, WO is much wordier, most obviously in the headlines and previewing, which are not broken up by different voices as NB's are. Moreover NB shows more concern to involve the listener by phrasing two of its brief and rather cryptic headlines as direct questions: 'Medical care by satellite?', 'And is it Techno RIP?'. On the other hand because WO's single question – about the future of the police – is longer and buried among much other headlining it seems more like an impersonal speculation than a direct address to the listener.

There are other stylistic differences. Whereas NB refers directly to the 'village vigilantes', WO dissociates itself from this racy journalistic coinage (even while making use of it!) by alluding to the '*so-called* village vigilantes'. In sentences which are otherwise almost identical, NB refers to men jailed for trying to 'sort out' a suspected thief, whereas in WO they merely 'kidnap' him – a less colourful if more precise description. We might describe NB's term as a colloquial euphemism, another piece of shorthand like 'shake up', and here meaning something like 'to threaten or assault, with a corrective intention'. Though both bulletins say that the jail sentence was 'reduced', NB is also prepared to repeat the less literary word 'cut'. Moreover its description of the crime is fuller and more colourful, rendering WO's repeated use of 'kid-napping' with 'dragging a youth into the back of a van and threatening him'.

On the other hand WO makes surprising use of the very formal relative pronoun 'whom', a word which now seems archaic even in many conventional literary contexts. And though in places less colourful, WO is careful in its attributions, repeating the precisely expressed judgements of the Prime Minister ('limited and pro-portionate') and the Lord Chief Justice ('grossly disproportionate').

We might sum up these presentational and linguistic differ-ences by saying that whereas WO essays an intellectual approach to its material by being thorough, accurate and precise, NB seeks the emotional involvement of the listener through an informal, terse style, direct questions and lively, concrete description.

CONTENT AND FORMAT

As with language and presentation, it is useful to begin by making one or two generalizations about the differences in content and format between quality and popular newspapers.

The former devote a large proportion of their space to serious, 'hard' news – that is, to occurrences of major importance in the spheres of politics, economics, technology, the arts, and so on, as well as to isolated events such as accidents, crimes and court cases. They also attempt to set the news in some form of perspective by grouping it into themes and subjects – headline news, further news, 'Home', 'Foreign', 'Financial', 'Arts' pages and so on; by using layout to distinguish the important from the less important items; and by locating features or 'background' articles on separate pages from those which contain the hard news items.

With respect to format, their pages are large, the headlines relatively small (with the frequent inclusion of lower-case lettering), they are characterized by little typographical variety and they contain a considerable amount of text, much of it divided into items of substantial length, and relatively few photographs and illustrations.

In contrast the popular newspapers seem less concerned to set the news in perspective than to demonstrate its interest to their readers or its relevance to their ordinary preoccupations. They devote a large amount of space to lighter, 'human interest' items and make no obvious distinction between these and the more serious items they include. They focus upon such subjects as accidents or crimes, dramatic court cases, news about pop stars, actors and other celebrities, and unusual stories involving people or animals. They also devote considerable space to sport, which like television and 'leisure' news, is slightly atypical in having a section to itself.

Their pages are of a smaller size ('tabloid') and rather fewer in number than those of the quality newspapers, and their format is spectacularly different. Their headlines are huge (there may be room for little other than headlines and a photograph on the front page) and mostly consist of block capitals; there is a large proportion of photographs and illustrations to text, and the latter is broken up into articles which are mostly short. These papers are also characterized by considerable typographical variety, for there are differences in print not only between articles but *within* them.

There is heavy print and lighter print, white letters on a black ground, black on white, white on grey, black on grey. Block capitals may occur within the text, and the items and photographs are framed by dots, borders, asterisks and similar devices. What is the purpose of this typographical variety? Print is a formidable medium for people for whom reading is not a frequent or congenial activity, and so its intrinsically authoritative nature will count for nothing if it remains unread. The typography therefore has two related functions. First it enables the text to advertise itself and make the business of reading more attractive. Articles begin in bold type and wide spacing to lure the reader into them and continue in closer, lighter print. The general effect of the changes is to break up the text into small and distinctive units. A whole article may be printed in bold to catch the eye amongst others in light, and vice versa.

The second function, especially common in the popular newspapers, is to make the business of reading, once undertaken, much easier by reinforcing – one might almost say, exaggerating – conventional punctuation. Key words are printed in block capitals or underlined, quotation marks enlarged and set in bold type, and so on. Since it remains impersonal the printed text retains an air of authority; but to the extent that it is no longer of uniform appearance but organized into shapes and shades which clarify, although they do not appreciably add to, its meaning it acquires an almost pictorial quality. The purpose of this typographical variety is, then, to make reading as inviting and easy as looking at pictures.

How can radio set about imitating these differences in content and format? The short answer is that it can match the visual resources of newspapers with its own acoustic resources. It can match the differences of size with differences of duration; words in different kinds of print with words in different tones or voices; dots, borders and asterisks with pips or musical jingles; and the photographs or icons of people and things with indexes – the sounds made by people and things.

But the correspondences are not quite that straightforward, for the sound of words on the radio and the image of words in print are not strictly analogous. Indeed, as was suggested in Chapter 3, print is a technological development of speech, which is the only 'natural' form of language, and the punctuation system of print is an attempt to fix meaning, which inheres not only in the words but in the inflections of the human voice. The typographical exaggerations of punctuation which occur in some newspapers are simply attempts to convey that meaning more clearly, they are not attempts to enhance or heighten it. So for the radio news-reader to try to reproduce them would be to reverse cause and effect, to imitate through speech something which is *itself* an imitation of speech.

But there are, as we have seen, other typographical devices which are to a great extent independent of the meaning. They are simply there to catch the eye, to relieve the impersonality of print without impairing its authority, and there may be as many as four different kinds of typeface in a single article. These could be, and are, matched by changes of voice among the newsreaders, but to nothing like the same extent since the voice is a live, personal medium and does not require the same measure of relief.

Indeed to match the number of changes in the typeface with the same number of changes of voice would make us conscious of the newsreaders to an extent which would compromise radio news's necessary attempt at a relatively *im*personal style of presentation. The amount of human 'presence' must be enough to make the reading of the news expressive and interesting, but not so great as to make us more conscious of the reader than of what is being read. Hence when a change of voice occurs in radio news it must be dictated by the logic of the news itself – by a change from one headline or story to another, or from one aspect of the story to another, including the transition from the actual text of the bulletin to a correspondent's report.

But not only must the acoustic resources of radio be more sparingly deployed than the visual resources of the newspapers, they are inherently more *limited*, for while most things in the physical world are visible many are soundless, at least for some of the time. A photograph of a vase in an exhibition, for instance, cannot be rendered acoustically since vases in these circumstances are silent. However, the vast majority of newspaper photographs consist of people, and people do, not infrequently, make noises. Of the ninety-six photographs which I counted in the *Sun* for 30 June 1993 all but seven were of people, as were all but seven of the ninety-one in the same day's issue of *The Times*.

Nevertheless the only meaningful noises which people make are words, so the radio equivalent of a newspaper photograph is the sound of a person speaking. But the radio equivalent of a newspaper text is *also* the sound of a person speaking – the newsreader reading the bulletin. Consequently what exist in newspapers as two separate codes, printed words and photographic images, can normally be expressed in radio only by the single code of speech, within which the only possible variation is the sound of different voices. In radio news, then, speech must be regarded as both typographic and photographic – the equivalent not only of the newspaper text but in many cases of its pictures.

With different exigencies to meet, then, in what way and with what success do WO and NB imitate the quality and popular newspapers? Superficially WO seems to fall well short of what quality newspapers provide. The ratio of quantity to time makes the provision of news in breadth or in depth seem impossible. Since the number of items to the duration of the news bulletin can allow for an average of only about 130 words per item the news coverage may be more reminiscent of the popular than of the quality press. Furthermore there is insufficient time for the grouping of the news into the 'Home', 'Foreign', and other sections which characterize the quality newspapers, and so such specialized forms of news must be allocated to separate programmes.

Nevertheless by being sedately paced over forty minutes and by 'packing' its news coverage on the one hand and extending its features presentation on the other, WO does succeed in conveying what is in radio terms a strong suggestion of news in breadth and in depth. With no apparent air of haste it compresses eight items of news, some of them containing recorded inserts or correspondents' reports, into a bulletin lasting less than six minutes and devotes its remaining thirty-five minutes or so to just five features, the longest lasting over eleven minutes and the shortest not less than three.

It is worth taking a closer look at the format of WO. The sedateness of its approach is partly established by the extensive headlining at the beginning, which incidentally points to the risk of drawing false analogies between radio and press news. From the fact that the presenter James Naughtie spends almost a minute in previewing the programme's news and features we might be tempted to see a parallel with the huge headlines of the popular papers, but a truer analogy would be with the table of contents which somewhat inconspicuously runs down the side or across the top of the front page of the quality newspapers. It can be so situated because in a spatial medium it can be perused at a glance, as can the contents themselves; but on the radio the contents must be declared at once and in some detail since the listener cannot otherwise know what is 'coming up'. Hence radio headlines are not closely analogous to newspaper headlines, and the length of WO's implies not sensationalism but quantity and depth – a perspective on the news and on current affairs.

This sense of amplitude and depth is created by two other aspects of the format of WO. The first is the strong presence, in addition to that of the presenter and newsreader, of what I will refer to by the generic term 'newsgatherers' – correspondents, interviewers, reporters, and in some other editions of WO, specialist editors such as the Political or Economics Editor. These are equally apparent in the newspapers but we must again beware of simple analogies. The impersonal, authoritative nature of print seems to allow the newsgatherer to take entire responsibility for the article he writes, for more often than not the whole of it is written in his name. The editor's presence is merely implicit: we are aware that newspaper articles are subject to editorial mediation, but there is usually no *evidence* of this mediation.

However, in radio news we have seen that the 'personal' nature of the medium makes a quasi-editorial presence unavoidable in the form of the newsreader or presenter: in news summaries or capsule news it is the *newsgatherers'* presence which is often merely implicit. But when the voices of newsgatherers are included in a programme like WO, it is interesting to see how the 'news purveyor' – a term I shall use to cover both the newsreader and the programme presenter if there is one – exercises her editorial status, indicating by the way in which she contextualizes the gatherers' reports what credence the listener should give them. She may make it clear that she is entirely dependent on a particular correspondent for the information and that she endorses it entirely. As Brian Perkins does in items (i), (ii) and (vi), she summarizes the item and the correspondent then provides the full details.

On the other hand the news purveyor may imply that her endorsement of the correspondent's report is only partial or provisional, that it should be treated as no more than a fragment of the total picture which has been, or will be, balanced with others. There is therefore a sense in which the role of each transcends that of the other, but we are never in doubt of the editorial authority vested in the purveyor: her words may imply that she trusts her correspondent's report entirely, but that in itself is an editorial judgement, a taking of full responsibility for what the correspondent says.

The nature of this relationship between news purveyor and newsgatherers is signalled in various ways in the broadcast itself. Though the purveyor delivers her words in an expressive, 'speech' tone we know from what we are told and/or from the fluency of pace and occasional 'literariness' of the language that it is not being extemporized. The newsgatherers normally deliver their reports in much the same way, but when events are of a dramatic or emotive nature and/or are still occurring their reports may be extemporized: but they are then 'legitimated' as news, set in perspective, by the voice of the reader or presenter, who in certain circumstances may interview the gatherer and thus treat him as a 'witness' of the news rather than as the initial 'judge' of it. She might also invite him to speculate about the nature or consequences of particular events, thus allowing a certain coherence or rationale to be given to the news, yet, since the speculations are not her own, maintaining the crucial distinction between fact and comment.

Because of his subordinate status to the purveyor the newsgatherer may even have a strong regional accent (unlike the genteel Scots of James Naughtie, for example, the Northern Irish brogue of the BBC's former Political Editor, John Cole, was a frequent object of parody); and whereas his reports may often be broadcast from the scene of the news itself, the reader will always read the news bulletin from a studio.

It is true that programmes such as *The World at One* and *Today* are sometimes transmitted from outside locations such as an annual party conference at Blackpool or a European Community summit in Brussels, but the news itself will be read in the home newsroom, or at the very least in a studio acoustic in these locations. A central paradox of radio (and television) news is that if there is one thing more vital to it than a sense of authenticity, of proximity to the events themselves, it is a sense of clear-sighted detachment from them – of this authenticity being mediated through the remote, sterile atmosphere of the studio. The final proof of this is the fact that whereas the former quality is dispensable, the latter is not. In news *summaries* we seldom hear newsgatherers or news actuality, merely the reader in what is always a studio acoustic.

If the newsgatherers do not *need* to be heard what, then, is the point of their strong presence in WO? There is a sense in which the impersonal, uniform nature of print is a limitation. It gives no hint of the eclectic nature of the information which goes into many of the articles. But the variety of voices and acoustics on radio news suggests the gleaning of its information from a multitude of sources and allows WO to show that whatever the quantitative limitations of its output its newsgathering operation is as extensive as that of the quality newspapers.

But even more important, the sound of newsgatherers on the medium seems to introduce an extra *level* into the production of the news and, indeed, exposes the mechanism of that production by making overt the processes of news collection and editorial mediation which are merely implicit in the news sections of the quality press. It involves a sequence of 'framing' which gives the listener a sense of being led deeper and deeper into the story.

For example, in introducing the fifth of the news features, which deals with the Turkish Cypriot reactions to the fugitive business-man Asil Nadir, James Naughtie frames it around the reporter Charley Lee-Potter, who in turn frames her report around a series of location interviews she conducted with the leader of the Cypriot opposition party, the editor of a local newspaper and the President of Turkish Cyprus. The variety of Lee-Potter's sources lends the story breadth, and the snatches of actuality from a local bar and a newspaper office lend it authenticity; but above all the double framing of the narrative, which can be expressed almost algebraically –

Presenter {Reporter (Opposition Leader + Editor + President)}

– lends the story *depth*.

Thus in its own way the programme achieves that sense of substantiality, balance and perspective which the quality press can achieve through the sheer quantity of its news coverage and its freedom to editorialize on other pages. Even a short piece such as item (vi), on the selection of the England cricket team, conveys this sense merely by incorporating a change of voice from the newsreader to the Cricket Correspondent and back to the news-reader. Moreover it is of course true that despite the vocal and often acoustic variety they help to provide, the newsgatherers are not part of the news, but *purveyors* of it along with the newsreader and programme presenter. Consequently they help to form a high ratio of reportage to actuality which mirrors the ratio of text to photographs in the quality newspapers.

In a study of television news it has been suggested that the
framework which this reportage provides for the 'voices in the
news' is somewhat analogous to the narrative framework provided by the author of a novel, within which we are 'privileged' to
hear the actual remarks of his characters: 'Even though the
dialogue "belongs" to the characters who speak it, it is *produced* by
the author' (Hartley 1982: 109). But the author in this context is to
be seen not as a fabricator but an *authority*, the guarantor of the
reality he is purveying.

The second aspect of the format of WO which helps to create a
sense of breadth and depth is the division of the programme into
hard news and what I shall call with convenient vagueness
'features'. Though they are also in a position to arrange their news
under subject headings such as 'Home' or 'Foreign', something of
this same division is apparent in the quality papers. On WO it is
faintly suggested by the opening announcement, 'forty minutes of
news and comment', and necessitates not only a newsreader
(Brian Perkins) but a programme presenter of similar editorial
status (James Naughtie). Moreover it mirrors in a structural way
the presentational distinction we have made between the newsreader's text and the newsgatherers' reports, since the Features
section is to some extent an illustration or amplification of the
News section.

In the News section we are apprised of the latest events in the
'serious' world of politics, economics, military affairs and general
human concerns. The WO Features section, as our outline shows,
may function partly as a background to those events (for example,
item (1) on the Baghdad missile attack, or item (2) on the selection
of the England cricket team), providing material which explains or
expands them or gives people's reactions to them where those
reactions do not in themselves amount to 'an event'.

It may also provide 'current affairs' – that is, cover issues which
are a part of contemporary life even though they may presently
lack 'hard news' content. Item (4), on the controversy about *News
at Ten*, could be included in this category, since the actual news
that the ITV companies intended to reschedule this programme
had broken several days before. But a better example would be
one of the special reports that WO sometimes runs – perhaps on
unemployment in a particular industry or region, or on the plight
of the Bosnian refugees.

Finally the Features section may leaven serious news with an item of a lighter, more frivolous nature. Our specimen programme contains nothing of this sort: item (2), on the England cricket team, is not exactly a frivolous matter, but we might notice in passing that although less serious than item (3) and possibly item (4), it precedes both and lasts longer than (4) – a reminder of our earlier observation that in radio news neither precedence nor length is an absolute guide to a story's importance.

We need to look more closely at how the Features section operates. I suggested just now that in its relationship to the opening news bulletin it parallels the relationship within the bulletin between the newsreader's text and the newsgatherers' more expansive reports. Its items may fill in details which were already known to news staff before the bulletin or they may be exploratory, speculative – seek to discover new details or dimensions if only in the form of people's reactions to the news. Indeed the Features section is largely an exercise in news *gathering* as distinct from news delivery.

This makes James Naughtie's role a complex one. I asserted earlier that a kind of editorial authority is vested in the news presenter along with the newsreader. Indeed Naughtie is more like the editor-in-chief in that he frames the entire news programme, of which the bulletin is only a part. Moreover it is Naughtie, and not the newsreader Brian Perkins, who reads the opening headlines. The news seems definitive, reading it an authoritative act. On the other hand the Features section, in which Naughtie replaces Perkins as the central presence, deals more in speculation and opinion than in facts, in investigation and enquiry rather than in certitude. In the bulletin the newsreader does not conduct interviews, that is left to the newsgatherers. But in the Features section Naughtie himself conducts several of the interviews. It is as if in the course of WO he 'regresses' from newsreading, the delivery of the finished product, to newsgathering, seeking the sources or raw materials of the news.

The effect of this is to 'unpack' the news bulletin, to turn it inside out and show how it has largely been constructed from the activities of interviewing, enquiry and speculation which take place in the Features section. Yet Naughtie maintains his quasi-editorial status because he frames, and thus legitimates, all the newsgathering activities in the Features section including his own, cueing himself in items (1) and (2) as the person who had conducted certain of the interviews before the programme began.

The 'regressive' tendency of WO, combined with the authority which Naughtie imposes on it, confirms our sense of the programme's depth.

But another aspect of his role reinforces our impression of its *breadth* because as a presenter in the Features section he integrates the items in two closely related and important ways. First, as in item (1), he pulls a story together from diverse sources – an apt reminder that news items are seldom if ever less than multifaceted. After a summary of the British political parties' reactions to the missile attack, he presents in turn some actuality from a speech by the US Vice-President; some remarks from a former national security adviser to President Bush; and interviews first with a Tory backbencher, second, with the Egyptian Chargé d'Affaires, and finally with the US Ambassador to Britain. What the presenter appears to be doing, then, is to take cross-bearings on the listener's behalf so that she can arrive at some composite notion of 'the truth'. (In its own coverage of the Baghdad story, this is something which NB also attempts very effectively, but WO's coverage, at three times the length, achieves breadth without running a risk of superficiality.)

However, as well as integrating different elements of a *single* story, Naughtie groups together *different* stories so that the listener can see latent connections and analogies. Something of this occurs at the end of the item on Baghdad when Naughtie invites the US ambassador (unsuccessfully) to see parallels between the Iraqi and the Bosnian situations; but the best example is item (3) in which the case of the 'village vigilantes' is linked to another successful appeal, that of Ivan Fergus, and both are then related to the future of the criminal justice system and the reorganization of the police.

This evokes the same sense of depth that we noted in item (5), where Naughtie framed a newsgatherer who in turn framed snatches of actuality and some interviewees: but here *two* newsgatherers are framed who in addition to giving their own reports frame between them three snatches of actuality and three interviewees, thus giving an additional sense of the item's range and diversity. Having had the news read to her at the beginning of the programme, the listener is thus enabled to 'read' it for herself – not only to hear it as a sequence of facts but to perceive causal and other connections within it.

Finally the closing headlines (6) acknowledge a reality beyond even the range of the Features section. Item (iv), on the singer Boris Christoff, was not dealt with in Features, while those two perennials, the City (v) and the weather (vi), were not dealt with in the news. Thus in structure as in presentation WO is able to evoke something of the substance and perspective of the quality press; but we might add that whereas our impression of its depth comes mainly from its method of presentation, the programme's two-part structure is largely responsible for our sense of its breadth.

In format and content NB differs radically from WO. It lasts a mere fifteen minutes, less than half WO's length, yet contains as many 'illustrated' features – a fair imitation of the bright, 'urgent' format of the popular papers. Such a feat of compression allows little time for headlining (half that of WO) and reminds us yet again that analogies between time and spatial quantity are not entirely straightforward. Although the compactness of the popular newspapers is well matched by the brevity of the programme, it does not follow that their huge headlines would be matched by lengthy previewing. Such headlines are, in fact, more quickly scanned than small ones, and NB gets much nearer to the spirit of its counterparts by moving as swiftly as possible into the first item.

Lasting a mere thirty seconds its opening sequence is a very effective radio equivalent of the front page of a popular tabloid. The headline, with its alliteration and crisp monosyllables, has the linguistic virtuosity of a newspaper headline, and the sound-bite of the woman outside the law court corresponds to the big photograph. Moreover the theme music which heralds the headline lends it an extra dramatic power equivalent to the sensationalist block capitals of a tabloid, while the 'Newsbeat!' jingle that follows the sound-bite is an acoustic version of a tabloid masthead. We then hear a rapid preview of the programme's content, which the readers give in alternating voices accompanied by the theme-music, thus evoking the visually varied puffs that are often placed under the tabloid masthead for certain features on the inside pages. Finally each of the readers identifies herself on the beat of the music – two 'news voices' which correspond to the variations in the tabloid text.

Much of the effectiveness of this opening sequence clearly derives from the theme music, a feature wholly absent from WO. We need to look more closely at its functions for the programme as a whole, all of which are prefigured in this opening.

The broad function of the music is to identify the genre of the programme, to remind us that what we are hearing is 'the news' as distinct from records or chat; and it does this by being staccato and repetitive, acting as an iconic index of various kinds of information technology – a typewriter, Morse telegraph, computer or teleprinter. Moreover there are other aspects of the music which declare that the news we are listening to is of *popular* rather than 'quality' appeal.

Since news presentation and reception entail an exercise of balance and judgement, are in a word dispassionate activities, and since music is commonly regarded as producing emotional effects, we might take its mere inclusion in NB as a sign that we are hearing popular rather than quality news. But the theme-tune of Radio 4's PM programme reminds us that music may characterize quality news too. However, the NB music includes that unmistakable sign of popular programming, the jingle, and quite aside from the connotations of the title proclaimed therein – 'Newsbeat!' – is very clearly in the rock idiom.

As well as establishing the general nature and tone of the programme the music and jingles also make a specific contribution to its format and sequence. Since they are heard at the beginning and end of each item they act as *frames*, reviving the listener's attention and thus increasing the appeal or intelligibility of the item by isolating it from the others. But in the directly informational sections of the programme the music does not merely frame, it *accompanies*, acting as a background to the preview, the news round-up in the middle, and the closing headlines and trails for *News 93*. Such a technique is not normally encountered even on those 'quality' news programmes which employ music as a framing mechanism, since it declares in effect that the news is an *emotive* matter. But in terms of our comparison with the newspapers we might see these accompanied sections as similar to those tabloid articles which are set off from the others by being printed on a different background.

Hence we can regard the music and jingles of NB as a form of radio typography, since they are 'redundant' sounds in the way that the dots, borders, rows of asterisks and different kinds of print are redundant images in the papers – there to embellish the text without appreciably adding to its meaning, and to create a sense of contrast and variety. A measure of the difference from WO is the fact that the latter has nothing more with which to strive for such effects than the voices of its newsreader and presenter.

But not only is there a sense of contrast and variety *between* the items; through its other resources NB achieves a considerable acoustic variety *within* each item. Reportage alternates with actuality, both of them involving several voices: but there are also alternations within the former which consists, in addition to the newsgatherers, of not one but two newsreaders. Just as the tabloids use chunking, asterisks, boldface and other devices to break up lengthy tracts of information and make them more palatable, so NB uses Maggie Shields and Tina Ritchie as alternating readers – an especially effective device for items such as the vigilante story (1) which require a measure of backgrounding, and for the opening and closing headlines and the mid-programme round-up (3).

On the other hand the actuality is equally varied, some of it live, some of it pre-recorded, and occurring in a range of acoustics: studio, locational and telephonic. And since its alternations with the reportage are frequent and no item lasts longer than a few minutes, we never hear more than snatches or snippets of anything. In item (2) on Baghdad, for instance, which runs for just over three-and-a-half minutes, there are more than ten changes of voice and six changes of acoustic – the alternations of Ritchie and Shields in the studio with the two ambassadors and Ken Livingstone in three separate locations, and with Michael Colvin and Tom Aspel in two different telephone acoustics. Indeed in terms of the production and editing techniques which must be used to meet its requirements NB is much more impressive than WO, just as, no doubt, the typographical demands of the *Sun* display the skills of layout staff much more than do those of *The Times*. Even its briefest sections, the preview and the one-minute news round-up, are enlivened by tiny sound-bites, voices caught like flies in aspic. In popular news, whether on the radio or in print, one gains a strong sense of the medium itself, of technology flexing its muscles.

To sum up, then, we can say that just as the popular papers are characterized by short articles in different kinds of typefaces, numerous photographs and illustrations, a number of typographical devices which enhance visual appeal, and by an overall compactness, so NB is characterized by brief spells of reportage delivered in different voices, lots of sound actuality or illustration, a number of jingles which enhance auditory appeal, and by an overall brevity – what we might describe as 'tabloid length'.

Two further aspects of NB's format must be noted – aspects which also distinguish it from WO and reinforce its similarity to the popular press. The first is that its newsgatherers have a much less prominent role than those in WO. To begin with, only two of them are named and neither has the same status as his 'quality' counterparts. Interestingly enough, the first, Michael Williams, reports for both programmes on the vigilantes' appeal, so we can make a direct comparison of his contributions.

In item (1) of NB he does not give a direct, uninterrupted report as he does in item (i) of WO's opening bulletin: indeed NB contains no reports of this kind. Nor is he cued as an interviewer. Instead he is informally addressed as 'Mike' by Maggie Shields and treated as an interview*ee* – an eyewitness of the events in court. Since he remains at the place where they occurred (in WO he apparently gives his report from the studio) – and occurred so recently that he is still improvising his account of them (note the hesitation 'er') – there is a sense in which he seems to be a *part* of the news rather than a gatherer of it. So whereas in WO Williams frames the events within a continuous monologue, in NB he is heard in a format which seems to place him *within* the frame of events, and which conveys the information to the listener not in one long slab but in two voices and in easily digestible morsels.

The second named newsgatherer, David Willis, behaves rather similarly. He is heard in item (4), ostensibly reporting on the British Scrabble Champion, but he is less of a reporter than a stooge, for in order to illustrate this story about a fifteen-year-old prodigy Willis also 'enters the frame' by giving the champion a game in which he is comically routed.

The remaining newsgatherers are either heard but unidentified – for example, the nameless female interviewers in items (5) and (6); or unheard and unidentified – those who asked the questions which have been edited out of the programme but whose responses are heard as isolated sound-bites (for instance, in items (1) and (2)). Of the fewer sound-bites which occur in WO most are framed within the newsgatherers' reports – for example, Currill's in item (3) and Lee-Potter's in item (5) – and thus seem to have been part of interviews which they conducted.

Hence the newsgatherers are much less of a presence in NB than they are in WO, but before discussing further their relationship to the other contributors to the programme I need to adjust my terms somewhat. I have so far referred to Maggie Shields and Tina

Ritchie as newsreaders, but since as we shall shortly see the line between news reading and news presentation is much more blurred in NB than in WO, I shall henceforth refer to them as news *presenters* and their activities as *presentation*.

What seems to happen in NB, then, is that instead of being used as an intermediate presence between the presenters on the one hand and actuality on the other, the newsgatherers are, if not eliminated altogether, treated either as unnamed, temporary presenters alongside Shields and Ritchie or as 'voices in the news', as a part of the events they are reporting on. In other words they are closely identified either with presentation or with news actuality.

This reduction in the role of the newsgatherers gives us much less of a perspective on the news than in WO, yet seems to bind presentation and actuality more closely together. Hence whereas WO uses its newsgatherers to show how the news is produced, NB seems to *conceal* this process. But it is not simply that we sense a closer connection between presentation and actuality, we are much more *aware* of the actuality than we are in WO: the first slice of it occurs as only the second utterance of the whole programme. Just as in many pages of the popular newspapers the text seems to be little more than ancillary to the numerous and often large photographs, so in NB the role of Maggie Shields and Tina Ritchie seems to be little more than to cue its many slices of actuality.

It might now be useful to summarize some of the points I have made. I suggested earlier that the news can be authoritatively delivered on the radio with nothing more than a reader with a recognizably RP accent, as is attested by the many summaries which consist of nothing else. But in WO this authoritative air is confirmed by creating a sense of depth and perspective – by demonstrating through the strong presence of correspondents, reporters and others its newsgathering and editorial processes. In the interests of brevity and vivacity, however, NB suppresses its newsgatherers and instead conveys its air of authority through authenticity – by a mode of presentation which is closely linked to actuality. And these differences of format seem to illuminate the basic differences between quality and popular news in any medium: for whereas the former broadly depends for its authority upon its 'literary' resources, upon the number and accuracy of its reports and the way in which they are set in context by editorial judgement, the latter draws its authority from its nearness to reality, from its pictures or sounds of the people in the news. To make a crude generalization: quality news relies on the strength of its reportage, on an approach to the world which is essentially verbal, that is, *symbolic*; popular news relies on its pictorial strength, on an approach to the world which is in the broadest sense *iconic*.

One other aspect of NB's format distinguishes it from WO and identifies it with the popular press: its integration of news and features, which reflects in a structural way the integration of presenter and actuality that occurs within each item. In WO we noticed the maintenance of a clear distinction between hard news and features, but in NB each of the main items is neither pure news nor pure feature but something in between. Much more, for instance, is packed into the NB item on the Baghdad missile attack (2) than is contained in WO's *news* item thereon (ii), but much less, despite the acoustic variety, than in the latter's *features* item.

NB's items are, then, shorter than conventional features but less abstract and summary than conventional news items, and might best be termed 'illustrated news items'. It is for this reason that I could not maintain a distinction in NB between the *newsreader*, who delivers the news, and the news *presenter*, who amplifies it and helps us to interpret it, but in the end referred to Shields and Ritchie simply as presenters.

What is the reason for this foreshortened perspective, for this conflation of the news itself with its background of illustration and reaction? It reflects an underlying assumption shared with the popular papers that the news consists not merely of 'events' to be perceived in a detached and clinical way, but of matters which must as far as possible be assimilated to the ordinary moods and concerns of the audience – its preoccupation with employment, money, sexuality, crime and so on. This explains the tendency in popular news towards an emotive or sensational treatment of serious events, but it also explains a greater predilection than in quality news for 'human interest' items – those which touch the heart, funny-bone, and sometimes the lower regions of the anatomy – and this predilection is apparent in NB.

Its choice of items makes a fascinating comparison with that of WO. Of the nine news items it contains, five are missing from WO including, however, two serious items in the news round-up (3) – one on Arthur Scargill (ii) and the other on South Africa (iv). NB gives extended coverage to five of its nine stories, treats them as what I have described as illustrated news items, and even the more serious of these might be introduced in 'tabloid-speak' to make them more appealing. For example, Ritchie begins item (5), on medical care by satellite, by declaring 'If you want to get an op, get a hat' – in which 'hat' is presumably slang for 'satellite dish'.

But a sizeable proportion of NB's coverage – about four-and-a-half of its fifteen minutes – is devoted to lighter fare, 'human' or leisure interests which will have an immediate effect on the listeners' moods and feelings: a surprisingly youthful Scrabble champion and pop music. Neither of these stories is included in WO, but it is not, of course, true that lighter stories are ignored in quality news, merely that they are more sharply distinguished from serious items. In contrast, the serious news round-up in NB is tucked between two of its illustrated news items and occupies only about a minute of the whole programme – a format which is also reminiscent of the popular papers, where a similar round-up is often provided on one of the inside pages.

Thus popular news is less concerned with perspective not only *within* its items, but *between* them. Serious and light stories are fairly freely intermingled, for in NB as in the tabloids the length and sequence of the items are even less reliable guides to import-ance than they are in WO. For instance, item (6), on Techno music, is half-a-minute longer than the lead story on the vigilantes (1), and the Scrabble story (4) precedes the more serious item (5), on medical care by satellite.

But what is perhaps most remarkable in NB is the concern not only to give its news-content a maximum appeal to its listeners, but to assimilate the programme as a whole to its broadcasting context, to emphasize to an audience not primarily interested in the news its relationship to the world of popular music and popular culture. We have already seen that this relationship is implied in the pun of its title 'Newsbeat' and in its jingles, which remind us in both rock music and words that it is basically a continuous pop network we are listening to: Radio 1. Moreover the voice that we hear in the jingles is deep and unmistakably American – appropriate enough when we recall that America is the cradle of modern popular culture, but quite extraordinary when we reflect that the voice also acts as an index of the *British* Broadcasting Corporation.

But NB further assimilates itself to the rest of the network's output by frequently ending with an item on pop music, making the point not only that 'the news' affects us as closely as pop music does but conversely – and as the popular papers do, too – that pop music, that most topical of subjects, is itself *part* of the news. After the Techno item and before the closing headlines, the final jingle 'BBC Radio 1 FM: the best sounds around' is nicely ambiguous. 'Sounds' could refer to the best news actuality, but it is also a reminder that Radio 1 is primarily a *music* network.

To sum up, then. For all the linguistic compression which the medium imposes, its inability to editorialize and its need to use voices not only for reportage but as actuality, radio news does succeed to a remarkable extent in paralleling and evoking the differences between the popular and quality newspapers. But we must now face a further question: what *advantages*, if any, does radio news possess over press news of all kinds?

Its advantages may to some extent be discernible in the comparisons we have been making. One of them is the presence of an authoritative 'news voice', the fact that radio news is a matter of speech. The potential *dis*advantage of this we have already noted: the very presence of a newsreader diminishes the required air of objectivity. Devoid of personal signs, print seems to be 'the truth' even when its language is value-loaded (something which quality as well as popular newspapers have frequently exploited in order to tickle the prejudices of their readers).

But given that *all* language is a personal product – the very choice of words declares the presence of an author – the radio voice can actually make the news more vivid and effective not in any crude, sensationalist sense but in the sense of giving news language its full measure of expression – of disambiguating not only through stress but also through voice tone such a statement as 'And the news from Fenner's is that Combined Universities won't be on the winning side yet again'; which on paper could mean either that Combined Universities have been losers many times in the past and are losers yet again or that they have been winners many times in the past but will be the losers this time. Though an advantage to radio in general this clarifying function of the voice is of particular importance in news, where accuracy is an absolute requirement, and in the frequent comparisons which are made between evanescent speech and permanent print it is insufficiently considered.

A simpler example of its power is provided by the title of Samuel Beckett's radio play *All That Fall*, whose visual ambiguity (noun – relative pronoun – verb: 'Everybody who falls'; or adjective – demonstrative pronoun – noun: 'The whole of that collapse'?) is instantly resolved when we hear it spoken; for the unstressed second word would leave us in no doubt that the first meaning is intended. Oral presentation can be used to belie or distort news content, but this is not to deny that it can, and should, enhance content when all allowances have been made for the fact that the news is always in some sense arbitrarily selected and partially treated. On the radio *due* stress and expression can be given to words which in the cold medium of print might be opaque, ambiguous – inadequate.

But the presence of sound is important with respect not only to the way in which the news is delivered but to news actuality, the people and events in the news; for it enables radio to have, in common with all the news media, its own special grasp on reality. Newspapers contain photographs of the world: we can *see* in the newspaper what radio can only *describe*. But radio has the *sounds* of the world. In contrast to the mere iconism of newspaper photographs, which are only *copies* of people and events, radio gives us an indexical sense of the news, the noises which those people and events actually make.

This indexical relationship therefore declares a *direct* connection; we are not presented with an illustration which is at one remove from reality. Hence the technical term for these sounds or noises, 'actuality', is well conceived. On the radio we hear the noises of the news, or at least the informed view or the eyewitness account 'straight from the horse's mouth' and often on location – outdoors, over the telephone – that newspapers can only report in the bland medium of print, a medium bereft of the inflections, hesitations and emphases of the living voice which contribute so largely to meaning, and also less able to evoke the location in which the account was given.

We might observe in passing that within the fifteen-minute NB programme outlined above, items on Baghdad, Scrabble and medical care were 'authenticated' by American, Iraqi, Indian and Scottish accents in various acoustics; while WO's items contained the voices of an Egyptian diplomat, a Welsh news editor and several Turkish Cypriots. Indeed an event can be particularly 'newsworthy' on the radio and gain much more public attention than it could through the press simply by being primarily a matter of sound. However extensive and eloquent it may be, the press coverage of the new release by the Techno band 'Alternate' could in one respect never equal NB's coverage since the latter includes the actual *sound* of its music.

A more frivolous example which springs to my mind is a 'silly season' item which BBC Radio Newcastle once ran about a Japanese professor who during a brief visit to the city learned to play the Northumbrian bagpipes. Essentially an 'acoustic' item, it would lose much in the newspapers and was most likely ignored by them – another reminder that the very *choice* of news item is determined not simply by its inherent importance but by how effectively the medium can convey it. A more serious example of the use of sound as a news resource is *Yesterday in Parliament* (BBC Radio 4), which comprises not only the presenter's links and the voices of the main speakers but the equally expressive background noises and reactions of the whole House.

But it could be argued that in stressing the difference between radio and newspapers and proclaiming the advantages of the former over the latter, I have merely demonstrated its similarity to television, except that television has the advantage over radio that it is endowed with pictures as well as sound. Our remaining task is therefore to see how radio fares as a news medium in comparison with television.

There is by no means universal agreement that television's pictures are a straightforward asset, for it could be said that they do not materially add to the news so much as illustrate it and slow down presentation:

> there are critics who argue that it is a bad medium for handling news . . . pictures take a long time to convey simple information and are often what is called professionally 'moving wallpaper'. Radio, these critics argue with force and considerable justification, is able to convey news in more detail without the distraction of pictures and – if speed is a valid consideration – more speedily than television.
>
> (Hood 1975: 35)

The question 'What is news?' is as knotty as any philosophical problem and to try to answer it would push us into deep waters I am keen to avoid. But it is at least arguable that news is primarily verbal, that however concrete the subjects with which it deals it is mostly concerned with the abstract relationships which exist within and between them and which can only be expressed in language.

This was brought home to me by a television news-flash which announced that mortar bombs had landed on a police station in Newry and that pictures would follow later. These consisted of shots of a damaged building and a fire-engine departing from it, and struck me as entirely dispensable. The cause of the damage and the reason for the fire-engine were not self-evident. To make sense they required *words*, all of which had been provided in the earlier news-flash; those words had not required the pictures. For a strictly intellectual understanding of the news words are entirely adequate. Indeed language is bound up with our very efforts to make sense of the world and images are seldom as explicit: even in newspapers, where the images are surrounded by text, they invariably need separate captions to explain their relevance.

One may go even further and argue that in certain cases the pictorial redundancy of television can *mislead* us as to the true state of affairs, or at least encourage us to draw false conclusions. One of the arguments against televising debates in the House of Commons, for instance, could not have been brought against radio: 'if the cameras showed only a few members in attendance during a debate, the public might think its representatives were neglecting their work, whereas in fact they might be attending meetings or talking to their constituents' (Paulu 1981: 234).

Certain members of the media audience are reassuringly alert to the potentially misleading effects of television news coverage, for in a recent survey 'Some discussants confessed to feeling more comfortable with a radio bulletin which was not dependent on the availability of dramatic pictures and could therefore order its priorities according to proper [sic] news values' (Barnett and Morrison 1989: 43).

Something of the mischievous redundancy of television can be felt at its *production* end, for its studios and cameras invite the broadcaster to make a 'spectacle' of himself, with the tendency towards irrelevance and artificiality which that implies. The somewhat 'spare' nature of radio technology, on the other hand, is less likely to dilute and distort the truth: the solitary microphone is more conducive to honesty. This point was facetiously made in a critical review of the highly successful BBC Radio 4 series, *In the Psychiatrist's Chair*:

Down at Portland Place, with a green baize table, a waxy beaker
of water, a stacker chair, a gang of technicians behind a glass
partition . . . the parallel between an interview and a private
confessional conversation may be plausibly drawn. On television, with heat, lights, make-up and visible cameramen
laocoonically wrapped in cable, the guest finds himself sub-
liminally invited by the medium to entertain. To be interviewed
on radio is like being asked to pause and tell them the truth; to
be interviewed on television is like being asked to lie quickly in
case people start switching off.

(Barnes 1983: 32)

If it is true that radio is a 'purer', more concentrated news medium
than television, then in terms of production it has another advantage over both television and newspapers, which is that the
link it provides from the occurrence of the news to the audience is
shorter and cheaper than that provided by the others, especially
the press with its lengthy processes of reportage, editorial mediation, composition, printing and distribution. This means that it
can provide 'newer' news than the press, including updates on
events which have been continuing over a span of time such as
wars or test-matches. As we saw in Chapter 2, the newspaper
proprietors recognized this advantage very early in radio's history
and took steps to prevent it, so that it was some years before it was
fully exploited.

One significant effect of this advantage which has emerged only
gradually, and largely as a consequence of local radio, is that the
medium has developed a whole new *stratum* of news, in that it can
cover events which are not only very recent but *ephemeral* – that is,
events which would have ended in the time it takes to go to press
and which the newspapers must generally ignore. One such event
might be the blockage of a motorway by an accident or the
presence of fog at a local airport.

But it is also true that radio is quicker and cheaper than full
television coverage: 'It is complicated and expensive to set up a live
television outside broadcast for a news item. All that radio needs is
a man and a telephone' (Herbert 1976: 26). This is all that television
needs too: we may, and sometimes do, hear an on-the-spot report
while our screens are filled with nothing more than a photograph
and a caption. But here television is a victim of its own visuality:
however redundant this or any other image would be, the medium

leads us to expect something more (Whale 1969: 19). What we have is quite adequate, it is televised radio; yet it is not felt adequate as *television*. I often think that the medium reaches its nadir with the Saturday afternoon soccer reports which are accompanied by pictures of the goalscorers' faces – not, it would seem, of the greatest relevance to their feats!

This means that in certain cases radio can cover events which would have to be overlooked not only by the press on account of their ephemerality, but by television on the grounds that for all their news-value they are not worth sending a camera crew out for, yet could not be broadcast without some visual accompaniment. It reinforces one's conviction that for all the glamour of television, news is quintessentially a *verbal* genre, and this verbal quintessence explains why, even in this visual age of television and teletext, news is part of radio's 'rump'. It is for 'newsic' – news and music above all – that people continue to listen in, for the 'chat' that people also listen to is merely an adjunct of the music; it can hardly be considered as a category on its own.

But the last and greatest advantage of radio news over television and press news is already familiar to us: that it is quick not only because the medium can forge a link between events and audiences more rapidly than any other can, but because there are many more circumstances in which its audience is able to attend to it at the *moment* of transmission. At the moment the newspapers arrive on the streets the aspiring reader may not be in a position to read a copy even if she is able to buy one; and when the news is broadcast on television the viewer may be nowhere near a set or in no position to watch it if she is. But radios are portable (or mobile) and cheap. They can be, and are, taken anywhere and attended to while the listener performs other activities.

Thus, given that the production of the news is *always* a selective matter (a matter which depends on such factors as the editor's political views and his general sense of what is important) the relatively condensed and synoptic way in which it has to be presented on the radio is in this respect a positive advantage, affording convenient and rapid assimilation. An early slogan of LBC News Radio was 'Read the newspaper with your eyes closed' (Baron 1975: 92). The first three words might equally have been 'Watch the television', for in certain vital respects radio news surpasses both.

SUGGESTIONS FOR FURTHER WORK

Here are two comparisons which might be fruitful:

1 Examine a single news story as it appears in each of the news media, noting particularly how radio's presentation differs from that of television and the newspapers.
2 Compare a morning news bulletin on a national radio station with the news coverage of a daily paper which seems to be targeting a similar audience. In its coverage of a particular story how effectively does the bulletin summarize the detail that is provided in the newspaper – or does it attempt a wholly different approach? How much of the bulletin consists of more recent news than the paper could include? Is there any evidence that the choice of news is determined by the medium for which it is intended – that is, does radio incline to certain stories because they have more 'acoustic potential' than others – or are stories included solely because they are 'important'?

In a more practical vein, listen to a BBC Radio 4 news bulletin, paying particular attention to the length and register of its items. Then take a newspaper story and rewrite it as an item for that bulletin, 'inventing' some actuality or a newsgatherer's report if you need to. In dealing with the often complex and profuse data of the news you may find it a formidable challenge to satisfy the conflicting requirements of brevity, accuracy and clarity!

Finally, listen to one or two of the 'news background' programmes on Radio 4 – *Analysis, File on Four, From our Own Correspondent, Special Assignment*, or even a more specialist programme like *Law in Action, Kaleidoscope* or *Medicine Now*. How far do they expand the limited content of the main news broadcasts? And is this *all* they do, or do you consider that they can offer something more than is offered by the similar background articles in the newspapers?

Chapter 6

Outside broadcasts: commentary on public events

Before I joined the B.B.C. . . . . I rarely listened to anything except concerts and running commentaries on sports events. These latter, which gave me a pleasure distinct from that which lies in *seeing* a game or race, should have provided a hint of radio's possibilities.

(Louis MacNeice, Introduction to *The Dark Tower*)

Outside broadcasts (OBs) consist of live coverage of an event which takes place outside the studio. Their various forms were categorized as long ago as 1929 (S. Briggs 1981a: 165) and in both radio and television they are extremely popular with broadcasters and audiences alike. Why?

They are a necessary, or at least desirable, proof that media messages can be originated in places other than the womb of the studio, an acknowledgement that radio and television not only serve the community but draw their raw material from it. One might expect that radio would have ceded outside broadcasting to television, which is in an obvious respect better qualified to do it. But precisely because its codes are limited radio has found it even more important than television to demonstrate its links with the 'real' world and has over the years more than maintained its OB output.

The most effective means of doing this is *commentary*, the improvised description or word-picture of an event. Thus commentary is even more referential or realistic than news because it is immediate and spontaneous – unscripted by a news editor – and occurs entirely *in situ*: it is not transmitted from a studio or newsroom. Commentary exists and is important in television as well as radio, but the differences in the two media mean that radio commentary is usually different in nature and always in effect from that of television. It is not simply the special abilities of a John Snagge or Richard Dimbleby which make them more memorable than television commentators but the difference in their *function*. In television the outside world exists as an icon or picture. It can be watched on a screen, where it engrosses most of the audience's attention. The commentator exists, as it were, off-stage: his role is largely secondary since his words are an elaboration of what we can already see. In radio the outside world exists as an index, if it exists at all. 'Effects' microphones are invariably installed to gather the sound of the action and/or crowd reaction, but as often as not it is inaudible or at best exists as a collection of distant and isolated noises – applause, shouts, the click of ball on bat. Beyond these the commentator must create the picture for us, and so his role is central. He acts as our eyes and to a large extent our ears.

This means that while all good radio commentators know the eloquence of a pause their commentary must be more nearly continuous than that of television. Its speed and style reflect the mood of the event and its language tends to be more explicit, creates its own context much more, than television commentary. It includes not simply a concrete description of the event but what has been described as 'associative material' (Evans 1977: 159) – other sense-impressions such as the smell of new-mown grass, the weather and the human 'atmosphere'; and also the historical background, those facts and causes beyond the event which remind the listener that there is more to it than meets the eye.

Primarily as a result of radio commentary a necessary new verb 'to commentate' has appeared alongside the traditional 'to comment'; for whereas 'comment' implies subjectivity – 'to express an opinion on something' – 'commentate' implies the more objective process of describing something as it happens. These functions are often quite sharply distinguished in live sports coverage, a commentator breaking off his *commentary* at intervals to invite *comments* from an expert sitting beside him. A somewhat similar arrangement occurs on television, except that since the action is largely self-evident the functions are less sharply distinguished: the commentator will not infrequently 'comment' as well as commentate. But within the total impression of an event which both media seek to convey the radio commentator must first create the picture or image of it which his television counterpart can take for granted – and however 'vivid' that picture may be it can never be iconic but merely *symbolic*, created in the opaque material of words.

Despite this apparent handicap radio commentary has always enjoyed a huge popularity, creating an impression in the minds of its devotees which is often more vivid than that made by the events themselves upon those who are watching them. It is not altogether surprising, then, that such commentary has maintained its popularity even in the age of television (Trethowan 1970: 8).

The two great BBC commentators were Richard Dimbleby on state occasions and John Arlott on cricket, and many people preferred to have test matches mediated through the commentary of the latter than through the television cameras. One likely reason for this is that unlike television or watching from the terraces, it left them free to do other things at the same time. Yet it is still listened to even by those who have time to view – the reason for which can only be that such people prefer words to images, signs which do not resemble the things they stand for to those which do. In brief, they prefer to *imagine* the cricket match than to *see* it. Nevertheless, as the following extract illustrates, radio commentary attempts to be as exhaustive and accurate as possible:

England vs. West Indies – Second Test Match
Transmission: 25 June 1963. Commentator: John Arlott.

England want 43 to win in 55 minutes . . . and Hall . . .
that little shower apparently wetted the outfield and for
the first time today a bowler has recourse to the sawdust
heap, Hall comes down . . . dries it . . . turns at the pavilion
5 end, comes up . . . great tigerish run, the leap . . . he bowls
to Titmus . . . Titmus covers up . . . it goes off the edge of
the bat and he takes a single to gully. (Applause)
A single to gully there, the ball didn't travel a third as
far as the batsmen ran. A very quickly taken single makes
10 England 192 for 5. And this is where one's almost afraid
to breathe for fear of rocking the boat: and these two
batsmen now faced with a tactical decision on almost
every ball. Two slips, leg slip, silly mid-on for Close,
Hall comes in, bowls to him and he plays that straight
15 up to silly mid-on, Worrell. Hall turns and walks back,
Close again goes out and prods the pitch. The trees
away in the distance heaving under this strong wind which,
in fact, would help Hall to swing the ball in to Close.

The wind is coming in from about cover point – say extra
20 cover. The trees heaving and bending under it, the light
murky: and Hall comes up again, past Umpire Phillips and
bowls to Close, Close a hook, he's beaten long leg, it's
through, it's four runs. (Applause)
Close is 50 and the people here are only sorry they couldn't
25 make ten times as much noise. An innings of remarkable
shrewdness, good judgement, courage and very sound
technique,
50 in 3 hours 15 minutes with five fours, his
first 50 in a Test: his previous best, 42 against the
West Indies at Birmingham in 1957: and now it's Hall
30 again from the pavilion end; in, bowls to Close and Close . . .
oh! tried to cut outside the off stump, through to the
wicket keeper and about six rows of members down here
fidget as if their ants were full of pants . . . pants were
full of ants . . . absolutely unable to stay still there. This
35 awful moment when you see a batsman play outside the
off stump at pace and it goes through.
196 for 5. 196 for 5. Hall comes in again, bowls to Close,
Close tries to turn that on the on side, takes it on the
thigh again as he turns, walks away with a little hobble,
40 still disdaining to rub . . . a very hard man this. He's
been hit, I would think, a couple of dozen times on
the thigh, he's resolutely refused to rub; he was cracked
once on the forearm . . . and I would think that that was
the first time in this innings that Brian Close has flashed
45 outside the off stump. And the reaction amongst the crowd
was almost terrifying, 196 for 5, then.
38 wanted and Hall comes in, bowls to Close, Close hooks and
again he's beaten long leg . . . leg slip but not long leg,
beautifully fielded by Butcher, they take a single
50 (Applause) – a Constantine-style sprint, pick-up and
and return, it's 197 for 5. Titmus 11, Close 52. England,
197 for 5, want 37 to win and there are 52 minutes left.
Well, still anybody's game but Close, I think, realizes the
position, he's hitting at everything on the leg side and
55 really, for the first time in this innings, since tea he's
been connecting with the ball on the leg side. He had one
or two swings before tea and never got a run from it; but this
time he's got two fours and two singles down to fine leg.

And Gibbs comes in, bowls to Close who goes down the
60 pitch, but checks the stroke, Worrell fields, and you
can hear the sighs come out of the spectators like
punctured bicycle tyres. Every time a risk is taken,
everybody walking the tightrope.
Gibbs to Close, tries to swing it, an appeal for LBW, not
65 out; taken by Close at slip and he appeals for it, Sobers
at slip, and he appeals for a catch. A few brows being
mopped though it's not a warm afternoon; and Gibbs comes
again and bowls to Close – a little short but Close, using
his reach, goes forward, smothers any turn and plays it
70 out on the off side. 197 for 5 and still with this very
economic field: eight men saving the one. Gibbs comes in,
bowls to Close, Close swings it on the leg side. (Roar of
crowd) Four again. (Applause) 200's up. It's been a long,
long road to home, this, and now England want 33. Gibbs
75 bowls to Close, and Close plays out on the off side, 201
for 5. Close 56, Titmus 11, and that grotesque tower away
in the distance suddenly catching the sun like a beacon,
the ground in bloom as Gibbs comes in, bowls, and Close
steers him to short third man and takes a quick single,
80 as Nurse closes in to field. 202 for 5, Close 57, every
Englishman in the ground with him. Every West Indian in
the ground after his blood.

Radio commentary entails a relationship between commentator
and listener which is complex and appears to operate at several
levels. At the first level there is the 'real' John Arlott and the 'real'
listener, who cannot know each other to the extent that they might
in circumstances of ordinary personal interaction. They are mutually invisible and physically remote from each other. Yet these
'real' individuals are, of course, the precondition of interaction at
any other level.

At the second level the commentator and listener assume the
minimal roles of 'mouthpiece' and 'hearer' respectively. The
commentator is the mere purveyor of actuality. He is as self-
effacing as possible, his primary duty is to events rather than to the
listener, he is interested only in what is happening 'out there'. He
is not present 'in propria persona', nor is he expected to be, but in
a sense pretends not to be present at all. Like the newsreader he
submerges himself in the reality he reports. John Arlott's language

in this passage is very largely referential, concerned with the objective world of deeds and facts – 'Hall comes in again, bowls to Close' (l. 37), and so on. In sum the passage consists of a description of every ball bowled, the number of runs England require to win, the physical and psychological duel between Hall and Close, the air of tension and excitement in the ground, the weather conditions. What confirm the existence of that objective world are the intermittent sounds of applause and Arlott's occasional unfinished remarks (l. 1), ungrammatical sentences (ll. 34–6) and errors of fact (ll. 65–6), which suggest that the events are putting him under pressure. In the sense that the commentator has no rhetorical design upon the listener but is presenting the facts on a take-it-or-leave-it basis, the listener 'pretends' not to be present, too. He merely eavesdrops on John Arlott's words as symbols of the action .

Nevertheless, as we saw in Chapter 1, the lack of resemblance between words and the things they represent means that however factual the events which the commentary describes they must be 'created' in the listener's mind, very probably in a form which is in many respects different from the reality itself, and are in that sense a 'fiction'. One broadcasting historian recalls that after hearing a particular OB 'I was taken to Rushmoor Arena to watch the Aldershot Tattoo, and was disappointed to find how small the spectacle seemed compared to the stupendous thing my mind's eye had seen' (Black 1972: 68). This is a disturbing reminder of the old philosophical dilemma that ultimately only words can explain the world yet do so by 'falsifying' it.

Thus however accurate John Arlott's account, the test match which the listener experiences is in the strict sense of the word *imaginary* and when he prefers this account to television coverage we must conclude that he is more interested in a fiction than in the 'truth'. We glibly refer to television as the truth since its photographic images seem to represent things 'as they really are': we are hardly conscious of the human agency (choice of camera locations, sequence of pictures, and so on) which is always involved. But in radio commentary the very fact that things are not 'apparent' in the words which represent them gives us scope to be much more conscious of the person who provides those words, and I would suggest that for all the commentator's objectivity there is a sense in which we become almost as conscious of him as of the events themselves.

In what way, then, do John Arlott's words proclaim his personality almost as much as they proclaim the events they describe? At the beginning of the extract he describes Hall's run as 'tigerish' (l. 5), a word which conveys to us something more than the objective nature of the bowler's action, for it is a metaphor which briefly superimposes upon that action the image of a wild animal and thus invests it not only with speed but with a primitive aggression, a suggestion of hunger and predacity. But at the heart of this as of all metaphors lies an incongruity. We would not notice the image if in most respects Hall were not quite unlike a tiger, and the incongruity thus declares the inventiveness of the commentator, his ability to sharpen our awareness of the familiar by discovering between objects connections which are unfamiliar.

We see this same inventiveness in ll. 17 and 20 when Arlott describes the trees in the distance as 'heaving ... heaving and bending', which is a buried metaphor and much more than such effete verbs as 'shaking' or 'waving' invests the trees with a kind of arduous, sentient life and suggests by implication the force of the wind which in helping Hall to 'swing the ball in to Close' (l. 18) may have a decisive effect on the match. In l. 63 Arlott describes cricketers and spectators alike as 'walking the tightrope', a momentary superimposition of images which the 'impersonal' iconic media would find hard to emulate! And when, facing Gibbs, Close changes his stroke at the last moment and Arlott avers that 'you can hear the sighs come out of the spectators like punctured bicycle tyres' (ll. 60-2) the comparison evokes the tension in the ground, but its bathos declares him, too, for he is momentarily detached enough from the proceedings to glimpse them in a comical light.

One or two other expressions highlight the commentator's sensibilities and his gift of words quite as much as the atmosphere of the match itself. He notices a 'grotesque tower away in the distance' (ll. 76-7), an observation and a description which are so idiosyncratic that we picture not only the object itself but Arlott observing it. Yet with an author's instinct he provides the tower with an aesthetic relevance to the events on the pitch. It suddenly catches the sun 'like a beacon' (l. 77) and this, together with 'the ground in bloom' (l. 78), which suggests not only the beauty of the summer but the colourfulness and excitement of the spectators, creates a sense of incipient celebration, is perhaps a portent that England will achieve a great victory.

Arlott concludes this phase of the action with a summary of Close's situation – 'every Englishman in the ground with him. Every West Indian in the ground after his blood' (ll. 80–2) – and like his previous expressions it is elegant enough to call attention to its creator as well as to its subject. The antithesis could hardly have been bettered had Arlott had the opportunity for a writer's premeditation.

But not only is Arlott's personality revealed in his choice of words – his distinctive epithets and his ability to find linguistic connections between the happenings in the test match and other, quite different, areas of experience; it emerges in his ability to find causal connections which exist within the match itself but are by no means obvious to everyone who is watching it. For instance even those who saw Titmus's quick single on television may have failed to notice that 'the ball didn't travel a third as far as the batsmen ran' (ll. 8–9), an arithmetical comparison which precisely conveys the pressures on the England batsmen to take risks.

Not only, then, do we have signs which do not resemble what they describe and are therefore just as likely to proclaim their author; they describe connections which may be partly visible within the photographic images of television but are by no means self-evident. They do not simply exist 'out there' but are made explicit by the commentator, and therefore declare his presence and percipience to an even greater degree than his use of metaphors and epithets.

Likewise, his subsequent observations that 'one's almost afraid to breathe' (ll. 10–11) and that 'A few brows [are] being mopped though it's not a warm afternoon' (ll. 66–7) confirm the existence of a tension within the ground whose cause is not at the moment wholly visible, as the last clause concedes. Lines 38–40 describe Close being struck on the thigh and hobbling away but disdaining to rub it. A spectator relying solely upon his own eyes might simply assume from this that Close was hit hard, but not very hard. He might have 'failed' to notice what Arlott perceives as a significant 'non-event', the refusal to rub, a perception which in its very utterance draws the listener's attention to the psychological as well as physical battle between Close and the West Indian fast bowler, Hall.

Finally in ll. 54–5 Arlott observes a change in Close's batting behaviour, 'he's hitting at everything on the leg side . . . really, for the first time in this innings since tea' and spells out the tactical significance: 'still anybody's game but Close, I think, realizes the position' – an observation which is at least partly based on visual data, but data which have been abstracted from a welter of other physical detail and over a period of time.

What Arlott is doing here, then, is conveying more than is conveyed by photographic images, he is 'reading the game'. His ability to describe a reality which is only partly visual, and to make connections between superficially disparate phenomena or between aspects of the past and those of the present, is essentially a human, an intellectual faculty. In all these remarks, no matter how objective they may seem, the mediating intelligence of the commentator is strongly declared. I do not, of course, mean to suggest that this cannot be done by television commentators, indeed they do very little else; merely that this reality is not established through images alone. But whereas on television it is done as an accompaniment to the events that the viewer can see for himself, it is done for the listener by the same person who has described those events to him, and very often in words which are an inseparable *part* of that description; and it thus makes the commentator a much more pervasive presence on the radio medium.

But in concentrating on the commentator's stock-in-trade of words we have so far ignored an obvious sense in which radio commentary is more personal than other accounts of the world: it is *voiced*. Newspaper accounts are also personal in the sense of being written by individuals, but as we saw in Chapter 5 the medium of print lends them an air of impersonality. By different means the radio presentation of the news also acquires an impersonal air, for we know that it is being *read* – a fact which suggests that it has originated elsewhere, been observed and set down by someone other than the speaker, and this deflects our attention from him. But commentary is improvised under pressure of events, as is clear from the variations of volume and pace in the commentator's voice – his alternating murmurs and shouts as the significance of the events changes, his fluency then hesitancy as he strives to keep abreast of them.

The effect of this is, as we have seen, to convince us of the realness of these events, but it also makes us very conscious of the commentator himself. When Arlott tells us that 'Close . . . oh! tried to cut outside the off stump' and then makes the mistaken reference to ants and pants followed by a correction (ll. 30–4) our awareness of what is happening on and around the pitch is indistinguishable from an awareness of the very human qualities of the speaker.

This awareness is heightened by two other factors. The first is that the commentator's presence is an unmitigated one. As we have seen, he can never leave events to speak for themselves as his television counterpart can, but must fill the entire medium except for a few isolated and often unintelligible sounds which exist, as it were, round the edges. And the second factor which may increase our awareness of him is the inherent quality of his voice – its timbre and accent. We observed that in radio news the invariable delivery in RP or near RP further minimizes the reader's presence, but when we read the above extract we must imagine the words as being spoken not only as if impromptu but in the gruff Hampshire burr which made Arlott's presence quite unmistakable.

Thus, as we saw in Chapter 3, radio language is a *binary* code in that *words* act as symbols of the objects they represent while *voice* is the index of the speaker. But we have seen in this chapter that it is also binary in the sense that words are also an index of the speaker, even when (as in our reproduction of John Arlott's) they cannot be heard: for his use of certain words in preference to others very much proclaims his personality – his level of awareness, command of language, emotional state, and so on. Anyone who doubts this indexical function of words may recall that when confronted with a piece of writing which we have not previously read we can often infer the identity of its author merely by discerning within it characteristics of style and vocabulary which we have noticed in his other writings. If such characteristics did not exist, we would never be able to enjoy literary parodies, such as Max Beerbohm's of Henry James. Linguisticians have a term for this characteristic mode of utterance, whether written or spoken: idiolect.

Let us sum up what we have suggested so far. No matter how accurately and objectively the radio commentator describes a particular event, his efforts will have two closely related and paradoxical effects: he will perforce create a 'fiction' from this event in the listener's mind and he will establish a strong sense of his own presence. Indeed we have noted that the radio OB differs radically from its television counterpart in giving us first-hand evidence of little else: through his voice and words the commentator is virtually the only thing we are directly aware of, so that he is quite literally a storyteller – the sole source and in that sense the 'creator' of the things he describes.

Our interest in these things is therefore indistinguishable from an interest in the commentator himself – specifically, in his creative intelligence, the way he perceives the events and transmutes them into something 'perceivable' by us. This is confirmed by the popularity of radio commentary among those who are present at the event as well as those who have the option of watching on television, where the commentator's role is merely ancillary. Using our own example we might say that our interest in the test match is much the same as an enjoyment of John Arlott's company, so that the relationship between the commentator as mouthpiece and the listener as hearer which we described earlier leads to a third level with which it is inseparably connected yet in extreme contrast: the commentator as 'personality' and the listener as his companion.

This sense of companionship between broadcaster and listener is not, of course, peculiar to commentary. It is generated by all personal presentation on the medium, and we noticed in Chapter 4 its particular importance to listeners to music radio. I suggested that we might distinguish two broad categories of music presenter: the 'personality', with an emotive, fairly free-ranging style of presentation and a limited and familiar play-list; and the more self-effacing, music-focused presenter.

It is not surprising that even those in the latter category should provide the listener with some degree of companionship since their language, however referential, also dwells along the 'I–you' axis and is implicitly conative. What any music presenter seems to be saying is: 'These are the records you might enjoy and even buy'. However, the strong sense of personality and companionship engendered by the commentator is perhaps rather more surprising since he seems much too preoccupied with events to consider what sort of effect they will have upon the listener. These are, as I suggested earlier, presented on a take-it-or-leave-it basis, for the commentator's words do not dwell nearly as much along the 'I–you' axis.

But the final point of importance is that however strong our sense of his personality in comparison with the events he describes the commentator is, of course, a 'fiction' too. I have just asserted that he is almost the sole reality we are aware of since we can hear him continuously, whereas the events have scarcely any existence outside the words which symbolize them. But the sound of his voice requires us to 'complete' him within our imaginations just as his commentary requires us to imagine the test match, and with little more likelihood of corresponding to the reality.

The late William Hardcastle, euphonious presenter of *The World at One* and an individual of some corpulence, once received a letter from a female listener who had just seen a photograph of him and was outraged to discover that he was not the slim and handsome figure she had quite naturally assumed him to be. But from the sound of a broadcaster's voice the listener will infer not simply his appearance but an impression of his personality which transcends that appearance. Many years ago an experiment was conducted to discover how accurately listeners could infer a broadcaster's personality from the quality of his voice. The results varied enormously from listener to listener and were substantially inaccurate (Pear 1931: 178–242).

However, in this experiment the subjects did not speak their own words but read a single passage from *The Pickwick Papers*, and we have been arguing that *words* quite as much as voice are an index of the speaker's personality: they suggest his educational level, intelligence, nature and mode of perception, and so on. But in the case of commentary at least, they are only obliquely self-revelatory, for the focus of attention is always upon the public event – the test match or the royal wedding; and the commentator's description thereof, delivered as it is in that blend of companionship and anonymity which characterizes the medium yet is quite untypical of most social interaction, may well give a positively misleading impression of his 'real' self. Nevertheless the important point is not how accurate the listener's impression is, but the fact that it is formed in a quite different way from – and on much less information than – the impression he would gain from direct experience of that person, or even from being able to see him on television.

We can conclude by saying that for all its concern to portray events as realistically and impersonally as possible, listeners tune in to the radio OB for a version of them which is in the strict sense imaginary, and for a concomitant sense of companionship with a commentator who is also very largely imagined. Since radio's attempts to deal directly with the outside world seem to lead inevitably to the creation of fictions, it is time to take a closer look at its dealings with the realm of the imagination.

SUGGESTIONS FOR FURTHER WORK

Plan a commentary on some public event near you – a local soccer match, student rag procession or vintage-car rally, for example. Research in advance the background and context: what has led up to the event and what, precisely, it will consist of; the relevant personal details of the participants; the topography of the venue (including a quiet vantage-point from which you will be able to observe the action). Take a tape-recorder along to the event and for about ten minutes conduct a running commentary, remembering to punctuate it with 'associative material' – relevant statistics, weather conditions, some description of the larger environment, and so on. You will find excellent guidance on all this in Evans (1977) and McLeish (1978). Finally play your commentary back to any people who were not present at the event and see what sense they make of it.

Part III

The imagination

Chapter 7

Radio drama

> The best in this kind are but shadows; and the worst are no
> worse, if imagination amend them.
>
> (Shakespeare, *A Midsummer Night's Dream*, V, i)

Since we have arrived in the realm of make-believe, we should
perhaps revert briefly to the more conventional distinction between fact and fiction and hint at the semiotic complexity which
such a distinction entails. Although radio involves us in acts of
imagination, in making fictions even when its concerns are factual,
the conventional distinction between fact and fiction is between
sign-systems or codes which refer to things that exist in the real
world, such as Boris Yeltsin or the Taj Mahal, and those which
refer to things that do not exist in the real world, such as unicorns
or Tess of the D'Urbervilles.

Though obvious enough in itself, this distinction creates semiotic complications, for if the word-signs of a newspaper are
symbols of the real things which they signify and the word-signs
of a novel are symbols of the unreal things which they signify,
there is a further semiotic relationship between the unreal and the
real, between fiction or make-believe on the one hand and fact on
the other; and it is one which is essentially *iconic*. Literature, as
they say, is a mirror of life.

In one way or another works of fiction reflect the real world and
are intelligible only because they do so. The events of Thomas
Hardy's *Tess*, though conveyed in verbal symbols, in some sense
resemble those which occur in real life. This is true of drama as of
novels. The characters and events of Shakespeare's *Othello*, even if
it is not based on actual history as many of his plays are, have a
broadly iconic relationship to the people and events of real life.

Having established the nature of the relationship which exists between the make-believe world of novels and drama and the real world, I now want to concentrate on what constitutes the *difference* between novels and drama. If novels create their fictional worlds through words, how do plays create theirs? One thing which might seem essential to drama is dialogue, which radio is peculiarly good at; but not all drama is characterized by dialogue or even monologue. There is the drama of mime, which reinforces the basic conviction that drama is essentially a *spectacle*, that one of the main things which distinguishes it from the signifying modes of most other arts, particularly literature, is *ostension*, whereby its fictional world is *shown* to the audience rather than merely described, explained or defined (Elam 1980: 29–30). The character of Othello is not merely conveyed in writing, as Tess is, but shown to us in the form of a dark-skinned man in Venetian costume.

However, this would seem to rule out the possibility of drama on the radio, for in its strict, literal sense ostension is impossible in such a medium. A radio producer put his finger on the difficulty many years ago: 'we are all accustomed, in everyday phraseology, to going "to see" plays, as opposed to going "to hear" them. In consequence the mere juxtaposition of the words "radio" and "play" must imply for many people a contradiction in terms' (Gielgud 1957: 85).

On the radio there can be no scenery, lighting, properties, costumes or make-up. At the very least, the absence of vision imposes huge restrictions on the *kinds* of play radio can do. Large cast dramas are next to impossible: in any one scene the listener can accommodate at best only four or five major speaking characters with distinctive voices. While one character is speaking it is not possible to show the listener any reactions she might produce in the other characters, to counterpoint what is heard with what is seen. No character who is present in a scene can stay silent for long, for if not regularly heard or referred to she 'disappears'.

Moreover no elaborate stage business is possible since its prerequisite is space, and our sense of space – of *proxemics*, or the physical position of the characters relative to one another, and *kinesics*, their moves and actions – is primarily visual. Stage business is shown or 'ostended' to us, so if ostension is a distinguishing characteristic of drama and radio is blind, we are again forced to ask how radio drama can be said to exist.

Even judged on its own, purely acoustic, terms the genre is

restricted. The technology of the medium compresses the vocal range available to the actors, making dramatic contrast harder to achieve because shouts must be distanced and/or muted and whispers slightly amplified. Moreover the sounds have to maintain a fairly unbroken flow to hold the listener's attention since there is no visual dimension to fill out prolonged silences.

Nor do the apparent deficiencies of radio drama end there, for its audience is not only blind but absent. Its members are not where the play is being performed but surrounded by the distractions of their own separate environments. In the conventional theatre the spectator, as Elam points out (1980: 95–6), initiates the communication process in a number of ways. By buying a ticket she sponsors, or commissions, the performance, makes a contract whereby she delegates an initiative to the actors. On the other hand she comprises with the other spectators an audience whose most significant signal is its mere presence. Its reactions exert a double influence – on the performance itself and on its reception. The spectators can influence the actors' performance and also one another through stimulation (for instance, by laughter), through confirmation (the spectator can find her own responses reinforced by others') and through integration (the spectator is encouraged in consequence to surrender her individual function to the larger unit of which she is a part).

But the role and circumstances of the radio drama audience are radically different, a point which was made many years ago (McWhinnie 1959: 33–6). Its members have not paid for their seats, so are unlikely to have a highly developed sense of occasion. But they are exacting in that they need not sit the play out, they can simply switch it off. Furthermore since they cannot use their reactions to influence or control the performance in any other way and are usually listening as isolated individuals they may feel that this is the only option left to them; for they not only lack the visual cues offered by actors on the stage, but cannot be influenced by the reactions of others in the audience. The business of understanding and judgement thus falls solely and squarely upon the individual listener.

Yet despite all these disadvantages, radio drama appears to be in a flourishing state: its variety and sheer quantity can easily be underestimated. It occurs not merely in the form of 'straight' plays and soap operas, such as *The Archers*, but in an 'applied' form – as an element in commercials, trailers, comedy shows and features –

and in 'characterized readings': narratives or storytellings. Thus it may appear in varied guises, as a comic or illustrative sketch, a monologue, a reading from a diary, journal or poem. The BBC's radio drama department has grown into the largest commissioner and producer of plays in Britain – around 350 every year, in addition to over 260 episodes of *The Archers* (Donovan 1992: 86).

How, then, does radio set about surmounting its limitations and create something analogous to conventional drama? Partly by a process of 'transcodification' – the replacement of one code or set of codes, in this case visual ones, by another, in this case auditory, the code of speech. We have already seen in the case of news and current affairs programmes that the spoken word is a relatively crude vehicle of communication. But in radio drama it has to carry extra freight, for as well as the dialogue itself it has to convey through dialogue, or at least through narration, almost all the other kinds of information that the theatregoer would be able to see for herself – that is, whatever the audience needs to know about setting, time of day, the stature, dress and actions of the characters, any physical objects they may make use of, and so on'. Hence transcodifiers – pointers such as 'Look out, he's got a gun!', which sound so contrived and superfluous in the visual media – are essential on the radio. Anyone present in a scene has to be identified – given speech, addressed or referred to fairly regularly so that the listener remains aware of her.

Of course it is important to remember that radio is not devoid of *all* the resources of theatrical drama: it has sound, including sound effects. But the role of sound is a complicated one: it seems to occupy a position intermediate between speech, the primary code of radio, and the purely visual codes of the theatre, which radio can convey only in a transcodified form. For present purposes I shall distinguish between *noises* – sounds which are extraneous to speech (the creak of a door, for example), and *sound effects* (SFX) – acoustic treatments of speech or sounds such as the fading up or down of speech or noises, or the addition of echo to a voice. Here we can see that the line between SFX and ordinary speech is a fine one, for the addition of echo to a voice may convey very similar spatial information to the sound of a raised voice.

Noises and SFX can be used as *environmental* indicators, acoustic means of depicting scenes or settings (birdsong can suggest the countryside, echoing voices and noises a dungeon, and so on) and scene changes (the fading up and down of voices is analogous to the rise and fall of curtains and/or the brightening and dimming of stage lights in the conventional theatre). They can also act as *spatial* indicators – ways of revealing proxemics, the physical distances between the various characters, and kinesics, their movements relative to one another and to the listener. Proxemic and kinesic information is most frequently and effectively conveyed by locating the actors at varying distances from the microphone and by moving the actors in and out of its sound-gathering areas. This means that a single sound effect, the fading out of a voice, is often used to convey both environmental and spatial information: it signifies either of two things which would be perceived to be quite different on a stage, the end of a scene or the exit of a character during a scene, but the radio listener would have no difficulty in distinguishing which of them was happening.

How does the listener know what these noises and SFX mean? John Drakakis describes them as 'really a kind of mediating system of "sound signs" which both [broadcasters and listeners] agree will conventionally represent particular kinds of experience' (1981: 30). This description is helpful if it implies that such sounds convey in radio drama what would primarily be conveyed by visual means in the theatre, and that our awareness of what is in effect their extended signification depends on a process of cultural familiarization. As we saw in Chapter 3, the sound of hooting may represent not only an owl but also by frequent association a dark, sinister setting, such as a graveyard at night-time.

But Drakakis's description is misleading if it suggests that the relationship between these sound signs and what they signify is arbitrary in the way that the relationship between *word* signs and what they signify is arbitrary. Both Drakakis and Erving Goffman ('Sound substitutes become conventionalized for what would ordinarily be conveyed visually', 1980: 163) seem to overlook the fact that in our perception of the world sound is a natural property even of those things which present themselves to us by predominantly visual means: it is not something which we *substitute* for its properties, as words are. And this is equally true of the predominantly visual world of the theatre. We do not simply *see* what is presented to us, we hear it. Our awareness of a stage murder derives not simply from the sight of one character drawing his gun upon another, but from the sound of a shot and the victim's cry, and our awareness of the characters' moves on to, around and off the stage stems not only from our sight of them but in however small a measure from the variations in the level of the sounds they make.

In this sense, then, the noises and SFX of radio are *not* what Goffman perceives as 'substitutes' or 'equivalents' of what happens in the visual world; they are a *part* of what happens. Their relationship to what they represent is indexical, not merely symbolic, and so to regard them as transcodifications is misleading. Hence the point I wish to make is that drama may be distinguished by ostension or showing, but ostension is partly a matter of *sound* as well as vision: we register the activities on the stage through what we can hear as well as what we can see. In certain cases, that of thunder perhaps, sound might even be the primary means of ostension in the conventional theatre, just as it would be in a radio play.

Radio dramatists and producers have long been aware of the ostensive possibilities of sound, as is demonstrated by the fact that there have been plays such as Andrew Sachs's *The Revenge* (1978) which have consisted only of sound effects – a term which, as SFX, I shall henceforth use to denote non-verbal and non-musical noises of any kind. Such plays might be regarded as a wordless but acoustic equivalent of theatrical mime. Nevertheless it has to be recognized that a substantial number of sounds are not easily identifiable in isolation, as we saw in the example of the rustled recording-tape in Chapter 3. Such sounds are capable of 'existing' on the radio, but to the extent that they have no intrinsic identity their status is much the same as that of visual phenomena, they can be 'revealed' to the listener only through the transcodifying process of speech. The rustling recording-tape is as 'unknowable' to her as are the dress of the characters, the time of day, the place in which the action is set, and so on, and only the words adjacent to that sound will enable her to know whether what she is hearing is someone walking through undergrowth, the swish of a woman's gown or the unwrapping of a package.

Indeed we also noted in Chapter 3 that it seems doubtful whether any radio sound is ultimately meaningful without the help of speech – even conventional, instantly recognizable, sounds are seldom very precise in their signification. Does birdsong, for instance, signify 'a garden' or 'the open countryside'? Do seawash and the cry of gulls mean 'the shore' or 'the open sea'? If the question is important it is only the narrative or the dialogue which will finally give us the answer.

We might attempt to summarize what is semiotically significant in a comparison of radio drama and theatrical drama by splitting the signs of the former into their component parts of 'signifier' and 'signified'. Anything which would signify itself in the theatre primarily by being seen (for example, a clock) cannot occur on the radio except as a signified which is identified by a non-visual signifier – either verbal ('That's a nice-looking clock') or acoustic (SFX: TICKING SOUND). Transcending their function as dialogue, words are the primary signifiers, identifying for the listener both the things which would be visible in the theatre, and sounds, which even when not difficult to recognize in themselves generally have an uncertain function. And sounds occupy an intermediate position in that they 'signify' or identify many of those things which would primarily identify themselves by being seen (the clock): but because sounds are often ambiguous or insufficiently expressive in themselves they need to be given identity or significance by words (SFX: CLOCK CHIMES. 'My God, is that the time? I'm late', and so on).

To put it yet another way, the most natural and obvious mode of ostension, and one which is possible in the theatre, is for an object to be *seen*. On radio this must be replaced by an equally natural if 'secondary' mode of ostension: the object must be *heard*. But if this is impossible or unhelpful the object must be rendered by means of an 'artificial' sign or signs – symbols called *words*, and this process is known as transcodification.

But of course this distinction I have been making between words and sounds is a false one. Words may merely *describe* what they refer to but they also 'show' the speaker, for in drama words are sounds also – the normal sounds made by human beings which have the advantage of being both intelligible in themselves and able to explain other sounds. Hence these words are not extraneous to the drama, made use of to remedy its ostensive deficiencies. As indexes of the characters who speak them, they are part of its ostensive apparatus.

Since ostension is not just a visual matter but a showing of any kind, many readers will by now be aware that it is much the same as our formulation of iconism at the beginning of the chapter, which implied a general resemblance to life and not merely a visual one. A brief recapitulation will be helpful here. We began by suggesting that the relationship between the fictional world of novels and plays and the real world is broadly iconic, but that whereas the fictional world of novels is created out of words – and there is therefore a *symbolic* relationship between these words and the world they describe – the fictional world of plays is *shown* to the audience. To be rather more precise, what the audience is shown on the stage is an image or icon of the fictional world of the play. Indeed the very notion of acting is iconic, since it is an attempt by one person to resemble or imitate another. The dark-skinned actor in Venetian dress is an icon of Othello, the wooden scenery an icon of the citadel of Cyprus, the handkerchief probably a real handkerchief but also an icon of Desdemona's handkerchief.

But the iconism does not end there, for it is a natural and inherent property of the objects in this fictional world not only to be visible but to be *heard* (Othello, like all human beings, makes sounds 'spontaneously' in the form of words and most, perhaps all, inanimate objects are audible if treated in certain ways): consequently the theatrical icons or images which 'show' them will be heard, too. In this sense, then, the principle of iconism and ostension applies to plays on the radio as well as on the stage because their speech and sounds are not simply indexes of the people and things that make them, they are a part of drama's broad resemblance to the world it represents.

Nevertheless while everything that we hear in a radio play is an act of ostension in that even if the only fully intelligible code is speech, that speech 'shows' the person or persons uttering it; not everything in the world it portrays is ostended. Those things which cannot directly reveal themselves through their own speech or sounds are merely transcodified from the visual medium to the symbolic, descriptive medium of words.

But at this point it is important to remember that ostension is not absolute in the conventional theatre either: we must not make the mistake of assuming that because radio plays are forced to describe what they cannot ostend drama is free from all such necessity in theatre, film and television. Words are needed not only to explain the purely visual phenomena and ambiguous sounds of the former but the images of the latter, for in our discussion of television news and OBs in Chapters 5 and 6 we saw that images often mean little by themselves. They may establish a great deal of the reality they portray, but are in themselves an incomplete guide to the causes, motives, attitudes and relation-ships which make that reality what it is. 'There is more to this than meets the eye' runs the cliché, fossilizing, as all clichés unfortunately do, the important truth it is meant to express; and the only accurate way to convey these 'invisible', or at any rate largely diachronic, factors is through words. If this were not true, the mime and the silent movie would be more prolific and expressive genres than they are, and the latter would never need its captions.

Thus, while I argued in Chapter 3 that words are the primary code of radio because they are needed to contextualize all its other codes, it could equally be argued that words are the primary code in *all* the media – in theatre, film and television as well as in the more obvious case of books and newspapers. But even things which could be ostended in the conventional theatre are often merely described, largely because the main concerns of the play-wright lie elsewhere. Battles, for instance, are frequently ostended in Shakespeare's plays, but in Act I of *Macbeth* the battles which gain the hero his rewards from King Duncan, and as it were provide a background to the play proper, are merely described, though this is not to deny that the descriptions ostend those characters, the Sergeant and Ross, who provide them.

Once again it might be helpful to review our assertions. Whereas literature conveys its world through description, the symbolic power of words, drama is characterized by ostension, by icons of its world which embrace not only images but also sounds (including the sound of words) and may even extend to smell. But ostension is seldom if ever absolute in drama. Some element of description is almost invariably present, and the difference between conventional drama and radio drama is merely one of degree: in the former there is likely to be a greater proportion of ostension and in the latter a greater proportion of description.

For this reason some of the contrasts drawn between the achievements of the two strike me as exaggerated. It is suggested, for instance, that because radio drama shows less and involves the imagination more, it can 'stage' a whole range of situations which are quite beyond the scope of conventional drama. Some situations are certainly beyond it, but not as many as might be assumed by those who are used to a diet of naturalistic plays; for not only is theatrical ostension limited in extent, it is highly variable in form.

A bridge, for instance, might be represented on-stage by an actual bridge or by a picture or cardboard cut-out of a bridge or by an actor on all fours. If the bridge is represented by a cut-out, a character in a play (a giant, perhaps) could carry it about the stage in a surreal fashion; if it is represented by an actor on all fours it could complain about those who walked across it or could instantaneously change into something else, a chair or a human being, and perhaps become part of a quite different scene. And as well as its powers of ostension, the devices of mime and verbal description make conventional drama equal to almost anything – underwater scenes, aerial battles, and so on. Pub and street theatre thrives, despite a lack of elaborate ostensive apparatus such as scenery, lighting and properties. Two actors on a bare stage might, with the aid of recorded traffic noises, convey the atmosphere of a crowded street simply by verbal references to such a street, by boarding, dodging or pointing to imaginary vehicles, being jostled by imaginary pedestrians, and so on. Indeed in the case of mime, wherein an actor adjusts himself to an object which is invisible, (for instance, when he pretends to pick up and carry a pane of glass), it can be almost impossible to tell where ostension ends and our imagination begins.

But as with mime so with theatre in general – the 'reality' of what is actually ostended vouches for the reality of what has to be imagined. In *Macbeth* it is not only the behaviour of the Sergeant and Ross but the strength of the entire dramatic illusion presented to us through images and sounds which helps us to believe in those rebellious 'kerns and galloglasses' whom we never actually see or hear. In this respect, then, the drama which is ostended to us is an *index* of that other part of the fictional world which exists around and beyond it.

Given this varying blend of ostension and description, of showing and telling, in both radio drama and drama in the visual media, what can radio 'convey' (a conveniently vague term which, along with 'present', I shall henceforth use to embrace both processes) which the conventional theatre cannot? Since it can ostend much less than conventional drama it invokes the audience's imagination to a much greater extent, and this ratio of ostension to description, which is a direct consequence of its blindness, gives radio a number of advantages.

From Chapters 1 and 6 we can already infer the most obvious of these – the fact that we can picture the visual phenomena of the play very largely as we would like them to be rather than having to accept them as they are. In the theatre the spectator may picture what is happening, or is referred to, off-stage but what is ostended to her on-stage allows little scope for her imagination to work. She may speculate about the personal background or inner being of the characters before her, but she is not free to imagine their actual appearance, to invent a moustache for one or change the build of another.

Something of this difficulty attaches even to those minimalist forms of theatre we have just been considering, in which the actors wear neutral attire, occupy a bare stage and render through mime and/or description every other visual phenomenon the play encompasses. Here, as we have seen, ostension and imagination may often be almost indistinguishable. When a character marches about the stage with a walking-stick resting on his shoulder, the spectator may furnish him with a soldier's uniform and rifle even as she watches him. But while she may *add* to what she sees she will not be able to 'abolish' it, to change the basic physique of that character.

In radio, however, we are free – forced – to imagine everything, even the actual dramatis personae who ostend themselves to us in sounds and words. However often we hear them, and in however much detail they are described, we will be required to picture them in our own way, together with further details of them which are *not* described. This is because words can never be as exhaustive or specific as a visual image (Scholes 1982: 66) – which is another way of saying that images are dogmatic, reductive. The relatively peripheral, or at any rate superficial, role which is afforded to the imagination by the visual media seems to be behind that variously attributed saying 'Television is chewing gum for the eyes' – that is, watching is an insipid, purely physical activity that does not engage the higher faculties.

But what is also of interest about the comprehensive role of the listener's imagination in radio is that it abolishes the conventional distinction between the actors (who perform) and the audience (who sit apart and watch) because the words, delivered by the actors who are a vast distance away yet through the paradox of technology 'closer' to us than they would be to a theatre audience, invade each of us alone and in our own surroundings and force us to take over some of the functions which would be performed on-stage. They make *us* 'construct' the appearance and movements of a character as much as or more than the actor who plays it, force *us* to build the scenery instead of the stage carpenter. Hence stage and auditorium become fused and are located inside each listener's head. But as we are already well aware, there are as many potential realizations of the play as there are listeners, and this, together with the fact that radio can accompany the listener wherever she goes, renders the play not so much an external event as the private and unique creation of each person who hears it. Within the generalities of language she can visualize the play as she likes it and carry it around with her; and this isolation from the rest of the audience, which we earlier noted as a handicap, is in this sense part of the advantage.

But radio is at an advantage over the theatre not merely because it affords a greater scope to the audience's imagination and an easier 'access' to its plays; it can convey settings and situations which the theatre can stage only with a certain amount of difficulty, and is in this respect more closely akin to film. Since the action is almost entirely in the listener's head radio can emulate the film camera in choosing settings which are virtually beyond the scope of the stage (the hero of Louis MacNeice's radio play, *He Had a Date*, 1944, was a man drowning at sea) and in switching between these settings with great speed and emphasis.

I suggested earlier, however, that it is possible to exaggerate the theatre's difficulties in establishing certain settings and instanced the way in which two actors on a bare stage might convey the impression of being in a busy street. Nevertheless the existence of two visible, palpable characters within a context of invisible and imaginary properties and scenery conquers the difficulty only in a somewhat stylized, artificial way which is likely to strain the audience's credulity. In sparing us from the need to see *anything* (though some aspects of the setting may be audible) radio can convey these situations rather more plausibly: if the voices are naturalistic we can assume everything else is.

Indeed the liberation of the listener from the need to see is useful even when what we would see in the play would be entirely naturalistic and 'believable'. The conventional theatre may be primarily a 'spectacle' in that it must first of all give us something to look at, but in its need to convey non-visual matters there are times when its visuality is if not exactly a disadvantage at any rate an embarrassment of riches. In contrast, it could be argued that radio has actually added to the potential of drama by being able to focus on certain aspects of the play which would normally be overwhelmed by the visual dimension.

One can take a simple example of this from the radio production of Raymond Briggs's *When the Wind Blows* (BBC Radio 4, 1983), in which an elderly couple have just survived a nuclear attack. The husband checks various domestic appliances, the fridge and the television, for example, to see if they are working. He reports, 'Nothing – all dead' and is echoed by his wife, 'All dead?' However vividly she may picture this scene, the listener is free from the need to *watch* it and therefore attends more closely to the words, to the possible nuances of the repeated 'dead' (as well as the appliances, those people who 'power' them – the engineers, broadcasters, and so on, and even the entire human and animal worlds), than she would if she were seeing the play in the theatre or on television. In this respect, then, 'Words, isolated in the velvet of radio [take] on a jewelled particularity. Television has quite the opposite effect: words are drowned in the visual soup in which they are obliged to be served' (Raphael 1980: 305). But the particularity of these words is even greater than if they were served up in a purely literary medium:

> When you have written for the page, you do not see your readers reading you; which is just as well as you could never tell if in their heads they were 'hearing' you properly. But in [sound] broadcasting you can, given the right speakers, force your listeners at least to hear the words as they should.
>
> (MacNeice 1964: 13)

For these reasons radio is good at creating drama out of situations in which there is literally nothing to see – the thoughts or conflicts which take place within a single character, for instance. These must also, of course, be conveyed in the conventional theatre, where dramatists tend to resort to monologue during which the character is seen on stage either talking to herself or staying silent while her recorded voice is heard. But neither convention is wholly satisfactory, for in the former the inner debate seems to be improbably externalized and in the latter there is an equally improbable dissociation of the character from her thoughts; so that in both cases the attempt to make the audience concentrate more on the words than on the spectacle seems self-defeating.

In the blindness of radio, however, the monologue is much more effective. Since an individual can scarcely exist outside the sound she makes there can be no misleading separation of a silent character from the recorded 'sound' of her thoughts as there can be in the theatre. This means, of course, that in radio monologue the character seems to be actually talking to herself just as she often does in a stage monologue. But given that it is improbable that anyone would conduct her internal debates in this external way, the improbability is rather less obvious on radio. We may *hear* the character talking to herself, but at least we do not have to *see* her doing so, and such is the tyranny of vision that the convention of a visible person using invisible properties and furniture seems a good deal more obtrusive than that of an invisible person voicing unheard thoughts.

If the latter is on radio no more than a voice, which we are able to accept as an index of her entire character as it would be revealed to us on the conventional stage; if this voice must not only convey her words but suggest all her other physical attributes – her height, dress, colour of hair; our belief is hardly strained if it also becomes the instrument of her unspoken thoughts. In any event the listener will regard the unnaturalness of the monologue as a small price to pay for the opportunity it gives her to inhabit without visual distraction the subjective world of a character, just as she can when reading a novel.

Indeed it has been pointed out that a radio dramatist like Louis MacNeice can present a character's mind by the daring expedient of splitting it into *different* voices (Gray 1981: 52–3). The problems such a device would pose for the conventional stage seem well-nigh insuperable: one character talking in two or more voices would be at best baffling and at worst ludicrous, and if the different voices were to be taken by different actors it would be difficult to convey the impression that these were meant to represent different facets of a single character rather than two or more separate characters. Only radio, it seems, can exploit this device without difficulties of staging, for 'It is in the nature of radio to establish connections that do not exist in space: such connections are entirely aural and not in the least visual, since they depend on a contiguity of voices, not of speakers' (Lewis 1981b: 103).

Thus, in a memorable phrase used by Ronald Hayman during a broadcast talk about radio drama entitled *The Invisible Performance* (BBC Radio 3, 1983), what radio is particularly adept at is the 'dramatization of consciousness' – a fact which renders the question of how it deals with spatial relationships, with those matters of kinesics and proxemics that are rightly seen as being central to conventional drama (Elam 1980: 56), as at once simple and inappropriate. In naturalistic drama the listener can visualize them with ease, and in non-naturalistic drama they simply do not exist. It is for this reason that certain technological advances can actually limit radio's unique potential by introducing irrelevant spatial considerations –

> by locating the characters in an arc from left to right, stereo in radio drama also deprives it of its special advantage as an immaterial medium not definitely located in space, able to move between dream and reality, the inner world of the mind and the outer world of concrete objects.

> (Esslin 1980: 184)

– and as a result of this technological advance radio drama has been criticized for a damaging tendency to become feebly iconic ('sound cinema') rather than exploiting its descriptive, symbolic powers (Raban 1981: 83).

But radio is at an advantage over the visual media in being able to convey not only what we do not want to see because it all takes place in the mind, but what we do not want to see because while it may exist in the material world it is literally invisible. On one of the BBC's long-playing SFX records (no. 21, 'Death and Horror') there is a track entitled 'Premature Burial' which depicts someone being buried alive. The listener's 'viewpoint' is evidently inside the coffin with the victim. She hears the superterranean sounds of the graveyard – the rooks cawing, the knell, the parson reading the obsequies – growing ever more muffled and distant as the gravedigger plies the shovel and earth rains down on the lid. At the same time the victim's heartbeat recommences and the track concludes with his panic-stricken groans and frantic attempts to claw his way out. This is an impossible perspective for a theatre audience and a difficult one for film spectators, but the real point is that radio can use sound to convey that which takes place in utter darkness. The slightest attempt by a film-maker to illuminate the situation would reduce the horror it is meant to impart, for however physical and 'external' the victim's predicament may be, the dramatic stage is really located *inside* his head. In the theatre we would observe his ordeal; in the cinema we would observe it very closely; but on the radio the experience becomes subjective – we *share* the unseeing, claustrophobic horror of the victim.

It is worth recalling that darkness was the shrewd choice of setting for the first play to be written especially for radio, *A Comedy of Danger* (1924) by Richard Hughes: its subject is miners trapped in a coal-mine and its very first line, 'The lights have gone out', places the characters on a par with the audience.

There are, of course, symbolic and effective ways in which the conventional theatre has attempted to present situations which are invisible or which take place in darkness, a notable example being Peter Shaffer's hilarious *Black Comedy*. Most of the play's action takes place during a power failure in someone's flat – a failure which is conveyed by flooding the stage with light. Conversely, during the brief periods when the flat lights are working, the stage – and the audience – are plunged into darkness! But for most of the play the audience can see what the characters are doing while they are 'blind'.

This device is an important, indeed an integral, part of the overall comedy, but like many good jokes it depends for its effect on its *in*appropriateness, its tacit admission that the one spectacle which the theatre finds it difficult to stage is the spectacle of darkness. Difficult, but not actually impossible. In theory it is possible to sit an audience in a blacked-out theatre and play it a recording of 'Premature Burial'. But in the conventional theatre, the audience's need to have something to look at is so paramount, so imperative, that it could not be expected to sit for any length of time in total darkness (just as the television audience cannot be expected to hear the news without seeing pictures, even though the news is not always a visual matter). In effect, such a measure would make the theatrical environment redundant: the audience would really be 'listening to the radio', and it is precisely because there is no such pressure on radio to provide something to look at that it would make a poor joke out of *Black Comedy*.

But the dramatic advantages of radio do not end even here. It can convey not merely what we do not want to see because it would distract us from what is being said, and not merely what we do not want to see because although it belongs to the material world it is invisible. It can also convey what we do not want to see because although a part of the material world in the play it does not exist as such in the world of our experience. It is an objectified fantasy of the dramatist and if reduced to a finite visual image would be unintentionally absurd.

In this case it would not be the theatrical conventions which would strain the audience's credulity but the subject-matter itself. This is well illustrated by the drama critic David Wade, who instances a play called *On a Day in a Garden in Summer* (1975) in which the main characters are not humans but dock plants in a garden. Its author Don Haworth perceives the medium's advantage in these terms:

> Obviously if you really thought about talking dock plants . . . it would be like a comic cartoon. The thing in radio is the value of the ambiguity of existence in this way; one is not always confronted with a picture of a plant, one doesn't think 'Well, where are their eyes, then?' One doesn't examine the naturalistic background, there isn't the embarrassing presence of something that is not a human being taking the human role.
>
> (cit. Wade 1981b: 230)

As Wade goes on to say (ibid.: 231) futuristic worlds, fairy stories, allegories, legends, myths and space odysseys are all liable to reduction by sight and therefore worlds of drama in which radio holds a virtual monopoly.

Finally, and perhaps most importantly, radio can convey what we do not wish to see because as a matter of dramatic necessity we must remain uncertain about the exact status of its existence. Does a person or thing continue to exist after it has been named or heard? Does a character exist in the material world or merely in the mind – as the figment of another character's imagination?

In these forms of drama silence has an important role to play since radio endows it with a peculiar potency. In what respect? Sounds, the very essence of radio, exist in time and constantly evaporate. If they are not renewed silence imposes itself. This also occurs in the theatre and cinema but is not important, since these media provide images which exist in space and which therefore endure through both sounds and silences. In radio, however, silence is visually unfilled and therefore absolute. Much more than in the theatre or cinema it is a quality which is noticed, heard, *listened* to. The difference used to be well illustrated by radio programmes which previewed new films by featuring unedited excerpts from their soundtracks. To the unseeing listener the pauses in the dialogue seemed pointless and interminable. Indeed, so threatening is silence to the radio medium that if it persists for more than a few seconds the listener rightly concludes that the station transmitter or her own receiver has either broken down or been switched off.

But silence on the radio does not simply consist of audible breaks in the sound-flow: there are also 'unheard' silences – for instance, the failure of a character to contribute to an un-broken dialogue even though her presence has previously been indicated. To counter the impression that she has departed or simply evaporated she must therefore be heard, referred to or addressed anew. In various ways, then, radio is positively besieged by silence – a silence which portends non-existence, annihilation.

These nihilistic tendencies also remind us that the relationship between word and thing in radio is rather more complex than we have assumed. We have so far assumed that however variously we may picture it, an object exists simply by being named; but we should note that its existence is unlike that of physical objects since there is a sense in which it ceases to exist as soon as the naming is concluded. Nevertheless this has its advantages: since radio's reality requires constant renewal, since it is susceptible to change and even annihilation, the medium is much better suited than the conventional theatre to the presentation of fluid, indeterminate worlds, especially those of absurdist drama. As Frances Gray points out (1981: 61–2) its lack of a consistent reality is itself absurd – a fact which abounds not only in absurdist but downright comic possibilities, as we shall see in the next chapter.

But even when radio presents a world which is internally stable and consistent, there may be things within that world whose ontological status is left deliberately ambiguous – and such ambiguity may also be suggested by heard or unheard silences. In Harold Pinter's play *A Slight Ache* (1959), one of the characters is the mysterious match-seller whom Edward and Flora ask into their home and to whom they open their hearts. He never speaks. Does he really exist, or have they invented him? This question is part of the play's *raison d'être* but is immediately and damagingly resolved if the play is staged or televised.

In this function silence again challenges our previous assumption that word and thing are much the same by demonstrating that a thing does not exist in radio simply because it is named; or rather, what is named may exist not as reality but as make-believe. We are unable to check that everything exists on the same plane and that is why, as Ronald Hayman pointed out in *The Invisible Performance*, radio is so much better than theatre at conveying confusions between subjective and objective reality. Moreover, and as will also be apparent in the next chapter, there is comic potential in the idea not only that an object may last for no longer than it takes to describe it, but that even when it does the description might be unhelpful and even misleading.

By now it should be clear that radio can combine ostension and description in various ways to produce drama which is at least as eclectic as theatrical drama. It is capable of presenting naturalistic plays, psychological dramas whose action is largely internal and invisible, fantasies, and those blends of realism and fantasy which make up absurdist and surreal drama. Such eclecticism is an effect of various characteristics of the medium which suggest that radio drama bears at least as close a resemblance to imaginative literature as to the conventional theatre – a resemblance which has frequently been stressed (Lewis 1981a: 8; Drakakis 1981: 28; Raban 1981: 81). It is worth reviewing some of the characteristics they have in common:

1 Both must rely on words since neither has visual images. Both involve the audience in a creative act by providing it with a 'text' from which its members make a complementary effort of imagination. The illusion is not externally preconstructed for them as it so largely is in theatre, film and television but internally realized by them: and because they are 'blind' media, both literature and radio can inhabit not only visible but invisible worlds, whether subjective or material, and make rapid switches of focus in time and space between speech and thought, consciousness and dreams. (It is also worth noting that the first ever radio play was written not by an established dramatist but by a novelist, Richard Hughes, whose theme – darkness – enshrined the novelist's perception that the imagination can 'see' where in a literal sense there is nothing to see.)

2 Both literature and radio drama address mass audiences, but whereas attendance at the theatre or cinema is a public, social experience, listening and reading are generally private, solitary experiences. The realization of the illusion and the judgement passed upon it are not only internal but individual matters, and to that extent may take an indefinite number of forms.

3 Both literature and radio drama are 'portable'. Books and radios are not in a fixed location like the theatre or cinema but may be carried around by the individual members of their audiences, and so their worlds can be more effectively 'entered into'.

Important as they are, the resemblances must not be pressed too far, for radio drama has non-linguistic codes too, and is therefore more 'fleshed out' than imaginative literature. As in the theatre, we can 'hear' the presence of the characters (as well as that of other phenomena) – and as in the theatre, the combination of text and voice can be much more evocative than text alone. Moreover radio drama can achieve its effects more concisely than literature – for instance, in its presentation of stream-of-consciousness, since whatever the subject thereof the voice and accent of the character who delivers it can convey her likely social position and previous history within a matter of moments (Rodger 1982: 136–7).

It seems most appropriate to locate radio drama somewhere *between* the conventional theatre and imaginative literature. In the theatre the characters are presented both audibly and visibly; in literature the characters are neither visible as such nor audible, but must be realized in the audience's head. In radio drama the characters are audible but the audience must picture them, so that what radio succeeds in doing is to combine the realism or 'concreteness' of the former with the imaginative flexibility of the latter.

But it is also important to guard against the notion that radio drama is simply the aggregate of literature and drama or that it is the mere adjunct of either. Certain of its effects are not to be found in books or theatres. It not only combines concreteness with imaginative flexibility but enhances these qualities by not making even the visual demand upon its audience that is made by the printed word. As a secondary medium accompanying its members while they are engaged in 'primary' activities it can therefore infiltrate their view of the world in a way which is all the more powerful for being only half-conscious:

> As soon as we hear a word in a radio play, we are close to the experience it signifies; in fact the sound is literally inside us. To submit to this kind of invasion, to allow another's picture of the universe to enter and undermine our own, is to become vulnerable in a way we do not when we watch a film or a play, where the alien world is demonstrably outside.
>
> (Gray 1981: 51)

This is attested by the gross 'framing' errors which have frequently occurred on the radio, with listeners sending flowers and wreaths to the studio after the death of a character in a soap opera. One such death – that of Grace Fairbrother in *The Archers* – completely upstaged the opening of ITV in September 1955 (A. Briggs 1979: 1013–14). In the theatre such errors occur much less frequently since the conventionalized markers are much clearer (Elam 1980: 89–90); nor, for the same reason, are they common among readers of literature.

SUGGESTIONS FOR FURTHER WORK

From a novel or stage play choose a short scene which could be adapted for radio, but which contains much important information that could not be conveyed to a listener in its present form. Rewrite the scene using transcodifiers which will convey this information as naturalistically as possible. Get your fellow students to act and record it, then find out how successful you have been by listening critically – preferably with your eyes shut, but certainly not with your script in front of you! Better still, play it to an uninitiated audience and ask for their reactions.

Chapter 8

Comedy and light entertainment

Seagoon	Thank yuckakabakkas, we're still in time – first I must get these bonds untied – have you got a knot?
Crun	Yes.
Seagoon	Quick, glue one onto my bonds and then untie them.
Bill	Listeners, as knot-glueing and untying has no audible sound we suggest you make your own – within reason, that is.

(*The Goon Show*, no. 141, 3 January 1956, 'The Hastings Flyer')

There are two factors which would appear to militate against comedy on the radio. The first is that comedy is often thought of as predominantly *visual*, a matter of facial expressions, gestures, postures and other physical business, and radio lacks this visual dimension. The nearest it comes to comic business or physical humour is in its use of SFX, and as we have seen even these are ambiguous without verbal identification.

The second factor is that listening to the radio is often a solitary activity, yet laughter is not the *normal* response of a solitary person. It is mostly a collective, social activity, and as we saw in our discussion of radio drama the isolated listener cannot look to the rest of the audience for guidance in, or confirmation of, his responses. Yet although the medium would seem to be an inherently unrewarding one, comedy has not only been hugely successful on the radio but achieved its success in a wide variety of forms.

Historically the problem of audience response was resolved almost before it was recognized. In the days of valve wireless sets listeners tended to listen in groups, and were thus in a position to influence one another's reactions. Moreover in the early days of broadcasting radio was seen in terms of comedy much as it was seen in terms of drama: as a mere channel or conduit for art forms which had already been shaped by the conventional theatre rather than as a medium which would act upon them to create art forms that were new. The first radio comedy shows therefore consisted of live relays from music halls in which the reactions of the theatre audience were audible – sometimes excessively so (A. Briggs 1965: 85), and which inevitably influenced the listeners. It is significant that in 1930, when the BBC had all but exhausted the available material in the commercial theatres and created its own studio-based 'music hall', it retained a live audience (Black 1972: 58–9) – and the live audience (or at any rate, an audience which could be heard) remained a feature of radio comedy and light entertainment throughout their heyday.

The theory was evidently that since comedy sets out to achieve a response which is vocal, that of laughter, the programme producer must prompt – one might even say, appropriate – the response of the remote and often solitary listener by means of separately recorded ('canned') laughter or the laughter of a live audience. This studio audience really becomes a kind of broker in the transaction between performers and listeners. It is the agent of the performers because it encourages the listeners to laugh aloud, making them feel they are part of a large assembly and thus able to give vent to a public emotion. And if live, it is also the agent of the listeners because it brings the best out of the performers by influencing the timing and delivery of their material.

But whatever the theoretical role of the studio audience, its actual effect on both performers and listeners has been somewhat variable. Some listeners have felt not so much that it is their agent or representative as that they are overhearing a show which is being addressed to someone else, that the audience is part of an event from which they are largely excluded. In this case, then, the presence of the studio audience is counter-productive, and the sound of its laughter, especially when prompted by something seen rather than heard, is likely to confirm the listeners' sense that their responses are being pre-empted.

The attitudes of performers to the studio audience have also varied. Benny Hill saw it almost as superseding that other, absent audience it is meant to represent. Although referring to television shows Hill's remarks are relevant in illustrating the comedian's need for an audible response even when he is actually performing for millions of people who exist 'elsewhere':

> To a great extent I'm guided by the studio audience. You say you are doing it for the people at home, but you are swayed a lot by the people in the studio. If you get coach parties who go 'who-hoo' when you say 'knickers' and who don't laugh at something a little more subtle, you find you are going that way.
>
> (cit. Nathan 1971: 166)

John Cleese, however, has come to regard the studio audience as more of a hindrance, an irrelevance. In *I'm Sorry I'll Read That Again*, which ran through 103 shows in eight series between 1965 and 1975, Cleese was a member of a cast who initially encouraged the live audience to hiss, boo and groan at various jokes. But in the end the cast was thrown by its boisterous desire for mere catch-lines and suggestive bits (Wilmut 1980: 126–7). This experience doubtless influenced Cleese's attitude towards the studio audience of the television series *Monty Python's Flying Circus*:

> We had a studio audience and were polite to it, but it was ignored. The incredible thing about a lot of television shows is that the directors are more concerned about the three hundred people in the studio than the ten million people watching. It stems from a lack of confidence and a belief that if you can make the studio audience laugh it is a successful show, no matter if it looks absolute rubbish on the box.
>
> (cit. Nathan 1971: 186)

Hill's and Cleese's attitudes together illustrate an ambivalence in broadcasting's approach to light entertainment which has been neatly summarized in terms of television:

> Previous live entertainments . . . have been seen in special places – theatres, bars, and so on, with an audience. What was going on was going on in the same place as the audience – the stage, the platform were there in the room with you. Television in contrast is watched at home, with a few people, even alone, and what is going on is going on somewhere else, is merely being transmitted to you. It is this last point that is important in any consideration of television, for producers seem seldom able to make up their minds whether television is simply a means of broadcasting other material or is an artistic medium in its own right.
>
> (Dyer 1973: 13)

In radio, at least, there have been two broad genres of comedy, which enshrine the two attitudes to the audience that I have just outlined. First of all there is the older genre in which the comedy is conceived largely in terms of what might loosely be called 'the traditional theatre', if not actually adapted or relayed from it. Such theatre is recognizable by its picture-frame stage and its depiction of settings by means of fairly elaborate scenery and accessories rather than the suggestive powers of actors using a bare set and simple props. Naturally the rate at which it can change these settings is relatively slow. It is theatre which we might broadly categorize as naturalistic, although it also provides space in front of its proscenium curtain for various 'non-dramatic' entertainers to perform their acts, such as comedians, singers and impressionists. In radio the genre is almost invariably characterized by the presence of a studio audience and implicitly regards the blindness of the medium as a negative quality to be minimized by a choice of settings which are naturalistic, or at any rate not outside the conventions of the traditional theatre.

In contrast, the newer genre sees comedy in terms of radio itself, regarding the blindness of the medium as a positive quality in its ability to liberate the listener's imagination. This means that the speed with which such comedy is performed and its settings changed, and the nature and scope of these settings, are of an order which transcends the conventions of the traditional theatre. On-stage, such comedy could at best be presented only in a stylized, impressionistic sort of way, and in some cases could not be presented at all. Since it does not originate in the conventional theatre, it may not always be characterized by the presence of a studio audience.

Indeed not only its early history but the entire development of radio comedy resembles that of radio drama, for in both the medium was perceived as being a means, despite its blindness, of relaying conventional shows and plays to a wider audience, and only subsequently as capable of creating, *because* of its blindness, forms which transcend those of the conventional theatre. And in radio comedy as in radio drama, the two broad genres co-exist to make for a surprisingly rich and diverse output.

Let us look at the older, more 'theatrical' genre first. One of its manifestations has been the telling of jokes and funny stories, which are the stock-in-trade of the 'stand-up' comic in the music hall, and have always been effective on the radio since they are essentially verbal and can often succeed without visual re-inforcement. This means that they are ubiquitous on the medium – frequently heard in shows that one would not regard as primarily 'comic'. But for many years they were the mainstay of such programmes as *Workers' Playtime*, a music and comedy variety show.

Another manifestation of this genre is situation comedy ('sit-com'), which seems to be based on the music hall sketch or on forms of comic drama which exist in the 'straight' theatre. In this type of show the jokes and facetious dialogue, though plentiful, are of less interest in themselves than the characters and situations which they illuminate. It is conceived in terms of the traditional theatre and transplants fairly easily to television, using naturalistic settings and requiring no special technical effects. The most famous BBC radio sitcom was *Hancock's Half Hour*, which was brilliantly successful throughout its run in the late 1950s. But such shows can commute so easily between radio and television that it is sometimes hard to remember which they were first written for: as well as *Hancock's Half Hour*, *Steptoe and Son*, *Dad's Army* and more recently *Yes, Minister* are examples of sitcoms which have been successfully broadcast in both media.

The first hint that radio might be capable of a form of comedy which transcends traditional stage presentation came as early as 1939 with Tommy Handley's show, *ITMA*, an acronym of 'It's That Man Again'. Although *ITMA* was conceived on the traditional formula of jokes and comic patter, Handley instinc-tively exploited radio's qualities of sound and speed to produce something which could not be matched by the traditional theatre. The show's main prop was a door which was fitted with various locks, bars and bolts. The sound of its handle being turned indicated a character's arrival, a slam his departure. This was the idea of scriptwriter Ted Kavanagh and was particularly suited to radio since, as Peter Black points out (1972: 113), it allowed the characters to come and go with the speed of imagin-ation. It is significant that even though *ITMA* was one of the most popular comedy shows in radio history the stage version of it, which was presented with the same cast, failed because 'Slowed down to the speed at which characters could move about a stage, its verbal acrobatics lost the key qualities of surprise and pace' (Black 1972: 112).

There is some evidence that the production team of *ITMA* were aware of themselves as pioneers. In his book on Tommy Handley, Kavanagh wrote

> My own idea of radio writing was an obvious one – it was to use sound for all it was worth, the sound of different voices and accents, the use of catchphrases, the impact of funny sounds in words, of grotesque effects to give atmosphere – every device to create the illusion of rather crazy or inverted reality.
>
> (cit. Took 1976: 30)

Producer Francis Worsley's experiments with the live audience included dispensing with it altogether (ibid.: 25), and writing towards the end of its years on the air he concluded 'ITMA is essentially a radio show *which is not meant to be seen* ... ' (Worsley 1948: 37).

This newer, radiogenic form of comedy was especially sensitive to the fact that word and thing are much the same on the radio, that its worlds can be created with the speed of utterance. To appreciate how it differs from the older, more theatrical genre one has only to compare the leisurely progress of *Hancock's Half Hour* with the rapid pace of *The Goon Show* or *I'm Sorry I'll Read That Again*. But it also recognizes the important difference which exists between visual and sound signs. The former are governed by the principle of permanence: unless they are changed they will persist. Sound signs are governed by the principle of change: unless renewed they will vanish. There is a conventional understanding in radio that although the signs vanish the things they signify will remain unless the nature of the subsequent signs indicates the contrary.

But the evanescence of its signs means that radio can achieve not only pace but easy and rapid changes of scene, just as for different reasons a film can: and it is not surprising that the newer, radiogenic kind of comedy should seize upon this potential and, indeed, show structural affinities to film. Whereas Tony Hancock often remained for the entire programme in the sitting-room of his house in East Cheam, the colourful yarns of *The Goon Show* took place in settings which succeeded one another without regard to the problems of time and distance; *Round the Horne* included quickfire imitations of romantic and science fiction movies; the various sketches of *I'm Sorry I'll Read That Again* were simultaneously changed and linked by the use of puns (Wilmut 1980: 133); and the satirical *Week Ending* consists of a sequence of comic episodes which follow one another like the items of a film news-reel. *Week Ending* is also notable for its lack of a studio audience – an affirmation, despite the fact that laughter is commonly a social activity, of belief in the comic possibilities of the 'solitary' nature of the medium, or more precisely, in the ability of the listener to appreciate jokes without the need for audible prompting, just as the reader of a humorous novel can.

One comedy series which is highly radiogenic yet in a category all of its own is *The Goon Show*, which was written by Spike Milligan and broadcast between 1951 and 1960, and is probably the most original and popular comedy show in the history of radio. Its origins and general character have been outlined in another study of radio (Parker 1977: 129–37), but it must be said at once that much of *The Goon Show* humour would have been funny in any medium – a fact which is suggested by the eclectic nature of its origins. *ITMA* was clearly an important influence, but the others were largely literary: Lewis Carroll, Stephen Leacock, S.J. Perelman and Beachcomber (Black 1972: 193). Aristophanes's satire has also been discerned and from the visual media, Holly-wood cartoons, the Marx Brothers, and the quickfire patter of English music hall comedy (Wilmut 1976: 99).

Nevertheless the Goon shows are of especial interest to students of radio because they are uniquely aware of the specifically *comic* potential of the medium's transient and uncertain reality:

> Their world shifts and changes. Objects appear when needed for a quick laugh:
> Dr Londongle   Silence – don't move, any of you, or I'll shoot.
> Seagoon   Fool – put down that tin of potted shrimps.
> Dr Londongle   And starve to death? Never.
> They disappear with equal speed, for in this world nothing is certain, not even the body itself. 'How dare you come in here when I'm changing me knees?' snaps a Colosseum gladiator.
>   (Gray 1981: 59)

What therefore distinguishes *The Goon Show* from other radiogenic comedies is that it uses the blindness of radio and the evanescence of its signs not just as a structural principle but as *part of the joke*. Taking the proposition that 'in Sound Radio we may go where we wish when we wish – all we have to do is to say so' (McWhinnie 1959: 38), the Goons pushed it with great gusto to its logical, and absurd, conclusion: for if we can go to East Cheam merely by saying so, then why not to the South Pole, the moon, or even up somebody's trouser-leg? And if the laws of time and space can be flouted then why can't other physical laws? In 'Tales of Old Dartmoor', for instance, Neddy Seagoon, the governor of Dartmoor Prison, is persuaded to take the prison to France – and does so simply by loading it on to a horse-drawn cart. A few words like 'Gee up' and SFX of hooves and creaking axles enable us to picture the achievement with speed and ease. In 'The Dreaded Batter Pudding Hurler' Bloodnok and Seagoon attempt to save their sinking ship by loading it into one of its own lifeboats and then board another lifeboat, at the end of which is a gas-stove. Inside its oven is an iron staircase which Moriarty descends, singing.

Hence *The Goon Show* creates its worlds through the symbolism of words just as movies create theirs through the iconism of images: but as we saw in the last chapter its achievement is not the merely descriptive one of literature, nor is it simply the narration of jokes and comic fantasies in the timeless fashion of the stand-up comedian: a substantial element of ostension is present, for the continual accompaniment of SFX suggests that its words refer to something 'actual', they confirm that a reality of sorts lies behind the language. The achievement has been usefully summarized thus:

> *The Goon Show* ... developed a form that set it off from any comparable undertaking, in that it used radio not as a makeshift or surrogate for the live, visual performance but as the authentic medium for an entertainment and for a humour whose effect lay entirely in language and its sound accompaniment. Conceived from the start in purely acoustic terms, it made its mark as 'really pure radio'. Grotesque and surrealistic as it was, it achieved so perfect a blend of language with the innate possibilities of radio that the listener, left to himself, would never regard the restriction to a single, acoustic medium as in any sense an impoverishment.
>
> (Priessnitz 1981: 36)

It has often been claimed that the Goons' tricks with physical laws are a unique form of humour, one which cannot be reproduced outside radio, and such tricks would certainly seem to be beyond the scope of a live performance medium such as the theatre. It is also a claim made by the Goons themselves. When Major Bloodnok commands 'Eccles, stand on my shoulders and pull me up', Eccles replies 'I'd like to see them do this on television' (cit. Gray 1981: 58).

The reference is clearly to live television – or at any rate to television as a substitute for live theatre, without special technical effects and to which radio sitcom transfers so comfortably. But for many years since then, developments in video technology have enabled television to match most of *The Goon Show*'s jokes with the physical world. Indeed the first show to make regular use of such jokes was *The Kenny Everett Television Show*, no doubt because Everett was a great admirer of Goon humour. But long before this they were also visually achievable by means of the animated cartoon, versions of which actually formed, as we have seen, part of the inspiration for *The Goon Show*: Spike Milligan apparently took the term 'goon' not from the description of their German guards by British prisoners of war but from a creature in a Popeye film (Nathan 1971: 49).

In almost all respects, then, vision can match the evocativeness of words and achieve the jokes performed on the radio, but it does remain true that radio has its own, inimitable way of realizing these jokes, or more precisely, gives each listener his own way, whereas the visual media can offer only single, finite, pre-emptive versions of them.

There remain, however, two comic effects created by words which do seem to be beyond the visual media, or at any rate which the latter could achieve only by making almost impossible demands on their audiences. Radio allows the Goons to assume Protean form. Usually of normal size Moriarty can, as we have seen, become small enough to descend a staircase inside the oven of a stove. At one moment a 'hairless midget', Neddy Seagoon might at another be enormous enough to be wearing trousers which afford total concealment to Eccles. It is true that all this can be achieved on film if not on 'live' visual media, but it might still make it hard for an audience to recognize any principle of consistency within such characters.

More significant is the fact that the characters may vary not only in their physique but also, within broad limits, in their roles. Roger Wilmut makes the interesting point (1976: 81) that all the Goon shows operate at three levels. At the first level there are the actors, Spike Milligan, Harry Secombe, Peter Sellers; at the second level there are the stock characters they play, Eccles, Seagoon, Moriarty, and so on; and at the third level there are the *ad hoc* roles these characters adopt in the individual shows. In most of the shows Neddy Seagoon is an adventurous single young man in the mould of the hero of a boys' adventure story, but in 'The Gold Plate Robbery', for instance, he becomes Lord Seagoon with a wife, Lady Lavinia, and in 'Call of the West' Harry Seagoon, a movie actor, playing the part of Double Captain Rapture, a sharp-shooting cowboy. Depending on the story-lines of the various shows these roles range in time and setting from the colonial wars of the past to the science fiction of the future.

The comic significance of all this lies in the irony which is generated between the various levels of the action. The story-lines of some of the individual shows may require the characters to behave as if they are meeting for the first time and do not recognize one another, but as Wilmut points out they often make asides which show that they really 'know' one another and are therefore only acting. In fact, the ironies resonate through *all* the levels, the frequent references to Seagoon's physical bulk being enriched by the audience's knowledge of Secombe's.

This multi-levelled action is not peculiar to the Goon shows: it is also discernible in other shows such as *Ray's a Laugh* (Took 1976: 94–5), but it does seem to be peculiar to radio. What is interesting is that whereas the listener's imagination is perfectly equal to such action, which combines for him the delights of familiarity with those of novelty, it seems almost impossible in the visual media, where its first two levels, which comprise the basic irony of dramatic impersonation – an actor disguised as a character and pretending to have no identity outside it, are so blatant, so insistent, that further levels of action and irony are likely only to confuse the spectator.

How can the imagination be equal to something which the visual sense cannot comprehend? Its workings are strange and difficult if not impossible to chart, but we might venture to suggest that although we often imagine more details than are actually described to us, in a normal state of consciousness we never imagine as vividly as we can see. We thus arrive at the paradox that with fewer materials to work with – its characters present only as voices and in other respects immaterial – radio is able to convey a reality both more complex in itself and richer in comic possibilities than the visual media can. The world we can imagine and the world we can see are not equal in scope or intensity, a fact which recalls us to the significance of radio's blindness.

Not surprisingly, it is a significance which the Goons were fully alert to, as is shown by Spike Milligan's frequent adoption of film themes for his story-lines; for these were not mere *imitations* of films but parodies of them – and parody relies for its effect not only on a resemblance to the original but on a fundamental, and therefore ludicrous, dissimilarity. This is made obvious in a Goon show entitled 'Call of the West', a 'wonder ear film' in the idiom of the cowboy movie. The show begins in the style of a Hollywood trailer, combining the extravagant language of the narrator, played by Peter Sellers, with western 'Gun Law' music and 'sound clips' of the stars as they will appear in the action.

Peter	(OVER MUSIC) See, hear and smell hairless-midget Harry Seagoon as Double Captain Rapture, hard-riding, hard-shooting, hard up cowboy.
Seagoon	(KENSINGTON ACCENT) Hello you 'orny critters.
Peter	This role calls for great audience imagination. See, feel and hit, Spike Milligna [sic] as the dying actor.

(Milligan 1974: 75)

Hence the joke which is fundamental to all *The Goon Show*'s 'film' stories lies in pretending that the radio medium is visual when it is not – that radio can provide a spectacle which is as literal and vivid as a film's. Of course the narrator's command 'See' is capable of a figurative sense, 'Imagine' – something which we can and inevitably do: but its repeated collocation with other verbs describing the primary senses 'hear – smell – feel' suggests that it is the literal meaning which is dominant here. Our imagination is invoked, but we are reminded above all that we are insuperably blind.

Let us explore the significance of this blindness a little more fully. We might begin by summarizing in semiotic terms the conclusions we have reached so far. Blindness forces radio to rely ultimately on a code or system of signs which are symbolic and do not resemble what they represent. And the lack of resemblance between the words and the things they represent has strangely contrasting implications. On the one hand it means that we are obliged to take the relationship between symbol (or signifier) and signified, word and thing, on trust: and as a result they tend to become closely identified on the radio. This is the basis of its expressive or 'pictorial' power – of Donald McWhinnie's confidence that 'we may go where we wish . . . all we have to do is to say so'.

But the lack of resemblance between words and the things they represent means that these things can never be as vividly realized as if they were represented by an image. Yet this, as we have just seen, can actually *enhance* the expressive power of the signs. It is precisely because the words evoking the multi-levelled characterization of the Goon shows do *not* resemble it, as images would, that it is much easier for us to comprehend and appreciate such characterization on the radio than it would be on stage or screen. Likewise, in the last chapter we noted various kinds of radio drama whose effectiveness depends upon our being spared from the need to *see*, however vividly we may imagine.

Yet on the other hand the lack of resemblance also means that the relationship between verbal signs and things is inherently looser and therefore a potentially uncertain one: as we saw in our discussion of *A Slight Ache*, the fact that something is named on the radio is no guarantee that it exists. Hence the blindness of the medium is significant not only as the precondition of its pictorial power but as the means of preventing it; not only because it promotes a close correspondence between words and things but because it can subvert it.

Once again, it is the Goons who exploit this negative function of the medium. I have been discussing radio as though its messages consisted only of symbols – words; but of course it is not a purely verbal medium, as literature is, it includes the indexical code of noises or SFX. Nevertheless I have stressed that words are the 'ultimate' or primary code of radio because as we saw in Chapters 3 and 7 the indexical relationship between noises and things is also an uncertain one and the uncertainty can be dispelled only by verbal clues – words. In radio we therefore run the risk of having obscure sounds interpreted for us by unreliable words. And in *The Goon Show* this is exactly what happens. The sound of clucking may lead us to infer the presence of a chicken, and then we may be told that what we are hearing is in fact a horse. But since we are aware that the relationship between words and things is itself dubious, merely a symbolic and arbitrary one, it is clear that however expressive or eloquent verbal and non-verbal sound signs may be, their only ultimate corroboration is vision. The inadequacy of the medium is exposed and the listener teased for his blindness:

Seagoon	. . . Taxi!
F.X.	BAGPIPES, RUNNING DOWN
Spike	Yes?
Seagoon	The Bexhill Gas Works, and step on it.
Spike	Yes.
F.X.	BAGPIPES FADE OFF
Bill	Listeners may be puzzled by a taxi sounding like bagpipes. The truth is – it is all part of the BBC new economy campaign. They have discovered that it is cheaper to travel by bagpipes – not only are they more musical, but they come in a wide variety of colours. See your local Bagpipe Offices and ask for particulars – you won't be disappointed.

('The Dreaded Batter Pudding Hurler', Milligan 1972: 29–30)

Of course, jokes which subvert the relationship between signs and objects are by no means peculiar to radio: simply watching a play or film does not mean that we can see everything its words refer to, nor that they (or the words of a book) refer to everything in the conventional way. But such jokes are bound to have a fuller impact in a medium where blindness is an absolute quality and we can *never* see what the signs refer to, yet where there is the sound of people and of other physical phenomena which is never present in literature.

This particular joke is a form of double bluff. What the listener assumes to be a taxi turns out to be bagpipes; but then the bagpipes do, indeed, possess the properties of a taxi. In fact the two objects are conflated so that the sound of bagpipes represents not conventional bagpipes at all but ones you can travel by, nor are these adequately conveyed by the term 'taxi'. Thus both index and symbol turn out to be inaccurate: the thing they purport to signify is neither recognizable bagpipes nor recognizable taxi.

Such exotic conflations can be achieved not only by juxtaposing words and sounds, but merely by counterpointing words which signify objects with disparate or incompatible qualities. In an exchange which I quoted earlier as an example of signs and things being much the same, what is described as if it were a gun turns out to be a tin of potted shrimps.

Spike Milligan's alertness to the comic possibilities of subverting the conventional correspondence between sound signs and objects is suggested both by the jokes played on the listener and by those which are generated among the characters themselves:

Seagoon	(WHISPERS) Blast, it's Grytpype-Thynne. Leave this to me, I'm a brilliant impressionist. (CHICKEN CLUCKING)
Grytpype-Thynne	A horse? There's no horses in this fort.
Seagoon	(WHISPERS) (DOG HOWLING)
Grytpype-Thynne	There's no chickens either.

('The Gold Plate Robbery', Milligan 1974: 137)

Sometimes such jokes are occasioned by a pun – one sign which refers to two possible objects. The listener is encouraged to understand it as referring to one object, only to discover that the other object is being signified:

Grams	SPLASH. SEAL BARK. BAGPIPES.
Seagoon	You imposter [sic], that's a seal. But why the bagpipes?
Moriarty	It's the Great Seal of Scotland.

('The Gold Plate Robbery', Milligan 1974: 130)

The splash and barking sound followed by Seagoon's remark leads us to interpret 'seal' as an amphibious mammal, and then the sound of bagpipes, acting here as a symbol of Scottishness, cues Moriarty's revelation about the true nature of the object. But the real point is that none of these sound signs corresponds to the reality they represent, imprinted wax discs normally manifesting themselves neither through splashes, barks nor bagpipes.

Occasionally too, there are sounds which do not merely purport to signify things that are normally soundless, such as the Great Seal of Scotland; they are unrecognizable as the sounds made by anything else.

Bill	It was the year 1907 and here is the orchestra to play it.
Orchestra	NEW MAD LINK ALL OVER THE SHOP. SINGING IN THE MIDDLE. SOUND F.X. IN MUSIC. FINISHES ON A CHORD.

('Battle of Spion Kop', Milligan 1974: 21)

In all the Goon shows there is an absurd confidence that the acoustic medium is equal to everything.

The inevitable effect of this dissociation of the signs from the things they signify or represent is to *blot out* those things, to draw the listener's attention to the fact that the signs are *only* signs, that all is mere artifice. Applause cuts in and then ends abruptly instead of being faded up and down naturalistically. Often, SFX are shamelessly 'milked' – or speeded up and slowed down to remind us that they originate not in the world but on a gramophone turntable. Moreover the characters themselves often confuse signs with that which they represent.

Seagoon Bluebottle, you keep me covered with this photograph of a gun. Right – let's go in –
F.X. DOOR KICKED
Seagoon Hands up!

('The Hastings Flyer', Milligan 1972: 169)

Their artificial nature is further emphasized by certain exaggerated claims which the characters make for them; for instance, by alluding to SFX as if they were not only auditory but visual:

Bloodnok Wait! Great galloping crabs, look in the sky.
Grams HELICOPTER
Bloodnok It's a recording of a helicopter – saved!

('Napoleon's Piano', Milligan 1972: 110)

Thus, although as we have seen elsewhere the SFX often confirm through their indexical role the 'reality' that words can only convey symbolically, they can also be used to confirm that the whole show is an invention – a bag of tricks. And this is true not only of sounds and photographs but of words. In purely verbal terms Bluebottle frequently makes the same mistake as Seagoon and Bloodnok by confusing his stage-instructions with the actions they describe:

moves right – puts dreaded dynamite under signal box for safety – does not notice dreaded wires leading to plunger up in signal cabin. Thinks. I'm for the dreaded deading alright this week.

('The Hastings Flyer', Milligan 1972: 169)

This is in the best tradition of clowning in its paradoxical impression of painful effort and insouciant ease. In an attempt to overcome the limitations of the medium and convey to us what we cannot see, Bluebottle involves himself in the most improbable dramatic irony, for he 'does not notice' the dreaded wires (comical enough since it is he who tells us he doesn't) and yet recognizes without doing anything to prevent it that he is in for the 'dreaded deading'.

Yet there is a sense too of Bluebottle cutting straight through the

Gordian knot: the limitations of the medium are magnificently ignored, and thus emphasized even as they are overcome. His achievement is at once fatuous and shrewd – fatuous because the actions he must perform require the visual ostension of the conventional theatre, and this is not the conventional theatre but radio, which is blind; and shrewd because if Bluebottle *had* performed these soundless actions instead of describing them we would have remained utterly ignorant of them. Hence on the radio words assume a greater reality than the things they describe. There is a sense in which reality shrinks to the dimensions of the signs because, as in literature, we can never see what the signs refer to; but the sense of shrinkage is even stronger here because unlike literature's the signs are only temporary, short lived. We noted earlier that in their power to set scenes and change them rapidly, words on the radio helped to evoke a vivid and dynamic world; yet in another way it is a world which dwindles to their own ephemeral nature and which has no existence outside them.

As we would expect, the Goons take this tendency to its logical, and ridiculous, conclusion. Not only are the signifieds reduced to the dimensions of the signifiers, but the artificial nature of the latter is further demonstrated by using signifiers which have no signifieds at all. *The Goon Show* is permeated with nonsense words – meaningless exclamations and strange noises. Though gibberish, many of them occur in sentences whose structure is conventional enough to remind us that they are still to be recognized as signifiers – ciphers to which, so arbitrary and artificial are signs in general, the listener may care to attach his own meanings:

> *Bill* I'm sorry I'm late but the flinn of flonn sclunned the nib of the Ploon.
>
> ('The Scarlet Capsule', Milligan 1974: 94)

The world has been reduced to symbols and these are nothing but noises – opaque and meaningless.

Thus we might summarize the achievement of *The Goon Show* by saying that whatever the themes of the individual shows (and they are many and various) it is fundamentally a joke about the possibilities and limitations of radio itself. It exploits our assumption that the correspondence of words (and sounds) to things will be a conventional one, and it does this partly by confirming it and partly by denying it; partly by activating the listener's imagination and partly by bumping him up against the blindness of the medium; partly by conceding that words are, indeed, things and partly by reminding us that they are sometimes mere signs. It uses the referential power of words and sounds to create full-blooded fantasies, and further, to present levels of characterization and action which would be beyond our ability to assimilate visually; and it also uses the precondition of blindness to frustrate the imagination and reduce everything to noises and tricks.

It could therefore be seen as combining the implicit recognition of radiogenic comedy that the medium can liberate the imagina-tion with the older, more theatrical genre's awareness that since the listener is blind his imagination may be misled and ought therefore to be tied closely to his familiarity with the naturalistic conventions of the stage. In a word *The Goon Show* uses its jokes to explore and illustrate the nature of radio, and on the analogy of the literary theorists' term 'metafiction' to describe novels which use the novel form itself to discuss or illustrate the nature of fiction (Waugh 1984: 1–7), we might coin for it the term 'metaradio' – though with the caution that it is not strictly analogous to Jakobson's term 'metalingual'. It will be recalled from Chapter 3 that Jakobson defines as 'metalingual' statements or communications which pertain to *code* rather than to contact or medium, though these are, as we have seen, largely determined by the nature of the contact.

But however we define in terms of radio the self-consciousness of such programmes as *The Goon Show*, it seems true to say that the success of any kind of comedy is bound up with the audience's sense of itself, and I would like to round off this discussion by returning to the listener's role in relation first to comedy and then to other forms of light entertainment.

In realizing or 'registering' the joke the listener acquires some of the creative insight of its perpetrator, and this flatters him. It gives him a sense of who he is – of his abilities and values. Hence in making him laugh, the comedy show invites the listener to view himself in a certain way and to identify with people of like mind. It has been pointed out that one technique of *The Goon Show* was to include just the punch-lines of lewd jokes (Wilmut 1976: 78). Evidently the purpose of this was not only to give the worldlier listeners a pleasurable reminder of the whole joke but to imbue them with the sense of being 'in the know', of belonging to an exclusive group.

Another comedy technique which was by no means peculiar to

the Goon shows or even to radio was the regular inclusion of catch-phrases, but although similar in effect to the punch-line the catch-phrase is in some ways the more interesting for being intrinsically *unfunny*. Yet it seldom failed to evoke tumultuous laughter and applause from the studio audience. Why? One explanation, though offered by someone who could claim to be an authority, does not seem quite sufficient:

> In a sketch in the first series [of *The Goon Show*] Milligan had propounded the theory that a catchphrase was simply a meaningless remark repeated until the audience was brain-washed into laughing at it. He illustrated this with a character opening a door, shouting 'More Coal!' and exiting again. It was demonstrated that on the first hearing, this was followed by dead silence; on the thousandth it was greeted by rapturous . . . applause.
>
> (Wilmut 1976: 94)

The catch-phrase seems to have evolved in order to remind the audience not of some joke which has originated elsewhere, as the Goons' use of punch-lines did, but of a character who is a part of the show in which it occurs. Catch-phrases were especially common in *ITMA*, and 'their power to fix a person in the mind's eye quickly made them an invaluable recognition signal, the aural equivalent of George Robey's eyebrows' (Black 1972: 116).

In other words, a phrase like 'Can I do yer now, sir?' was a slightly more artful form of self-identification than 'Hello, it's me, Mrs Mopp, again'; and the laughter that it prompted in the audience-members, whether sitting in the studio or listening at home, was a way of expressing their recognition and appreciation of the character who used it, and thus of declaring their own membership of a kind of club or group. Moreover unlike a more conventional form of self-introduction the catch-phrase not only made characters comically repetitive and mechanistic, but gave the listeners something they could import into their own daily lives in order to make or renew contact with fans of the same show. As Peter Black puts it: 'the secret of the catchphrase's appeal . . . remains, simply its easy availability. It put within everyone's reach, on a very simple level, the national vice of using quotations' (1972: 117).

Its overall effect is thus very similar to that of delivering isolated punch-lines, except that the listener can use it as a kind of cultural badge or password – as a means of making a connection between himself and others who do not simply have a broadly similar sense of humour but who actually listen to the same, specific show. Since the catch-phrase is not in itself funny ('He's fallen in the water!' was regularly uttered by Little Jim, alias Spike Milligan, in the Goon shows) the studio audience's delighted response to it might well infuriate the uninitiated listener; but it is not surprising that so many producers of comedy shows – even those in the newer, radiogenic style – should think it worth running the risk of alienating him by retaining the studio audience. In so narrowly conative a genre – where the object is to persuade the remote and isolated listener to laugh – there is a pressing need to represent him in the medium, to make his putative laughter audible within it. But even in comedy shows without a studio audience, the jokes imply a highly developed sense of who the listener is, and thus give him a kind of presence on the medium which seems much more insistent than in other types of programme.

A similar effect is striven for in the more traditional type of radio quiz game, which is almost invariably characterized by the inclusion of a studio audience. If the listener and the audience are given the answers to the questions, as they were in the long-running series *Twenty Questions*, they can then savour the panel's wit or stupidity as it tries to guess them. The pleasure here seems very similar, if not identical, to the voyeuristic pleasure of dramatic irony in the theatre, where the audience experiences a corporate sense of superiority or self-satisfaction through knowing what those involved in the action do not know.

But in most of these games, such as *The Gardening Quiz*, *My Music*, *Screenplay* and *Brain of Britain*, the answers are withheld from the listener and the studio audience, just as they are from the panel of contestants. This means that the sympathy between listener and audience is if anything greater than it is in comedy shows since the latter is never, as it sometimes is in comedy, in a privileged position: the contestants' efforts that the audience applauds are much more exclusively a matter of sound than the efforts of comedians to get laughs, and therefore more readily endorsed by the listener at home.

Nevertheless the listener's role is much less passive than in comedy because the challenge which the questions pose to his knowledge or intelligence seems much more insistent than that posed to his sense of humour by jokes. It is usually easier to

understand jokes than to answer questions, but even more important to one's self-esteem to attempt the latter, though the satis-
faction at having answered a question correctly seems analogous
to that of 'getting' the joke.

The difference, however, is that the 'star' performers of quiz
games, the contestants, are not the perpetrators of the questions as
the star performers of comedy shows are the perpetrators of the
jokes; they are the *recipients*. This means that the listener identifies
not only with the studio audience but with the panellists – which
moves him vicariously to the centre of the action. And not only
does he identify with them, he competes against them – which
means that when he matches any of their achievements he is
logically if not actually as much the object of the studio applause
as they are. All this gives him not just a heightened sense of his
identity and abilities *vis-à-vis* the studio audience and performers,
as it does in comedy shows, but a greater involvement in the
action – a sense of himself as participant, performer.

However, in recent years there has been an interesting development in radio light entertainment from quiz games which
simply test the panellists' knowledge, such as *Round Britain Quiz*,
to those which test their ability to combine knowledge with comic
improvisation, such as *Just a Minute*, *I'm Sorry I Haven't a Clue* and
The News Quiz (all BBC Radio 4). These are not so much quiz
games pure and simple as blends of quiz game and comedy show.

The reason for their development may be a feeling among radio
producers that purely factual quiz games can be more clearly and
interestingly presented on television, with its resources of flashing
numbers, gauges, meters, and split screens which can juxtapose
frowning contestants with a ticking clock or the smug faces of
those who know the answers. In radio something more inventive
is perhaps needed in order to transcend the lack of vision, and
certainly the comic flights of fantasy of some of their panellists
have made these hybrid shows enduringly popular – even when,
as in the case of *The News Quiz*, which can be watched as *Have I
Got News For You* (Channel 4), they have subsequently been stolen
by television.

In general terms the audience satisfactions afforded by these
shows are clear enough. In active vein, the listener can pit his
knowledge against that of the panel, and more passively, enjoy its
comic conceits. In the latter role, he again becomes part of a club
that 'gets the joke' and shares the values on which it is based; and

since the humour is often satirical there is a strong sense of those whom the joke excludes: its explicit victim but also, by implication, those who do not understand or appreciate it.

Certain other forms of light entertainment on the radio, such as music request programmes and 'meet the people' shows, give the listener even more of a presence on the medium by taking him, or at any rate the 'common people' of whom he is one, as part of their actual theme. The titles of such programmes, which date from the height of radio's popularity, reflect their concern with a homely, workaday world outside the rarefied atmosphere of the radio station – *FAMILY Favourites, HOUSEWIVES' Choice, Down YOUR Way* and so on.

In music request programmes the object is not simply to play music which the requester/dedicatee likes (most such listeners can play their own on a domestic cassette or CD player), but to associate him with it by naming him on the air. By this means he and all the other listeners who are potential requesters/dedicatees can feel a personal stake in the station's output, a sense that it is not the preserve of professional broadcasters. Gaining a similar effect by different means were the original version of *Down Your Way* and Wilfred Pickles' famous *Have a Go*, both of them now strangely reincarnated in *The Radio 1 Roadshow*. In *Down Your Way* a sequence of presenters which included Richard Dimbleby and Brian Johnston visited small communities, interviewed the inhabitants about their lives and jobs, and played their favourite music. *Have a Go*, which in 1947 commanded an audience of 12 million, travelled around the country ostensibly as a quiz game involving local people, but really as a way of capturing the vitality of ordinary folk (Black 1972: 179–81). The show's epigraph, as announced every week by Pickles, was 'to bring the people to the people', and before the advent of the instantaneous phone-in it was probably the most effective way in which radio could give the impression of being a two-way medium – accessible to, and energized by, its audiences. It is time to look at these audiences in more detail – their requirements and the potentially active and passive nature of their roles.

SUGGESTIONS FOR FURTHER WORK

1 Write a short comedy sketch, or two or three pages of dialogue consisting not only of jokes but a humorous situation or

character, in order to see if it is possible to be funny without benefit of visual clues or of comic business other than that which is audible. (One useful approach might be to parody a radio commercial or a well-known programme.) Can you use the medium itself as part of the joke? Be warned that material often 'feels' hilarious when you are writing and recording it but may sound less funny when played back: so play your recording to an objective audience and pay even closer attention to their reactions *while* they are listening than to the comments they make afterwards.

2 Write a critical commentary on, or analysis of, a radio quiz game such as *The News Quiz* or *My Music*. The absence of a distracting visual dimension may enable you to concentrate on the following questions. What assumptions do these games make about the knowledge and intelligence of the panellists? Even more important, what assumptions do they make about the knowledge and intelligence of the listener? How far do they reflect and foster the widespread belief that knowledge has no value other than as a commodity or status symbol? What assumptions do the jokes make about the awareness, attitudes and values of the listener? Finally, and more broadly, is there such a thing as 'pure' entertainment – or in order to entertain must the entertainers always be doing something else too?

Part IV

The listener

Chapter 9

Phone-ins

That the man in the street should have anything vital to contribute to broadcasting was an idea slow to gain acceptance. That he should actually use broadcasting to express his own opinions in his own unvarnished words, was regarded as almost the end of all good social order.

(D.G. Bridson, *Prospero and Ariel*)

It was suggested at the end of Chapter 3 that the purpose of the phone-in is to attempt the ultimately impossible feat of providing feedback for the audience, and that its dominant function is therefore phatic and metalingual. It creates the illusion of radio as a two-way medium and is concerned to verify that the station or channel has an audience and that this audience is capable of understanding and responding to the message which the station transmits.

Nevertheless it has to be added that this function may not always be self-evident. Let us imagine a phone-in which includes a call from a mother who is tempted to batter her baby. Her call produces an immediate response from a social worker who may be a studio guest or the next telephone caller, and an on-air discussion ensues during which the mother's problem is solved. In this case the station has been acting as a switchboard. For the mother it provided a way of getting something done, and as a result she and the other callers and listeners may regard the station as a genuine welfare agency. But however happy it may be to be regarded in this light, the station's prior concern is that when it has a phone-in on this or on no particular topic its audience will declare its presence and understanding by, in a corporate sense, making itself heard on the medium. If the solution of the mother's problem maintains or increases audience responsiveness, well and good: but it is only the means to what is purely a radiogenic end. It is worth adding that the London station Sunrise Radio has achieved this end by using its phone-ins to arrange marriages for its listeners, most of whom are Asian (Donovan 1992: 203).

Broadcasters have always been at pains to give themselves and their listeners a sense of the latter's presence on the medium, and we saw in Chapters 4 and 8 that this is an important function of much radio light entertainment. A considerable amount of language on the radio is phatic in its intention and, generally speaking, the less formal the style of presentation the more openly that intention can be declared: 'We can't go over to Roker Park now, but we'll bring you that report later in the programme, OK?' Since this language involves an element of pretence or make-believe – that the listener is capable of direct and audible feedback – it is particularly appropriate to light entertainment. Music presenters addressing an audience which consists largely of isolated housewives use a flirtatious direct address which implies that they are talking only to a single listener and that she is visible and making an audible response. 'How are you? You're looking nice today.'

BBC Radio 1 presenter, Steve Wright, used to take the process a stage further in his afternoon show: when he read out 'Another True Story' or some sensational item from the newspapers he played in the reactions of recorded voices, 'Ooh! Wow!', which were evidently meant to represent those of his listeners. But this is merely a comic illustration of a need which is imperative in all broadcasting: to remind the broadcaster that she has an audience, even though she cannot see or hear it, and to encourage that audience to keep listening. Even the announcer's or newsreader's formal greeting 'Good morning' is an expression of this need. As Erving Goffman points out, the broadcaster must talk *as if* responsive people were before her eyes and ears. She must be 'response-constructive', which might extend to inventing dialogue in which she either pauses for the listener's putative reply or conducts both sides of the conversation, one side in a disguised voice to represent that of the listener. But 'In both cases the timing characteristics of dialogue are simulated' (Goffman 1981: 241).

The phone-in was regarded as such a major development in broadcasting because for the first time it gave the viewer or listener a presence on the medium which was *audible* – not as the result of her having a letter read out on the air or going into a studio or attending an outside broadcast in her neighbourhood, but spontaneously and away from broadcasting equipment, in her own home or local telephone box or at her place of work.

Paulu (1981: 219) implies that its origins are American. In Britain it made its début on a local station, BBC Radio Nottingham, in 1968, but it was pioneered at network level by a producer named Walter Wallich and first heard on Radio 4 in 1970 as *It's Your Line*, presented by Robin Day. This was soon followed by *Whatever You Think*, another programme with a title that stressed the role of the listener, and both were succeeded by *Tuesday Call*, which now takes the form of a personal invitation to *Call Nick Ross*. Since a discussion programme like *Any Questions?* is bound to produce immediate reactions in its audience it was logical that its counterpart *Any Answers?*, which had previously consisted of listeners' letters, should switch to a phone-in format in 1989 (Donovan 1992: 203).

The phone-in was also taken up by television, but it has been especially important to radio because as we are well aware the radio message differs from that of television in being entirely invisible and thus more easily disattended or misunderstood. This means that its phatic and metalingual needs are particularly pressing. Phone-ins on television are fairly infrequent, partly no doubt because there is nothing to fill the eye while the caller is speaking; but they are ubiquitous on the radio – not uncommonly as programmes in their own right and even more often as an element in others, such as talk and music shows. It therefore seems no exaggeration to say that the phone-in is highly radiogenic – peculiarly suited to the medium; nor is it surprising that a genre which involves a complex of channels or contacts between studio-based broadcasters, callers and the silent audience, should attract considerable academic attention (for example, Higgins and Moss 1982: 1–27; Kress 1986; Hutchby 1991; Brand and Scannell 1991: 210–15).

We began by looking at the function which the phone-in has for the broadcaster, a function which we have regarded as the dominant one in view of the fact that it is the broadcaster who initiates the communication act; but it is also important to consider its function for the caller. It is complementary to that of the broadcaster, an opportunity to influence the radio 'text' or message by making an actual contribution to it. The caller may avail herself of the phone-in to make suggestions about the station's output or to voice criticisms of it: but even when she wishes to discuss something quite unrelated to the radio station or merely phones in to advertise or bid for goods in a 'swap shop', she modifies its output merely by her presence on the medium.

As far as the caller is concerned, then, we might broadly define the function of the phone-in as being 'emotive' in Jakobson's sense of the term – concerned to reveal one's own personality and interests – and perhaps conative too, a means of influencing others; and this overall function seems to assume one or other of three main forms which shade into one another but which I shall nevertheless distinguish as the *expressive*, the *exhibitionist* and the *confessional*.

The *expressive* phone-in

The caller's purpose here is to air her views on some issue or topic, and if the caller so wishes it gives her 'for the first time some chance of challenging the power of the media men and interested parties to impose their view of events on the community at large' (Evans 1977: 56). Using the graphic Australian term 'talk-back' Higgins and Moss describe the significance of this type of phone-in in rather more formidable terms: it is 'a counter-hegemonic discourse phenomenon – as it is one of the few ways people can find to give public expression to private and perhaps dissonant viewpoints in a culture otherwise saturated with approved meanings' (1982: 1). Other media analysts take a similar view: such phone-ins 'represent an attempt to accommodate the mounting pressure from excluded and under-represented groups for greater access to scarce communications facilities' (Murdock and Golding 1977: 38).

In the terms of our own discussion of radio we might describe this type of phone-in as an opportunity for the listener to counter, if she wishes, the 'bardic' tendencies of the medium. As was pointed out in Chapters 3 and 5, radio language has to be relatively simple because of the nature of the medium: but of course the use of relatively simple language does not always imply an inability to extend ideas and knowledge, a fact confirmed by much spoken output, including schools broadcasts, on BBC Radios 3, 4 and 5. Nevertheless, as a mass medium with audiences which are highly heterogeneous in terms of background, education and taste, radio frequently succumbs to a tendency to rehearse the conventional or collective wisdom. The expressive phone-in gives the listener of minority or unorthodox views a chance to challenge or modify that wisdom in language which is spontaneously oral, and therefore likely to be fairly intelligible to the other listeners.

Two further points are worth making with respect to the expressive phone-in. The first is that since the arrival of television, politicians have largely abandoned the hustings and availed themselves of its influence to address the people in such a way that they cannot be directly questioned or criticized by them, but only by their representatives, the interviewers – and the latter may not always ask the questions many people wish to put or may not press sufficiently hard for answers. Television, then, has in some respects enhanced the rhetorical powers of politicians and, which is much the same thing, protected them from direct and immediate feedback. But it could be said that the phone-in has partly rectified this situation: it is a challenge which no electioneering politician can afford to ignore – and yet it is a way of putting him back on the hustings by forcing him to face objections to his own arguments. Among the international leaders whom callers have been able to question on *It's Your World* (BBC Radio 4/World Service) are Margaret Thatcher, Rajiv Gandhi, Benazir Bhutto and Kenneth Kaunda (Donovan 1992: 140).

The second point is that although network radio has provided the phone-in with some of its more conspicuous achievements it is most prevalent in local radio, an important reason for which seems to be that the caller regards herself as having to compete with fewer other callers to gain access to the medium, and as having a better chance in her neighbourhood than nationally of influencing opinion to get things done. In this sense the phone-in would seem to be a happy adjunct to local radio because it has been suggested that the latter was in the first place a general institutional attempt to make the medium two-way (Smith 1974: 151).

The *exhibitionist* phone-in

The caller's aim here is not so much to vent her opinions on a particular topic as to project her personality, to become a performer. The programme presenter – on this occasion less a chairperson than a controller of ceremonies – encourages the caller to tell jokes, sing songs, or simply talk about herself and her interests. In a phone-in quiz the caller is invited to answer questions, perhaps in competition with other callers, and for the audience at large the object is simply entertainment, sometimes of an unscheduled sort where the caller behaves in an exhibitionist fashion even when there is nothing in the manner of the presenter or the nature of the programme to encourage her to do so.

The *confessional* phone-in

In this type of phone-in the caller's primary aim is to express her individual needs or problems and get advice. This may seem a rather extravagant description when the caller's problem is no worse than a blocked drain or green-fly on the roses. But it has to be acknowledged that the mixture of invisibility and companionship which radio provides (see Chapters 1, 4 and 6) – a mixture which is even more potent than in television, where the presenter, at least, can be seen – usually elicits problems of a more personal nature. The caller then 'confides' – opens her heart or behaves like a patient, and the role of the presenter and/or her studio guest(s) is correspondingly that of therapist, confessor, confidante or counsellor. It is not surprising that in 1975, when the phone-in had become well established in British radio, LBC launched a programme presented by Phillip Hodson which offered sex therapy (Donovan 1992: 125).

Above all, the caller can treat the presenter as a friend, someone whom she can hear and talk to without the embarrassment of visual confrontation, and it is possible to regard not only confessional but all types of phone-in as therapeutic in their effects. When the caller wishes to air her views or to reveal her personality even more directly, the presenter, heard but not seen, facilitates this act of self-exposure before an audience which is (happily) both *un*heard and *un*seen. It is interesting to note that after several phone-ins whose titles have stressed the position of the listener/caller – *It's Your Line*, *Voice of the People*, and so on – the BBC's current offering, *Call Nick Ross*, though every bit as expressive and non-confessional as its predecessors, stresses in its title the person to whom the caller will talk.

The blindness of the medium seems to have a therapeutic function

not just for the caller in any kind of phone-in but for the professional broadcaster in any kind of radio. Invisible herself, the
latter must in some respects find it easier to communicate with
an unseen and unheard audience than with those whom she
knows personally – and it might not be too far-fetched to evolve
a pathological theory of the effective broadcaster as the innocuous,
socially acceptable version of the anonymous phone-caller. It is a
paradox that many popular broadcasters seem to be shy intro-
verts whose personalities can be transformed by the presence of a
live microphone.

But to return to the phone-in. While it is true that its basic
function is phatic and therefore that the callers are members of the
audience in the broadest sense of that term (for even a caller who
is not a regular listener to the station must, at however many
removes, be a recipient of its message to know that the phone-in
exists), there are many other members of the audience who are
'present' at the phone-in but only in the silent, passive role of
listeners, and it is important to examine its function for them.

The listeners' attitude to the caller would appear to be a
profoundly ambivalent one. In the first place there is a strong
sense of identification. The telephone acoustic proclaims that she
is 'one of them', a member of the audience challenging the
monopoly of the professional broadcasters. The 'voices' elsewhere
in radio are there because in some way *accredited* – the eyewitness,
the celebrity, the expert, the person in the news. In the phone-in
the caller is on the air as a result of nothing more than picking up
a handset and dialling a number, and she is in this sense representative of the listener irrespective of whether the latter sympath-
izes with her or with her views.

Thus in a curious way the medium is inverted – turned inside
out. The audience members become the broadcasters: they are, as
it were, enabled to reflect themselves. For the individual who is
merely listening to the phone-in there is not only the likely and
conventional pleasure of hearing a discussion – what Higgins and
Moss describe as 'argument as theatre' (1982: 117) – but an
impression, however misleading, created by those phoning in of
innumerable *other* listeners who approximate to the community at
large. The title of the BBC's phone-in, *Voice of the People* (Radio 4),
was evidently meant to confirm this impression of breadth and
representativeness. More recently the network has gone even
further and joined with the World Service to present an inter-

national phone-in entitled *It's Your World*: but as we have just seen the phone-in is particularly popular in local radio, where audiences often have a more tangible sense of communal values and are enabled to respond to and influence developments in their immediate neighbourhood.

But the radio phone-in also exerts a contrary effect upon the listener – one which distinguishes it from its television counterpart. On television the distinction between callers and 'official' broadcasters remains clear-cut, and the continued ascendancy of the latter is proclaimed by the fact that they can be seen while the callers cannot. In the radio phone-in there is, despite the difference in acoustic between telephonic and studio voices, a substantially greater sense of parity between callers and broadcasters. Noting in a *Sunday Times* article that 'radio has many strengths beyond the power of television' Alan Brien instanced the phone-in as providing 'a direct, intimate, practical kind of "access" which . . . camera-dominated studio confrontations can never match. A discussion between public and pundits gains when both are equally invisible' (cit. Evans 1977: 57). Hence, because all the parties in the phone-in are invisible there is the paradox that however 'unaccredited' the caller may be, she acquires a kind of authoritativeness merely by being on the air, she becomes a broadcaster, a performer, on a par with those in the studio.

But this inevitably creates a feeling of detachment in the listener, the apartness that she normally feels when listening to a discussion between 'professional' broadcasters. In this respect her role is like that of the eavesdropper, and her sense of this is sharpened by the telephone acoustic, which, combined with the frequently confessional nature of the discussion, gives her the powerful impression of listening in on a crossed line, of overhearing words which are being addressed to someone else. Indeed an indication of how near the phone-in comes to being a private medium is the fact that if it encounters a crossed line the radio station must immediately ring off, since under the terms of the Wireless and Post Office Telegraphy Act it is illegal to listen in to a private telephone conversation.

Something else which often occurs in a phone-in is that a caller who reveals a problem is immediately followed by another caller who can help her – a social worker or clergyman, perhaps – and the station will then connect them on the air. The listener thus finds herself listening in to a discussion which is *entirely* conducted in a telephone acoustic.

All this makes her a bit like the aural equivalent of the voyeur, and we are again reminded of the effect of dramatic irony in the theatre, except that the caller is a performer with even less sense of her audience than she would have on a stage or before a microphone; for she is not in a studio but on a private medium, the telephone, and the listener complements her pretence of talking to just one person but in fact wishing to reveal herself to a mass audience, by a kind of pretended absence – by giving no hint of her awareness of the discussion but by listening in all the same. Thus the phone-in is capable of unique effects within radio, for it is a half-private, half-public medium in which one element of the audience becomes part of the performance and involved in a complex and unusual relationship with the other element.

The presence of two 'audiences' creates an equally complex and shifting role for the third party in the phone-in, the presenter, and it is not altogether surprising that the latter sometimes concentrates on one at the expense of the other, for practical purposes regarding either the callers or the listeners as her 'target' audience. Phone-ins which concentrate on the caller are often virtually unmediated by the presenter and without an agenda: the callers simply telephone to discuss almost any subject they wish and within broad limits the presenter allows them to say what they like. The listeners to such phone-ins are important to the extent that they are able to hear what is being said, but as far as the presenter and the station are concerned whatever interest it may have for them is incidental, or at any rate secondary, to the purpose of publicizing the phone-in facility to would-be callers. Nevertheless relatively few stations will conduct phone-ins which are so completely indifferent to their listeners' needs, if only because it is from the ranks of these listeners that their future callers must come.

At the other extreme, phone-ins which concentrate on the listener are usually based on a firm theme or agenda and highly mediated by the presenter. The caller is still, of course, their *raison d'être*, but once she is on the line and the station has demonstrated to itself and to the outside world the physical fact that it *has* an audience, the presenter will concentrate on fulfilling the needs of that unheard but larger and therefore more important section of the audience who are listening.

The presenter of this type of phone-in is normally distinguished by presence of mind, wit, articulacy and a readiness to 'squash' the caller as soon as she ceases to be interesting, and the calculation is that the listener will be satisfied wherever her sympathies lie. If they lie with the presenter and/or if she is primarily interested in the theme under discussion, she will be pleased by the 'extinction' of a tedious caller; and if they lie with the caller she will 'love to hate' the presenter and keep listening in the hope that a subsequent caller will get the better of her. But phone-ins of this sort do run some risk of deterring callers and even alienating the listeners. During the 1980s two presenters who were renowned for their unpleasant and even brutal treatment of phoners-in were Brian Hayes of LBC and James Whale of Radio Aire, both providing grim reminders that restricted access-time, a telephone acoustic, and an instantaneous censorship mechanism always place the caller at a potential disadvantage (Kress 1986: 415).

As we might expect, the great majority of phone-ins are conducted by a presenter who provides at least 'the semblance of personal interaction with the caller, yet at the same time uses the medium to entertain the wider listening audience' (Higgins and Moss 1982: 19). She tries to balance her duty to the individual caller, who needs to have her say, with her duty to the listeners at large, who need to hear something of interest. The task is a difficult one, especially in phone-ins of a confessional nature. As McLeish puts it (1978: 142–3), how far are private and individual problems of general interest? And in what circumstances do they transcend that interest? Conversely, is it proper, even with the implied assent of the caller, to exploit private problems for public entertainment? Sometimes the presenter may be required to silence not only the boring or offensive caller for the sake of the listeners, but the rashly self-revealing caller for her own sake – even when what she says may be of immense fascination to the listeners.

Such questions properly belong to the realm of professional ethics rather than media analysis, but if we discount any studio guests, who are in any case somewhat peripheral to the phone-in itself, it is worth repeating that the interests the presenter must balance lie entirely within the audience and not partly with the audience and partly with a separate category of 'official' broadcasters.

We can conclude by suggesting that the phone-in is of importance to the student of radio in three main respects. First it represents a synthesis of private and public media since it is an individual, 'point-to-point' mode of communication which is overheard by a mass audience of indeterminate size. Indeed it could be seen as an advance towards that elusive goal, 'access' radio, since it makes the medium at once a private channel of expression and a public forum.

Second, the phone-in represents a kind of inversion of the radio medium. The programme is *about* its audience, which in a way and to an extent otherwise unknown in the medium gains a sense of itself as a varied yet corporate entity, the 'consumers' of the radio message who are both separate from, yet on a par with, the 'professionals' – the broadcasters, pundits and personalities. And third, the phone-in demonstrates that the radio audience can use the medium in many different ways, some active and some passive, and that the relationship between callers and listeners is a complex and varying one.

We must now look at one or two of the ways in which this audience and its uses of the medium may be more closely analysed, and at some of the problems which such analysis faces.

SUGGESTIONS FOR FURTHER WORK

Listen to several callers from as wide a range of network and LR phone-ins as you can. Are the phone-ins 'free-for-alls'? If not, can you detect the principles according to which the callers are selected? Are they chosen to provide a balance of opinions, genders, social backgrounds, and so on? What can you infer about the callers' motives in phoning in? Make a preliminary grouping of the callers according to the expressive–exhibitionist–confessional classification I have offered above. You may soon find it too narrow for the range of callers you hear, or too broad for the finer distinctions you perceive between them. Can you therefore classify them in more useful ways?

Hutchby (1991) analyses some phone-in discussions on current affairs to show how they are 'managed' by the presenter. Make an off-air recording of a similar discussion, and listening to it very carefully, see if you can analyse it in the same way.

Chapter 10

Audiences

Oh! Oh! You radio!
Oh! what I owe to you my radio:
I listen in and you dispel the gloom,
For you bring all the stars into my room;
Oh! Oh! You radio!
You're the most entertaining friend I know,
You give me music, dancing, joys I never knew
Oh! radio I'm radiating thanks to you.
                    (Theme-song of Radiolympia Exhibition, 1936)

'Audience studies' is a subject rich in questions and well-nigh barren of answers. Its methodological difficulties are huge, and as I hope to show later, they are in some respects greater in the case of radio than television. This fact makes the subject demoralizing for many of its students and even, for its critics, somewhat disreputable.

Let us take a look at its difficulties. Those of definition and relevance seem truly overwhelming. When we discuss the question of the influences which the media exert, what do we mean by an 'influence' and how can we measure it scientifically? In considering the viewer or listener who may or may not be influenced, what factors in her character and background (psychological, economic, environmental, and so on) are relevant, and to what extent? How far can the audience researcher take for granted her powers of self-knowledge and/or self-expression? If two listeners approve of a programme, one because she 'enjoyed' it, the other because it was 'interesting', are they expressing different reactions or merely the same reaction in two different ways? And if the latter, is that reaction felt in equal measure by both?

An inevitable consequence of these difficulties is that researchers' findings often contradict one another. Rosengren (1974: 282) cites two investigations of soap operas: one blaming them for reducing the listener's social and environmental awareness, the other commending them for increasing it.

Another consequence is that many are inconclusive. Researchers cannot, apparently, show a clear correlation between the amount of exposure to the media and the extent of their influence (Golding 1974: 11), or demonstrate whether the media have effects upon society or are themselves social products or effects (McQuail 1983: 176–8). And a third consequence is that many findings would seem to be perverse – at odds with the promptings of what we loosely term 'instinct', 'gut feeling' or 'common sense'. For instance, the fact that all societies impose at least some restrictions on the showing of violence on television suggests that for most of us there is a self-evident connection between violence on television and violence performed in real life. Yet audience research has failed to demonstrate such a connection and in some instances even impugned it.

On the other hand when research findings do conform to common sense they seem to be redundant and little more than statements of the obvious. When the Yale Communication Research Program found that 'people who value their membership in groups highly will be least affected by communications which advocate positions counter to the norms of the group' (Lowery and De Fleur 1983: 172), scientific observation was hardly distinguishable from platitude. Whether it reaches or fails to reach conclusions, then, audience research gives the impression of applying scientific methods to a subject which is not susceptible to them and has therefore been attacked for its use of 'scientism' and its naively quantitative approach (Smythe 1972: 20–1; Burgelin 1972: 324). The broad effect of these difficulties has been described thus:

> Research findings have too often seemed negative or slight in importance, there has been little development of theory, and the accumulation of general findings has seemed slow and inadequate. The initial excitement of trying to discover the 'effects' of the new communications media gave way to a growing realization of the conceptual and methodological complexity of such an enterprise. The process was educative, but to some, depressing.
>
> (McQuail 1972: 11)

Nearly twenty years after this was written, little headway had been made (Cumberbatch and Howitt 1989).

Before the problem of audience effects can be tackled, researchers must *analyse* the audience – in radio terms, discover how many are listening and what their social identity is. Yet even so simple an objective as this hides another complex question: what constitutes a listener?

Someone who owns, or has access to, a radio set?

Someone who listens to a whole programme? (But 'programme' is itself a problematic concept since there is a difference between a programme which is meant to be listened to attentively and continuously, such as a play or documentary on BBC Radio 4, and a three-hour music show on Virgin 1215 which presumes, or at least allows for, casual and intermittent listening.)

Someone who listens to a minimum proportion of a programme (say, 50 per cent)?

Someone who listens for a minimum amount of time in the day (say, half an hour)?

Someone who listens for several hours a day but whose listening span corresponds to no complete programme, possibly because she switches between stations?

The question of audience size is further complicated by the practice of off-air recording – cassetting or 'time-shift' listening – which means that the total number listening at the time of transmission will not amount to the total audience, not only because some members of that audience may listen at another time but because some of them may listen to the transmission *several times over*. This must be particularly true of the many who illegally record pop music from the radio in order to listen repeatedly to the hits they would otherwise have to buy.

To meet some of these difficulties broadcasting researchers have found it useful to adopt more than one concept of the audience: there is the 'average' audience for a programme's duration; 'reach', the number of people who listen to at least a part of, for instance, a sequence programme such as *Today* (BBC Radio 4); and the 'core' audience which stays with the entire programme.

Once it has been decided which concept of the audience to adopt and the number of listeners to any given programme computed, the question of their social identity may seem easier to determine. But those audience analysts who represent differing professional interests may define this social identity in several different ways: by age, gender, racial or political composition, and so on. The more useful of these are outlined by McQuail (1983: 150–5), among them the following:

1 The audience as a mass. This focuses on its overall size, its heterogeneity, anonymity, lack of social cohesion and geographical dispersion. Foremost among those in radio and television who think in terms of 'mass audiences' are the network controllers and station managers, even though the expression is sometimes used to imply 'low taste'.
2 The audience as a cohesive class or professional group – pre-existent to the media, not created by them, and so while served by them not dependent on them. This audience is alert, self-aware and largely autonomous. It might be characterized as part or all of 'the informed public' – a perspective which can be of particular use to programme planners and producers.
3 The audience as a market – the actual or potential consumers of a product or service. It is not a self-conscious or interactive group but could be a population area (e.g., Greater London) or a social category (e.g., housewives).

It is important to stress that these views of the audience are merely abstractions for particular purposes and are not mutually exclusive: many – most – of its members could be included in more than one category. Nevertheless researchers have been able to build up a reasonably clear picture of who listens to the radio and when. The method they use is to question a small sample of a station's total potential audience, since sampling 'is based on the predicate that conclusions about large populations can be inferred from data about a limited number of them' (Silvey 1974: 44). This essentially quantitative method is much easier to conduct than effects analysis and is of great help to broadcasters and advertisers alike. It can tell them which stations and programmes are most listened to, the identity of those who are listening in, and what their listening routines or habits are.

In Britain, for instance, Radio Joint Audience Research (RAJAR), the measurement system agreed by the independent and BBC stations, has shown that many more people listen to BBC Radios 1 and 2 than to 3 and 4 (Wroe 1993b: 1). Although the recent arrival of national commercial radio may have altered the picture some-what, it is also true that before 1991 middle-class listeners pre-ferred Radios 3 and 4, while working-class listeners inclined to Radios 1 and 2 and ILR (Seymour-Ure 1991: 126). Nevertheless the *amount* of listening was highest among the higher social grades and showed no female bias (ibid.: 152).

It has been found that listening also decreases with age (ibid.). However, as listeners grow older they graduate from music to speech radio. This is perhaps because they grew up on speech as part of a radio diet of mixed programming which existed before television became the main medium, or because the available music stations do not cater sufficiently for older tastes (Barnett and Morrison 1989: 30, 35). Not surprisingly in view of their waking and sleeping hours, teenagers and young adults listen little in the mornings and a lot in the evenings (ibid.: 11).

Finally it is apparent that whereas the attachment of television viewers is to programmes rather than stations or channels, for radio listeners the opposite is true (ibid.: 20–1). There are two reasons for this. First, since television replaced radio as the main mass medium most radio stations no longer provide 'programmes' as such. The sound medium is now used very largely as back-ground, as an accompaniment to other activities; and as we saw in Chapters 2 and 4, this use is best served by a range of 'formatted' stations offering streamed and essentially unvarying output rather than self-contained programmes. Second, and as we also saw in Chapter 2, audiences find it harder to twiddle the tuning-knob on their radios than to jab the channel-change button on their television sets. Having fixed upon a radio station, they therefore tend to stay with it through thick and thin.

An overall profile of daily listening has also been discerned (Seymour-Ure 1991: 151). Radio's peak time is in the early morning, when people get up, have breakfast and go to work. Women continue to listen in quite large numbers through the morning. The afternoon audience steadily declines, builds again for an hour or so in the late afternoon rush-hour, and then succumbs to television except for a late rally at bed-time.

But knowing how big an audience is at any given time, and even what percentage of it consists of professional people or potential purchasers of double glazing, is not enough, if only because it gives broadcasters and advertisers no clue as to how such an audience may be retained, or preferably enlarged. As R.J. Silvey puts it of his early days in BBC listener research:

> however useful as a substitute for the box office, there were functions quantitative data could not fulfil. Knowing the size of a programme's audience told one nothing about that audience's listening experience, what it was about the programme they had liked or not liked or why they felt about it as they did.
>
> (Silvey 1974: 113)

One might even argue as Silvey does elsewhere (ibid.: 185) that there is no virtue in audience size for its own sake, what matters is the measure of the audience's appreciation: a small audience might have been delighted with what it heard, a large audience disappointed. BBC Radio 3 is a minority station – indeed its listeners are almost too few to measure: yet they are the loyalest and most appreciative of any (Barnett and Morrison 1989: 21).

One way to discover what listeners think of the programmes is simply to rely on their unsolicited correspondence, as the BBC did during the first fourteen years of its existence. But this is an atypical reflection of audience attitudes because correspondents are atypically literate people and, moreover, people with atypically strong feelings ('Disgusted of Cheltenham'). Correspondence thus tends to reflect not the audience as a whole but only its more literate members, or rather only those more literate members with unusually strong feelings about the programmes (Silvey 1974: 29–31).

But just as the number of people listening to a programme is a poor guide to their feelings about it, so feelings are a poor guide to the programme's effects or influence. A listener might, after all, enjoy violence or pornography on the radio and yet be harmed by it: conversely a programme about death and coping with bereavement might make painful listening, yet be of moral benefit and practical help to the listener.

Effects analysis, the consideration of what the media – in our case radio – do to their audiences and what they make them think, is a subject laden with theories, all of them plausible, most of them conflicting, and none of them proven. When the question 'What effect do the media have upon their audiences?' was first put during the inter-war years it was assumed to be a simple one with an obvious answer: they exerted a persuasive and pervasive effect, transmitting simple and deliberate messages to which their audiences reacted in direct, predictable, uniform, and often dramatic ways (Lowery and De Fleur 1983: 23, 366–7).

Since media messages were thought of in almost ballistic terms – fired off as if from a gun and with almost equally inevitable results – this has sometimes been termed the 'magic bullet' or *stimulus-response* theory of audience behaviour. Lest such a theory seem laughably naive to the modern reader, I must hasten to add that there were good reasons for adopting it during the 1930s. First of all, the media were newer and fewer than they are today: scepticism about their messages was not natural in an age less inured than ours is to the clamorous and conflicting voices not only of newspapers and radio but of multi-channel television. And there were other reasons:

> There was the seeming ease with which World War I war-mongers and Fascist regimes in Europe of the 1930s had manipulated people's attitudes and bases of allegiance and behaviour. That impression was compatible with theories of mass society, current at the time the study of media effects began to take shape, which postulated that the dissolution of traditional forms of social organization under the impact of industrialization and urbanization had resulted in a social order in which individuals were atomized, cut off from traditional networks of social relationships, isolated from sources of social support, and consequently vulnerable to direct manipulation by remote and powerful elites in control of the mass media.
>
> (Blumler and Gurevitch 1982: 242–3)

A dramatic vindication of stimulus-response theory seemed to occur in the USA in 1938 with Orson Welles's radio adaptation of H.G. Wells's *The War of the Worlds*. The mock news bulletin with which it began announced an invasion by creatures from Mars and caused widespread panic. According to some accounts, over a quarter of the estimated 6 million listeners believed what they heard, and a number of those living near the supposed invasion site got into their cars and fled.

As Schramm points out (1971: 45), the affair dramatically illustrated three points: first, since persuasion seems to work better when it is hidden rather than overt, the importance of the broadcast *not* being perceived as manipulative; second, the effect of a threat against which listeners could think of no defence; and third, the use of a 'contractual cultural norm' – of a medium, radio, which was normally trusted as a reliable news source. But it has been pointed out that one limitation of stimulus-response theory is that 'we are limited to inferring that a message has had an influence only when we are able to observe a *change* or *difference* in the response chosen as the indicator of effects' (Roberts 1971: 359).

Since a number of effects analyses made between 1946 and 1961 by the Yale Program of Research on Communication and Attitude Change seemed to suggest that media messages did *not* appreciably change audiences' views, or at least that there were no simple ways of achieving or predicting attitude-change through the media (Lowery and De Fleur 1983: 148–75, 367–70), stimulus-response theory gave way to new and often overlapping schools of thought. The first held that media effects are negligible (Cumberbatch and Howitt 1989: 4); the second that the media are more effective in *confirming* the beliefs and attitudes of their audiences than in changing them.

Many of the findings on which this second line of thought, known as *reinforcement* theory, is based are summarized in Schramm and Roberts (1971). From two major studies of voting behaviour in US elections Berelson, Lazarsfeld and McPhee concluded that the media strengthened rather than challenged the political opinions of their audiences (1971: 655–77). Lazarsfeld and Merton suggest (1971: 560–77) that while the media confer 'status' on certain issues and social movements by publicizing them, these originate within society itself, whose various elements the media help to cement. Their general finding is that the media change opinions only if their audiences are predisposed to change, otherwise the effect is one of reinforcement (cf. also Silvey 1970: 312). It is at least noticeable that while the media seem generally unable to change political and religious beliefs, their influence in the world of popular culture seems enormous (McQuail 1977: 87). Presumably because they want to be, audiences are highly susceptible to media messages relating to pop music, fashion, buzz-words, and even to the deeper, moral values that are implicit in this world – values which relate to sexuality, gender, race, and so on.

Reinforcement theory has been adopted and adapted by modern Marxist thinkers, who argue that those who control the media, and who therefore have an interest in maintaining the status quo, preclude any changes of attitude in their audiences by what is known as an 'agenda-setting' function, by transmitting messages which reinforce the 'dominant ideology' and limit the audiences' ability to see issues in any other terms, or indeed to see any other *issues*, than those 'on the agenda' they prescribe (Lowery and De Fleur 1983: 380–1). Put simply, the media may not succeed in telling us what to think, but they do succeed in telling us what to think *about*: one of their roles is to act as 'gate-keeper', to debar from public scrutiny those issues or stories which may be inimical to the political establishment. This seems to have led Raymond Williams (1974: 122–6) to dismiss most effects studies as misplaced, since they are insufficiently concerned with social, political and cultural *causes*. But in his discussion of the audiences of radio soap operas, Murdock uses the reinforcement and agenda-setting theories to suggest that in a deeper and subtler way than was at first envisaged, there is perhaps some truth in the old stimulus-response theory after all. At the conscious level listeners may not be crudely vulnerable to media messages in the sense that they will think whatever they are told to think; they may be

> active rather than passive, participants rather than dupes. Even so, it is activity that remains confined by the limits set by the imaginative and ideological world presented by the serials . . . . [They] do indeed appear as vehicles for dominant and largely conservative values. Although the audiences were mainly working-class, the serials concentrated on the doings and attitudes of the upper class and the better-off sectors of the middle class. They therefore provided a powerful conduit for the downward transmission of dominant views and assumptions.
>
> (Murdock 1981: 156)

As Blumler and Gurevitch point out (1982: 249) it then becomes important to see whether the conservative views and values which the media foreground as suitable for public consumption are similarly foregrounded in the minds of their audiences. Moreover, if it is true that audiences are seldom consciously persuaded, either because they have already been prejudiced at a deeper, ideological level or because they are instinctively resistant to overt attempts to influence them, a logical development in audience research is from theories of reinforcement to those of *cognition*, to an examination of how much information audiences glean from the media (ibid.: 248).

The other line of thought which succeeded stimulus-response theory – one which runs parallel to reinforcement theory, from which it is in some respects indistinguishable – is the *uses and gratifications* approach. Since the effects of the media upon audiences seemed to be minimal yet 'consumption' of the media remained vast, this approach switched the focus of research from what the media do to people to what people do with the media, the *uses* to which they put them and the satisfactions or *gratifications* they obtain from them. We might note in passing that the notion of an active audience which the uses and gratifications theory presupposes seems vindicated by the popularity of the phone-in; for the phone-in, as we saw in the previous chapter, depends upon an audience which is prepared to impose itself upon media output to the extent of originating it.

There are many helpful summaries of uses and gratifications theory (e.g. McQuail 1983: 82–3; Lowery and De Fleur 1983: 374–5; Fiske 1990: 151–6), but its basic assumption is that the message is much more a matter of what the audience makes of it than what the broadcaster intends and that for the former there are four main kinds of gratification:

1 Diversion – the need for escape from life's routine and problems, for emotional release.
2 Social integration – the need for companionship, to form relationships with others.
3 Self-awareness – the need to compare personalities to oneself, programme content to one's own situation.
4 Surveillance – the need for information about the world.

The classic uses and gratifications study was conducted by Katz, Gurevitch and Haas (1973: 164–81), a summary of which may be found in Fiske (1990: 19–20). They drew attention to the fact that the potential media 'consumer' consciously discriminates among the media and their characteristic forms of content according to her psychological and social needs and her physical circumstances, all of which vary in time.

For instance, it was discovered that the need to establish rapport with one's family was best served by television, and with friends by television or the cinema. But since newspaper *content* was an important basis of conversation with friends, it was clear that the choice was not simply between media, but sometimes between media and messages. Since the print media are generally more conducive than the electronic media to the transmission and retention of abstract and complex material, it is not surprising that the researchers found that the former were preferred by the more educated, the latter by the less educated. Of the main needs listed – for knowledge, 'escape', aesthetic pleasure, improving self-confidence and strengthening social ties – not one was best served by radio, despite the almost universal ownership of sets.

In exploring the ways in which the five main media catered to audience needs the researchers perceived an interrelationship or 'circumplex' between them, in which the position of one medium *vis-à-vis* another depends on the closeness of the needs which they gratify. If we begin, arbitrarily, with the book then its 'next of kin' is the newspaper, from which the interrelationship runs to radio, television, cinema, and so full-circle back to the book. Thus if we lack books we are likely to seek gratification either from newspapers or the cinema, whose functions most nearly match their own: we are less likely to switch on the radio or television.

The study is open to question, particularly its claim that in most cases we seek gratification from a medium rather than from its content. It is true that as a way of strengthening their social ties people will sometimes decide to go to the cinema irrespective of what film is showing, and very probable that the better educated prefer print to electronic media. But in Britain radio would almost certainly afford more gratification to the educated classes than it does in the USA or Israel (where the study was conducted), since with BBC Radios 3 and 4 Britain has a much stronger tradition of catering to their needs.

Thus content seems to be a rather more important source of gratification than this study implies, though this is not to deny that the consumer's choice will naturally be constrained by the fact that some media are better at providing certain kinds of content than others. It has been pointed out that radio, for example, is good for music, news, politics, and some women's interests, but less good for sport (except cricket), fashion and sex (Seymour-Ure 1991: 158). Nevertheless choice often transcends the individual media. The study suggests that if she lacks books the consumer is likely to seek gratification in the 'adjacent' media of newspapers on the one hand and cinema on the other; but I would suggest that kinds of content rather than choice of medium would be foremost in her mind, and that without books she would be every bit as likely to seek gratification in radio or television as in newspapers or the cinema.

Another objection to the study is that the gratifications it lists seem somewhat arbitrary and ill-defined. We might think of others it does not include, and in discussing those which we derive from books, for instance, we surely need to distinguish between the gratifications afforded by fiction and those of non-fiction. On the other hand the study seems to overlook the possibility that improving self-confidence, strengthening social ties and acquiring knowledge are gratifications which are in some respects indistinguishable from one another, as are those of 'escape' and aesthetic pleasure.

Nevertheless the study was important because while it conceded that certain gratifications are common to a number of media its contrastive descriptions of the latter (public/private, electronic/print, and so on) sharpened awareness of their distinctive characteristics, the kinds of content they typically carry, and the social circumstances in which they can be resorted to. It reminds us that listeners and viewers are not separate and rival species but that the listener at 9 am is a viewer at 9 pm – that audiences are capable of discriminating quite consciously between the different media. Indeed it has since been pointed out that during major political crises such as the Kennedy assassination, the variety of the media and the public's attitude towards them are a force for calm rather than panic, since the public tends to seek verification from more than one medium, whereas panic is the natural consequence of rumour and ambiguity (McQuail 1977: 86).

Nevertheless I would argue that the study is of particular interest in respect of radio. If uses and gratifications theory is applicable to the other media, if it is indeed true that in pursuit of our various gratifications we select a particular medium rather than particular content, it will be especially true of radio. However much we may adapt them to our psychological needs the other media first require an adjustment from *us*, in the sense that we must suspend most other activities in order to attend to their messages. But radio, being non-visual, is different. Locked into some primary activity such as driving or cooking, we resort to the medium almost irrespective of its content because there is *no other medium we can attend to*. Consequently we adapt radio to our *physical* circumstances and requirements in the way uses and gratifications theory argues that we adapt all the media to suit our *psychological* circumstances and requirements.

The study also enabled important distinctions to be drawn (Katz, Blumler and Gurevitch 1974: 24) between the gratifications to be derived from the *content* of a medium ('I enjoy listening to *Desert Island Discs*'); from *exposure* to the medium *per se*, which might consist as much of 'dial twiddling' as listening to individual programmes ('I enjoy listening to the radio'); and from the social *context* which typifies the exposure to the medium ('I enjoy listening to the radio while I'm shaving').

Again these distinctions seem especially relevant to a secondary or background medium such as radio. Moreover the study's account of the inherent characteristics of the various media gave theoretical justification to attempts, some of which had already been made, to examine the effects of one medium in isolation from all the others. In 'Listening to radio' (1964: 239–49) Mendelsohn had already pointed out that listeners do not greatly distinguish between different kinds of content, whether informative or entertaining, but use radio to 'structure' their day and as a 'companion'. It provides material for conversation, and its importance lies less in the amount of time people listen to it than in the psychological needs which it gratifies.

In this and a later study of housewives and radio (Hobson 1980: 105–14) it was stressed that radio gives the isolated listener a feeling of community not simply with the broadcasters but with the *other* isolated listeners, two different needs for social contact which do not seem to have been distinguished by Katz, Gurevitch and Haas. The experience of many listeners would, I suspect, echo Mendelsohn's and Hobson's findings and confirm that our attitude to radio is 'utilitarian' in a way that our attitude to television cannot be. We certainly use television to fulfil our psychological and social needs: followers of soap opera, for example, respond to the medium in an active and critical way, closely relating its content to the preoccupations of their everyday lives (Hobson 1982: 119–36). But as we have just seen, it also requires them to *suspend* their lives during the time that they watch it. Radio, on the other hand, makes no such demand: because we continue with our lives *while* we are listening, its content is, as it were, transplanted into our own existence and adapted to our own purposes.

In the previous edition of this book I illustrated this through my own use of the medium between 8.45 and 9.15 on weekday mornings – a time during which I drove to work, dropping my daughter at school on the way. For the first part of the journey we listened to BBC Radio 1, after which I would turn to the 9 o'clock news summary on Radio 4, then to the beginning of *This Week's*

Composer on Radio 3 – a span of three stations and three programme boundaries in about half an hour.

I suggested that all this chopping and changing, indisputably
an 'active' attitude to the medium, served a number of needs
and gratifications, most of which are recognizable in terms of
the studies we have looked at. There were the self-directed needs
for self-confidence and aesthetic pleasure, and the more 'out-
ward' needs – to find out what time it was and what was
happening in the world. But the importance of my *situation* was
also noted, not simply that of being about to 'face the day' but of
listening to a *car* radio rather than a portable set: for the simple
fact that like most car radios mine had push-button tuning,
whereas tuning on most other sets requires rather more dexterity,
meant that I hopped between stations much more than I otherwise would have, and was therefore able to extend the range of
gratifications open to me.

However, the fact that my listening spanned programme boundaries was even more significant than the spanning of stations. I
began by hearing the last fifteen minutes of a Radio 1 show which
had been on for nearly two hours, then listened to a complete news
bulletin of five minutes' duration, and concluded with the first five
or ten minutes of a programme that would last for another forty-
five minutes or so. Thus, if I had stayed tuned to a single station, I
could still not have heard any complete programme other than the
news summary on Radio 4.

My account has a coda. Although I am sure that at this time of
day these stations are every bit as good as they ever were, I no
longer listen to any of them; and the reason is simply that my
current routine consists of a succession of varied activities that
cannot be accompanied by the radio. My point, then, is that radio
is 'appropriated' by the individual much more than is any other
medium because the attention she is able to give it is dictated not
so much by the programmes it offers her as by the highly variable
yet often rigid circumstances of her own life.

I should not have inflicted an account of my own use of the
medium on the reader if I had thought that it was particularly
idiosyncratic: or perhaps it is truer to say that *everybody*'s is. The
demands made by the housewife, the student and the company
representative will differ in time, and in amounts of time, from
each other's; yet they will all be alike in being determined largely
by the exigencies of their lives and only in the second place by

what the individual stations provide. Nor can these exigencies necessarily be foreseen or altered by the listener herself.

Let us take the case of the company representative who in a typical working day travels a hundred miles from her base to visit three or four of her customers in a single town. For the two hours or so of her initial journey she can listen to her car radio without interruption, perhaps hearing two complete programmes on Radio 4. But then she arrives at her first call, and irrespective of the point which the present programme has reached, she must switch off: the day is short, there are several customers to visit, and the length of her visits will vary. Thenceforward her use of the radio will be in short snatches and at unforeseeable intervals between visits. In terms of the programmes that radio has traditionally provided, this use of the medium is almost nonsensical: the programme planners would have a headache in providing for our company 'rep' alone, quite apart from all the other people listening at times and for spells which are equally arbitrary. Yet in an age of transistor portables and car radios, such casual and desultory listening is also inevitable.

A glance at the schedules of almost every radio station in Britain confirms that broadcasters are well aware of this. With the notable exception of BBC Radio 4 which still offers a miscellany of 'built' programmes, the typical output of a station is, as we noted in Chapter 4, of a single, uniform kind – usually a music format – and carved into two- or three-hour chunks which are distinguishable from one another mainly by their changes of presenter. Even the conservative and highbrow BBC Radio 3 is virtually a classical format station: music accounts for more than three-quarters of its total output (BBC 1992: 28), much of it broadcast in sequences of programmes each lasting about two hours.

However, even the streamed output of Radio 3 is not altogether satisfying for the intermittent listener since unfettered by the need to provide advertising breaks, it generally broadcasts classical works in full and thus usually imbues her with a sense of having missed, or being about to miss, a great deal. As we also noted in Chapter 4, the best mode of presentation for format radio is *segmentation* – the division of the output into self-contained 'bites' each lasting no more than a few minutes. We observed that segmentation is ideal for broadcasters and advertisers because it homogenizes the output, making the commercial breaks and informational elements seem all of a piece with the music. But I wish to make the point here that segmentation is also ideal for the *listener* because it allows her amid the many other demands of her life to drop in and out of radio content without feeling that she has missed anything of major importance. Even in all-news formats segmentation works well since it usually consists of a repeated sequence of bulletins, interviews and short features which allows the listener to 'step aboard' at any time.

Unlike Radio 3, BBC Radio 1 does adopt a segmented mode of presentation: we referred in Chapter 4 to its rapid succession of records, chat, competitions, trails, non-commercial adverts, and so on. But audience analysis (as we have seen, a more fruitful line of inquiry than effects analysis) suggests that even Radio 1 cannot give the individual listener exactly what she wants. Experience suggests that she requires output which she can not only tune into and out of as her circumstances allow, but which always approximates to her particular musical tastes. Yet pop music is no longer the monolith that it was, and she may have to wait some time before she hears something she likes:

> [Pop] may be youth music but its ever-lengthening history precludes it from an exclusivity of appeal based on age. Increasingly, Radio 1 finds itself in a similar position to that of the Light Programme in the early 1960s, obliged to cater for all ages and a broadening range of specialist tastes within a single network.
>
> (Barnard 1989: 62)

In one respect this is reassuring and would seem to give yet another lease of life to the old concept of public service broadcasting. We noted at the end of Chapter 2 that Radio 1 intends to provide much more information on matters of social concern – unemployment, education, counselling, and so on – and in so doing seems to be offering a new notion of 'public service' in place of the old mixed programming pattern. But increasingly too it must provide a range and mixture of music within the pop genre to satisfy pre-teenagers at one extreme and the middle-aged at the other – a third notion of public service.

Radio 2 is in a somewhat similar predicament, poised as it is between fans of early rock, traditional jazz lovers, country and folk enthusiasts, 'sweet music' devotees, and 'swing', mainstream and big-band addicts; and both stations, together with those community stations whose appeal is to a locality rather than a special interest group, try to solve this problem by targeting different audiences at different times of the day. But as I mentioned earlier, listeners seem very loath to tune into a station merely for that part of the output which suits them and then tune out again. Barnett and Morrison show that the listener is notoriously loyal to one station (1989: 15) and will go to almost any length to avoid re-tuning (ibid.: 96). And in any case, why should she be expected to do this if another station – Virgin 1215, perhaps, or one of the ILR stations such as Jazz FM – will give her exactly what she wants at almost any time of the day?

All of this suggests that, in radio terms at least, the public service concept of catering for a range of tastes may have reached virtual exhaustion. Radio 1 (and soon, perhaps, Radio 2) faces a stark choice. Either it must continue as a 'broad church' and run the risk that its entire audience will be divided up and lured away by the more specialized independents (most local and community stations offer chart or ethnic music, while older listeners are being tempted by the 'adult' rock of Virgin 1215); or it must specialize in only one kind of pop music – and thus attract censure for no longer catering for a spread of listeners that is the sole justification for a universal licence fee.

To sum up, then. The listener is undeniably 'active' in the sense that she has no need to adjust to the daily schedules that radio provides: on the contrary, she imports it into her own daily schedule and often in a casual, fitful way – at unpredictable times and for unpredictable spells. But predictability must characterize its output, in the sense that its structure should be familiar to her and its content should accord with her tastes, and she must not be made to feel that her use of the medium is causing her to miss out on anything of great importance.

But the listener is active not only in the fact that she uses the radio on her terms rather than the medium's, but in the ways that she interprets its verbal content. It has long been known, for instance, that different listeners will use a single media message to gratify their differing psychological needs (Johnstone 1974: 36). These uses might be termed 'variant decodings' of an intentional nature: the solitary person might use a soap opera to reinforce her private fantasies, the gregarious person might use it as a topic of conversation, but they are 'intentional' in the sense that the scriptwriter provides for both uses within the content.

On the other hand there may be variant decodings of an unintentional nature – unintended by the broadcaster or the listener or both (McLeod and Becker 1974: 141–2). A broadcaster's programme categories may be at variance with the psychological categorizations of the listener: the former may, for instance, conceive of *The Archers* as a drama series, while the latter perceives it as a features programme about farming made on behalf of the Department of Agriculture. Sometimes the message may not correspond to the *listener*'s intentions, as when she switches on a programme entitled *Animal Farm* in the expectation of an agricultural documentary but instead hears, and enjoys, a dramatization of George Orwell's political allegory.

Finally there may be 'errant decodings' in which listeners misunderstand media messages or consciously distort them to make them more palatable (Cooper and Jahoda 1971: 287–93). Such decodings could, of course, be used to support the 'magic bullet' theory of audience effects, for the *War of the Worlds* broadcast was one such decoding. But the uses and gratifications theorist would probably argue from the fact that listeners misinterpret so many more messages to their advantage than to their disadvantage that their role is a good deal less passive than magic bullet theory would imply.

Still, errant decodings do indicate the respect in which uses and gratifications theory and reinforcement theory are at one: regardless of the intentions of broadcasters listeners will hear what they want to hear:

> Occasionally . . . a broadcaster may aim at a pigeon and shoot a crow; he may fail completely to meet the need he intended to gratify, while in fact gratifying a need of an entirely different kind. A notorious case in point is the broadcaster who intended, by a word-picture, to satisfy the homebound listener's desire to visualize a Naval Review but who, instead, succeeded triumphantly in satisfying the need to be entertained.
>
> (Silvey 1970: 303)

For these reasons it is important for audience researchers to distinguish media *effects* – any of the consequences of programme output – from *effectiveness*, a programme's ability to achieve a given objective (McQuail 1977: 70).

Much uses and gratifications theory suggests, then, that broadcasters have little influence over their audiences – or to put it another way, that audiences are busy and alert but that among their more predictable responses is the ability to resist media effects. Robert Silvey is one of its most eloquent exponents since he was the first Head of BBC Audience Research and studied listener behaviour for over thirty years. His descriptions of the ordinary listener, naturally wary and critical, mostly active but proof against persuasion even when she is not, make reassuring reading (1970: 305–8; 1974: 166–7). Silvey points out that the listener is not a mere receptacle. She *becomes* a listener through an act of choice: she selects certain kinds of output rather than others. She is not obliged to switch on, and once her radio is on she can switch it off. She can reject or disagree with what she hears, and her natural human inertia will make it easier for her to resist the pressures to change her views than succumb to them. Challenge is stimulating but also discomforting: she is more likely to want to relax and be entertained than to think. Consequently she can simply reduce the amount of attention she gives to the broadcast, to the point of ignoring it altogether. Or she may practise selective perception by listening to some parts and ignoring others. Or she may consciously or unconsciously distort its message to fit her own preconceptions. And if all else fails, she can simply forget what she has heard.

Nevertheless, uses and gratifications theory remains open to certain criticisms: not everyone agrees on the nature of the uses to which the listener puts the media, nor on the amount of gratification she seeks from them, nor on the extent to which she is proof against their effects. What precisely is meant by 'uses' and 'gratifications'?

> A host of studies has attempted to set forth lists of the needs satisfied by media content, or typologies of motivation and functions involved in attention to mass communication. Unfortunately, such lists and typologies vary greatly from one investigator to another. No agreement exists ... why people select particular content, what needs a given form of content satisfies, or how such gratification leads to behavioral consequences.
>
> (Lowery and De Fleur 1983: 375)

Mendelsohn adopts a similar argument (1974: 306), pointing out that the listener's 'needs' in relation to the media are not always self-evident but reflected in a variety of ways. The criterion of 'need' does not adequately explain the different use patterns to which the media are put, nor the presumable difference in the gratifications afforded by these different kinds of media experience. Why, for instance, does one listener in search of diversion turn to a Samuel Beckett play on Radio 3 and another to *The Archers* on Radio 4 – what is the difference in these two forms of gratification which the single word 'diversion' hides?

Elliott discerns even more radical problems in the concept of 'needs' (1974: 255), alleging that unlike 'deficiency' needs such as hunger, they are merely 'growth' needs which have been learned through social experience, including experience of the media. We must then talk of the media gratifying needs they have helped to create. In any case, as Golding avers (1974: 10–11), these needs and gratifications may be extremely hard to articulate even for the listener herself, a point developed by Lowery and De Fleur:

> One might raise the objection that such [listeners] may not be aware of the underlying motivations that draw them to particular kinds of content. What they claim in lay terms may have little to do with their 'true' motivations because these motivations may not be understood at the conscious level. One can also ask whether age, sex, socioeconomic status, and other such common variables of social research are the ones that should be given priority in gratifications research. The answers to these issues are not at all clear.
>
> (1983: 375)

But it is not even beyond dispute that audiences are as active in their uses of the media or as resistant to their messages as researchers like Silvey suggest, and it is in this respect that radio is a medium of peculiar significance to effects analysis.

We have already seen that radio is unique in being a secondary medium and that this is what enables it to be used in a casual, desultory way that television cannot: we can slip into and out of its content as our circumstances dictate, and with little or no reference to programme structure. Nevertheless we have assumed that while the radio is on, the listener's attention to it is both uniform and close even though she is likely to be doing something else. Earlier, I painted a self-portrait of someone who even while he was driving was constantly monitoring radio content to the extent of changing stations every few minutes, and I have suggested that such listening behaviour is not atypical. But I have not sufficiently stressed that our use of radio is variable not only in the odd and arbitrary times we resort to it but in the amount of attention we pay to it *while it is on*, and it must also be typical listening behaviour to disregard it almost entirely and treat it as 'background'.

Of course television may be treated as background too, and is in a surprisingly large number of households, but since a large part of its message is visual we can say that in such circumstances it is being ignored. This means that unlike television's, there is some doubt as to who radio's actual audience *is*, and we have returned to the question we posed at the outset: in respect not only of duration but attentiveness, what constitutes a listener?

> Having taken over the word ['audience'] from the theatre, cinema, or concert hall, where it has a meaning, we have overlooked the fact that it cannot be applied to broadcasting in a similarly precise way. The audience for a performance of a play is the people who were present in the theatre when it was performed. They are in a sense a 'captive' audience. But the people who are exposed to a broadcast are not similarly captive. Some of them, it is true, may remain in their chairs throughout, enthralled from start to finish by what they hear . . .; some, though present in the room, may virtually ignore the broadcast their set is receiving . . . . Is the listener who reads a newspaper to the accompaniment of a radio discussion part of its audience or is he not? . . .
>
> The answers to such questions as [this] depend, of course, on how you choose to define the term 'audience'. You may choose to define it conservatively, confining it to those who have given the broadcast their full attention throughout, or you can define it generously, including all within earshot, or indeed you can choose any point along this continuum. But whatever your decision, be assured that it is highly relevant to the question of audience size, for if a broadcast's audience is deemed to include all within earshot it may be many times larger than if it is deemed to exclude all but the fully attentive.
>
> (Silvey 1974: 179)

Not surprisingly, this is a can of worms which the modern RAJAR surveys decline to open: its questionnaires do not distinguish between primary and secondary listening, nor in any other way seek to measure the respondent's attentiveness. To count as a listener she must simply be within earshot of her radio for a minimum of five minutes in any one quarter of an hour.

On the face of it, uses and gratifications theory would seem to be vindicated by the suggestion of 'mind over medium', of many, perhaps most, listeners exercising even more than viewers their freedom to pay scant attention to radio's messages or even to ignore them altogether. But to describe such listeners as 'conscious' or 'active' in their use of the medium seems misleading, to say the least. It has long been known, for instance, that the time at which they listen is far more important to most listeners than the nature of the programmes they are listening to:

> Without any change in the content of a programme, the size of its audience could be radically altered simply by transmitting it at a different time or by changing its placing; put it immediately after, or even immediately before, a programme which had a large following and its audience went up. Even a mere change of title could make a difference. No series of Chamber Music programmes ever attracted a substantial following until someone thought of leaving those fatal words out of the billing and calling it simply *Music in Miniature*.
>
> (ibid.: 113)

Of course the times at which people listen are not always a matter of pure choice, but when the choice is between their usual station and their favourite programme the facts are more telling. In 1966 *The Archers* lost a million listeners simply by moving from the Light Programme to the Home Service (Wade 1981a: 101), and programmes originating on BBC Radio 3 invariably attract bigger audiences if they are re-broadcast on Radio 4.

All this paints a disturbing picture of an inert majority of listeners who switch on at a fixed time and to a fixed station irrespective of programme content, and who in so far as they exercise any preferences are easily duped out of them by mere changes of title. Nevertheless, as we have seen, some uses and gratifications theorists such as Silvey would regard this inertia as itself part of the weaponry with which the listener resists media effects: it is not so much that she is duped as detached – not greatly affected by what she hears, provided that it does not take up too much of her attention or try too hard to challenge her views, and as long as it affords her some general sense of routine and companionship.

But the evidence is profoundly ambivalent. She may hardly be listening, but unlike the television, which she experiences while disengaged from most other activities and which she is therefore much more likely to recognize as extraneous to her personal situation, her radio is on simultaneously with her primary activity. This means that whatever their proportions relative to each other it is often hard to separate first-hand experience from vicarious, 'radio' experience: 'Where did I hear that story? Did someone tell me at work or was it Simon Mayo on Radio 1?' It may be that precisely because it is ignored radio is capable of strong effects, that its content can infiltrate the listener just because her conscious faculties are primarily engaged elsewhere and her mental defences therefore down. This is a plausible challenge to the conventional view that the most influential media are the visual ones: there seem good reasons for arguing the opposite, that they are the more resistible for being perceived consciously and being perceived 'out there', as separate from the events of our own lives.

By their very nature the existence of unconscious media effects is, of course, almost impossible to prove: as soon as we assert their existence we are open to the objection that if we are sufficiently aware of them to discuss them they cannot be 'unconscious' at all. Perhaps the best we can do is to appeal to personal experience. How often do we find ourselves humming a song which we detest and do not remember having heard, yet which we could only have got from the radio? How often are we aware of knowing something as a result of listening to the radio, but which we remember hearing only by reference to the *primary* activity we were engaged in at the time, for example shaving or cleaning the car?

Speaking for myself, there are certain songs I always vividly associate with particular streets because it was while driving along those streets that I first heard them on the radio. Of course it is a moot point whether I was paying much less attention to the music than to the driving: I can only assert that I was hardly aware of the music at the time.

But if we grant that radio has discernible effects even upon the inattentive listener, how much more, or less, influenced is the attentive listener? If the former is open to strong but unperceived effects, the latter is surely highly resistant to them, critically alert to everything she hears and ready to change stations to get what *she* wants rather than what the broadcasters may wish to foist upon her. Against her, any would-be propagandists may be virtually impotent. On the other hand it could be argued that since she is listening harder she is more open to influences than the less attentive listener. They are likely to be the influences or effects she desires. She will probably, as the reinforcement theorists suggest, be seeking confirmation of her prejudices. But in so doing she will be more susceptible than the listener whose prejudices wither away because she never listens hard enough to content which would strengthen them.

It might be helpful to conclude with a summary of our findings. Radio is almost invariably a secondary medium: we listen to it while doing something else, quite often for spans of time which do not correspond to programme spans. Furthermore, we may vary the amount of attention we give to the radio even while it is switched on. We may be almost completely engrossed by what we hear, or we may be barely conscious that we are hearing anything.

This seems to have implications for both audience and effects analysis and for uses and gratifications theory. It means first of all that the very *identity* of the radio audience is much more problematical than that of the television audience: or to put it another way, because other media make a more absolute claim on our attention the distinctions between media consumption and our other activities are much sharper. When we watch television we can do very little else. Of course television may also be treated as mere 'background', but since a large part of its message is visual we can say that in these circumstances the audience is not strictly an 'audience' at all. We cannot make such confident assumptions about the radio audience. Nor, assuming we can measure an effect or influence, can we attempt to identify our audience as those who are most affected or influenced by its messages, for we have also seen that there is no simple correlation between the amount of exposure to the medium, or the measure of attention the listener gives to it, and the extent of its effects upon her. Indeed there is some, albeit subjective, evidence that because it is more integrated into everyday life than are the other media its effects are greater, that the medium is the more influential for being less perceived.

Hence effects analysis is an even more complex matter in radio than in the other media, for whatever else may be said about television, we can say that its direct effects will be found only within the ranks of those who have been paying attention. We cannot say the same about radio; its effects may be found among the inattentive, too.

All this lends credibility to uses and gratifications theory yet also demonstrates its limitations. The fact that we make radio subserve our physical situation in a way that is not possible with the other, visual media gives some ground for believing that we also adapt the media to our psychological requirements. On the other hand if we can describe all those who treat radio as secondary as 'using' the medium, from those who listen closely to those who are virtually ignoring it, the concept of use has been over-stretched and tighter definitions are required. Moreover uses and gratifications theory obscures, but does not dispose of, the old problem of effects and influences, for the fact that even the most inattentive listener is in some sense using the medium does not preclude the possibility that it might be 'using' her, too – that she might be subject to its influence in almost subliminal ways. It would appear that radio's distinctive role in the field of audience studies is simply to add to the complexity of its problems!

SUGGESTIONS FOR FURTHER WORK

Devise a questionnaire to find out about your fellow-students' use of the radio (or that of any other section of the community). This might include versions of some or all of the following questions. Do you possess a radio set of your own? Do you normally listen alone? Are you normally doing something else while you are listening? If so, what main activities does your listening accompany? At what times of the day do you listen and for how long? Do you listen primarily to a station or to a particular kind of output? What sort of gratifications does the station/output provide? Are there any kinds of output which radio does not currently provide but which you feel it could and should provide? And when you have an equal choice between watching television and listening to the radio, do you ever choose the latter? If so, why? The questionnaire might include further questions which enable you to compare the respondents' consumption of radio with their consumption of other media – television, newspapers, cinema.

When the questionnaire has been completed, examine the overall profile of listener identity/use that it gives you. You might then imagine that you are the manager of a radio station that seeks to appeal to a significant number of your respondents. *Either* imagine that it will be an all-music station and draw up a twenty-four-hour schedule of output, detailing the kinds of presenter you would use at specific times of the day and the style and content of presentation you would expect from them, the kinds of music that would be played, and other elements – news, travel reports, phone-ins, competitions, and so on – that might be included in the output.

Or imagine that the station will provide a diet of distinct, mixed programmes and draft a single day's schedule of what these might consist of.

Finally draw up a list of the kinds of advertiser who you think should be particularly interested in reaching your target audience and compose a letter or prospectus soliciting their custom.

Conclusion

Throughout the previous chapters we have attempted to identify the distinctive characteristics of radio by discussing the different kinds of output, and audience uses, which would appear to illuminate them. It seems fitting to conclude our discussion by addressing two further questions: of what use or significance are the findings we have reached, and what, briefly, is the medium's future?

The significance of our findings would seem to range from the theoretical to the practical, but it must also be said that part of this significance pertains to things *outside* radio – that in some ways the medium is not so much of interest in itself as for the light it throws upon the ordinary means by which we perceive the world or upon the more 'conventional' ways in which its messages are conveyed.

It may not, for instance, be too pretentious to suggest that radio's broadest theoretical significance is philosophical – that the faculties which it deploys and denies tell us something about *epistemology,* or the way in which we normally know of the existence of things and are able to make sense of them. We discovered that radio is a blind medium whose codes consist only of noise and silence, and that among these codes only that of words is ultimately intelligible and able to make meaningful those of music, sounds and silence. The epistemological significance of this lies in the fact that our discovery included the perception that the faculty through which we make sense of the world is primarily visual, that of sight; whereas since images are seldom self-explanatory the faculty through which we *communicate* about it is primarily verbal, that of words.

Similarly, our comparison of radio with the other mass media in order to identify the advantages and limitations of the former is also of significance for the insight it afforded us into some of the special characteristics of the latter. The comparison showed that the blindness of radio distinguishes it not only from film and television, but from the print media. Like radio, print lacks the iconic signs of film and television, which display the reality to which they refer; but its symbols are, at least, visible in themselves.

Nevertheless since the comparison involved looking in some detail at the different forms which certain kinds of content assume in the different media, we could assert that it threw almost as much light on the distinctive features of newspaper and television news, televised outside broadcasts, theatrical drama and certain narrative modes of literature as it threw upon their corresponding forms in radio.

Since neither context nor message is visible in radio and its primary code is that of words, it follows that this code must be a *spoken* one; but since speech exists in time and is therefore always evanescent we also discovered that radio is of limited efficiency in conveying highly complex ideas and information, a potential problem in news and documentary broadcasts.

Nevertheless Ong (1982) has pointed out the artificiality of the distinction between speech and writing, orality and literacy, and therefore by implication the worthiness of speech as an object of study. Among our other discoveries was that radio involves particularly sophisticated uses of speech – utterances which take spontaneous forms but which are scripted, a phenomenon known as 'secondary orality'; and forms of talk which are ostensibly interpersonal and intimate, yet function as an impersonal, mass mode of communication (Montgomery 1986; Scannell 1991).

Another consequence of the fact that radio's primary code is oral is that its words can never be distinguished from the presence of a speaker: it is therefore a *binary* code. We noted, then, that however limited their ability to convey abstract ideas, words in their descriptive function can exert a powerful effect on the listener's imagination, in some respects more so than literary words can because they are enhanced by the inflections of the human voice – and what they describe may also be partly realized through SFX.

Nevertheless the imaginary world which is evoked is not the simple counterpart of the one we can see. It is both less and more than the visible world: less in the sense that it is generally less vivid, more in that this relative lack of vividness renders the listener capable of grasping a more complex reality than could be assimilated visually. The listener is therefore grateful for the opportunity to picture what is being described, but for not having to *see* it when he wishes to concentrate on the non-visual aspects of the message.

Moreover the lack of vision not only stimulates the imagination, but may mislead it in the sense that it allows the arbitrary relationship between words and things to be undermined. As we saw in the chapters on drama and light entertainment, radio is thus well equipped to pose ontological questions, present fantasies and indulge in comic deceptions.

We are now, of course, discussing those things we have learned about radio which are of a more practical significance – and among these is the fact that as a binary code speech evokes the *speaker* in addition to the subject of her speech, and to a much greater extent than writing evokes the writer. Hence the imagination is power-fully involved in radio not just in respect of what is being described but of who is describing it, and as I suggested in Chapters 1, 4 and 6 this evocation of the speaker is the basis of radio's pervasive though partly 'fictional' sense of personal companionship.

The last important consequence of radio's blindness is one which we have extensively discussed: it is very largely a *secondary* medium in that the great majority of its audience are likely to be doing something else while their radios are switched on. This means that the circumstances of its reception are curious and even unique. For the (usually solitary) listener the companionship of the presenter, the 'reality' of the world of a play, or the emotional power of a piece of music are strangely superimposed upon, and variously 'colour', his primary activity, whether he is driving, cooking or eating: they do not *replace* it as they do when he watches the television or reads.

But the term 'secondary' disguises a *range* of listening postures: his role is even more complex and variable than that of the 'consumers' of the other media. He can listen closely or treat the radio as mere background (an attitude which can be seen as both more and less active than that of the television viewer) – nor is there any clear correlation between the degree of his attentiveness and the extent of the medium's influence upon him.

The secondariness of the medium is at once its great advantage and disadvantage, for the evidence suggests that radio is used more than ever before, but listened to less. For such a medium we might conclude that there are two kinds of content which seem ideal. The first is news, since as we noted from our investigations in Chapter 5 news in any medium appears to be primarily verbal, and so the very latest events can be conveyed to the listener without requiring him to take his eyes from what is his primary activity. Second, we can infer from our discussion in Chapters 3 and 4 that music is highly suitable for a medium which receives fluctuating attention, for since it does not 'refer to' things in the way that words do it does not force, though it may encourage, the exercise of the listener's imagination.

We noted that in practice music radio is always combined with some measure of personal presentation in order to satisfy the listener's need for explanation and companionship; but it is true too that such output is mostly segmented in nature, thus giving the presenter's talk an inconsequentiality that is also appropriate for secondary, sporadic listening. Moreover our discussion of segmentation led us to conclusions about the cultural contexts of radio and the ways in which its listeners use it – an instance of the way in which media analysis can illuminate the larger concerns of cultural studies.

So, despite its inherent disadvantages and despite continuing technological developments in other media, radio's secondariness gives it certain unconquerable advantages, and thus an assured future – which is a partial answer to the second question we posed at the beginning of this chapter. Furthermore the technological developments within the medium itself offer healthy and exciting prospects. As we saw in Chapter 2 they are partly responsible for the broadcasting deregulation that is taking place and for the consequent growth in the number of stations – a growth that will bring with it a greater editorial freedom for broadcasters and a wider choice for the listeners.

The great majority of these stations will offer formats, mostly of music, but not necessarily all of them: recent proposals for some London franchises included a station for women and a comedy channel. Moreover the new stations at community level are already providing opportunities for do-it-yourself broadcasting, blurring the very distinction between broadcasters and audiences by widening access to production and presentation, and thus bringing about a measure of de-professionalization in radio that is much overdue.

Finally in the realm of receiving technology, RDS will soon

increase the amount of information the listener can obtain from his radio and enhance his autonomy by enabling him to 'shop around' among stations and types of content much more easily than ever before. When we notice the small box in our car or kitchen, whose appearance is so unassuming yet whose present and future power seems so formidable even in this televisual age, the exuberance of Lord Reith's description seems more than ever apposite: it is, indeed, a miraculous toy.

Bibliography

Armes, R. (1988) *On Video*, London: Routledge.
Barnard, S. (1989) *On the Radio: Music Radio in Britain*, Milton Keynes: Open University Press.
Barnes, J. (1983) 'Interviewer with the judo touch', *Observer*, 31 July.
Barnett, S. and Morrison, D. (1989) *The Listener Speaks: The Radio Audience and the Future of Radio*, London: HMSO Books.
Baron, M. (1975) *Independent Radio*, Lavenham: Dalton.
Barthes, R. (1977) *Image – Music – Text*, (trans.) S. Heath, Glasgow: Fontana.
BBC (1969) *Broadcasting in the Seventies*, London: British Broadcasting Corporation.
—— (1977) *Handbook 1978*, London: British Broadcasting Corporation.
—— (1984) *Annual Report and Handbook 1985*, London: British Broadcasting Corporation.
—— (1992) *Guide to the BBC 1992*, London: British Broadcasting Corporation.
Berelson, B.R., Lazarsfeld, P.F. and McPhee, W.N. (1971) 'Political processes: the role of the mass media', in Schramm, W. and Roberts, D. (eds) *The Process and Effects of Mass Communication*, Urbana, Ill: University of Illinois Press, revised edn.
Bernstein, B. (ed.) (1971) *Class, Codes and Control*, vol. 1, London: Routledge & Kegan Paul.
Black, P. (1972) *The Biggest Aspidistra in the World*, London: British Broadcasting Corporation.
Blumler, J.G. and Gurevitch, M. (1982) 'The political effects of mass communication', in Gurevitch, M., Bennett, T., Curran, J. and Woollacott, J. (eds) *Culture, Society and the Media*, London: Methuen.
Brand, G. and Scannell, P. (1991) 'Talk, identity and performance: *The Tony Blackburn Show*', in Scannell, P. (ed.) *Broadcast Talk*, London: Sage Publications.
Bridson, D.G. (1971) *Prospero and Ariel*, London: Gollancz.
Briggs, A. (1961) *The History of Broadcasting in the United Kingdom: Volume I – The Birth of Broadcasting*, London: Oxford University Press.
—— (1965) *The History of Broadcasting in the United Kingdom: Volume II – The Golden Age of Wireless*, London: Oxford University Press.

—— (1970) *The History of Broadcasting in the United Kingdom: Volume III – The War of Words*, London: Oxford University Press.

—— (1979) *The History of Broadcasting in the United Kingdom: Volume IV – Sound and Vision*, Oxford: Oxford University Press.

—— (1985) *The BBC: The First Fifty Years*, Oxford:Oxford University Press.

Briggs, S. (1981a) *Those Radio Times*, London: Weidenfeld & Nicolson.

—— (1981b) 'From cats' whiskers to cathode rays', *Sunday Times Magazine*, 16 August.

Brown, M. (1990) 'The sets that suffer from radio inactivity', *The Independent*, 7 March.

Burgelin, O. (1972) 'Structural analysis and mass communication', in McQuail, D. (ed.) *The Sociology of Mass Communications*, Harmondsworth: Penguin.

Cardiff, D. (1980) 'The serious and the popular: aspects of the evolution of style in the radio talk, 1928–1939', *Media, Culture and Society*, 2.

Chapman, R. (1992) *Selling the Sixties: The Pirates and Pop Music Radio*, London: Routledge.

Cooper, E. and Jahoda, M. (1971) 'The evasion of propaganda: how prejudiced people respond to anti-prejudice propaganda', in Schramm, W. and Roberts, D. (eds) *The Process and Effects of Mass Communication*, Urbana, Ill: University of Illinois Press, revised edn.

Croft, S. (1991) 'Breakthrough for digital radio', *Broadcast*, 22 February.

Cumberbatch, G. and Howitt, D. (1989) *A Measure of Uncertainty: the Effects of the Mass Media*, London: John Libbey.

Curran, J. and Seaton, J. (1991) *Power Without Responsibility*, London: Routledge, fourth edn.

Donovan, P. (1992) *The Radio Companion*, London: Grafton.

Drakakis, J. (1981) Introduction to Drakakis, J. (ed.) *British Radio Drama*, Cambridge: Cambridge University Press.

Dugdale, J. (1993) 'Breaking up is hard to do', *Media Guardian*, 26 April.

Dyer, R. (1973) *Light Entertainment*, London: BFI Television Monograph, no. 2.

Elam, K. (1980) *The Semiotics of Theatre and Drama*, London: Methuen.

Elliott, P. (1974) 'Uses and gratifications research: a critique and a sociological alternative', in Blumler, J. and Katz, E. (eds) *The Uses of Mass Communications*, London: Sage Publications.

Ellis, J. (1982) *Visible Fictions*, London: Routledge & Kegan Paul.

Esslin, M. (1980) *Mediations: Essays on Brecht, Beckett and the Media*, London: Eyre-Methuen.

Evans, E. (1977) *Radio: A Guide to Broadcasting Techniques*, London: Barrie & Jenkins.

Fink, H. (1981) 'The sponsor's v. the nation's choice: North American radio drama', in Lewis, P. (ed.) *Radio Drama*, London and New York: Longman.

Fiske, J. (1990) *An Introduction to Communication Studies*, London: Routledge, second edn.

Fiske, J. and Hartley, J. (1978) *Reading Television*, London: Methuen.

Fornatale, P. and Mills, J.E. (1980) *Radio in the Television Age*, Woodstock, NY: The Overlook Press.

Gielgud, V. (1957) *British Radio Drama, 1922–1956*, London: Harrap.

Gillard, F. (1964) *Sound Radio in the Television Age*, BBC Lunch-time Lectures, second series, no. 6.

Goffman, E. (1980) 'The radio drama frame', in Corner, J. and Hawthorn, J. (eds) *Communication Studies*, London: Edward Arnold.

—— (1981) *Forms of Talk*, Oxford: Basil Blackwell.

Goldhamer, H. (1971) 'The social effects of communication technology', in Schramm, W. and Roberts, D (eds) *The Process and Effects of Mass Communication*, Urbana, Ill: University of Illinois Press, revised edn.

Golding, P. (1974) *The Mass Media*, London: Longman.

Gray, F. (1981) 'The nature of radio drama', in Lewis, P. (ed.) *Radio Drama*, London and New York: Longman.

Gregory, M. and Carroll, S. (1978) *Language and Situation*, London: Routledge & Kegan Paul.

Harris, P. (1970) *When Pirates Ruled the Waves*, London and Aberdeen: Impulse Books, fourth edn.

Hartley, J. (1982) *Understanding News*, London: Methuen

Hawkes, T. (1977) *Structuralism and Semiotics*, London: Methuen.

Herbert, J. (1976) *The Techniques of Radio Journalism*, London: Adam & Charles Black.

Higgins, C. and Moss, P. (1982) *Sounds Real: Radio in Everyday Life*, St Lucia: University of Queensland Press.

Hobson, D. (1980) 'Housewives and the mass media', in Hall, S., Hobson, D., Lowe, A. and Willis, P. (eds) *Culture, Media, Language*, London: Hutchinson.

—— (1982) *Crossroads: The Drama of a Soap Opera*, London: Methuen.

Hood, S. (1975) *Radio and Television*, Newton Abbot: David & Charles.

Hutchby, I. (1991) 'The organization of talk on talk radio', in Scannell, P. (ed.) *Broadcast Talk*, London: Sage Publications.

Jakobson, R. (1960) 'Closing statement: linguistics and poetics', in Sebeok, T.A. (ed.) *Style in Language*, Cambridge, Mass: Massachusetts Institute of Technology Press.

Johnstone, J.W.C. (1974) 'Social integration and mass media use among adolescents: a case study', in Blumler, J. and Katz, E. (eds) *The Uses of Mass Communications*, London: Sage Publications.

Katz, E., Blumler, J. and Gurevitch, M. (1974) 'Utilization of mass communication by the individual', in Blumler, J. and Katz, E. (eds) *The Uses of Mass Communications*, London: Sage Publications.

Katz, E., Gurevitch, M. and Haas, H. (1973) 'On the use of mass media for important things', *American Sociological Review*, 38.

Kress, G. (1986) 'Language in the media: the construction of the domains of public and private', *Media, Culture and Society*, 8.

Kumar, K. (1977) 'Holding the middle ground: the BBC, the public and the professional broadcaster', in Curran, J., Gurevitch, M. and Woollacott, J. (eds) *Mass Communication and Society*, London: Edward Arnold.

Lazarsfeld, P.F. and Merton, R.K. (1971) 'Mass communication, popular taste and organized social action', in Schramm, W. and Roberts, D. (eds) *The Process and Effects of Mass Communication*, Urbana, Ill: University of Illinois Press, revised edn.

Lewis, P. (1981a) Introduction to Lewis, P. (ed.) *Radio Drama*, London and New York: Longman.

—— (1981b) 'The radio road to Llareggub', in Drakakis, J. (ed.) *British Radio Drama*, Cambridge: Cambridge University Press.

Lewis, P.M. and Booth, J. (1989) *The Invisible Medium: Public, Commercial and Community Radio*, London: Macmillan.

Lewis, P.M. and Pearlman, C. (1986) *Media and Power: From Marconi to Murdoch*, London: Camden Press.

Lowery, S. and De Fleur, M. L. (1983) *Milestones in Mass Communication Research: Media Effects*, New York and London: Longman.

MacCabe, C. and Stewart, O. (eds) (1986) *The BBC AND Public Service Broadcasting*, Manchester: Manchester University Press.

McLeish, R. (1978) *The Technique of Radio Production*, London: Focal Press.

McLeod, J.M. and Becker, L.B. (1974) 'Testing the validity of gratification measures through political effects analysis', in Blumler, J. and Katz, E. (eds) *The Uses of Mass Communications*, London: Sage Publications.

McLuhan, M. (1967) *Understanding Media*, London: Sphere.

MacNeice, L. (1964) Introduction to *The Dark Tower*, London: Faber & Faber.

McQuail, D. (1972) Introduction to McQuail, D. (ed.) *The Sociology of Mass Communications*, Harmondsworth: Penguin.

—— (1977) 'The influence and effects of mass media', in Curran, J., Gurevitch, M. and Woollacott, J. (eds) *Mass Communication and Society*, London: Edward Arnold.

—— (1983) *Mass Communication Theory*, London: Sage Publications.

McQuail, D. and Windahl, S. (1981) *Communication Models for the Study of Mass Communications*, London and New York: Longman.

McWhinnie, D. (1959) *The Art of Radio*, London: Faber & Faber.

Mansell, G. (1982) *Let Truth Be Told: 50 Years of BBC External Broadcasting*, London: Weidenfeld & Nicolson.

Mendelsohn, H. (1964) 'Listening to radio', in Dexter, L. A. and White, D.M. (eds) *People, Society, and Mass Communications*, Glencoe: Free Press.

—— (1974) 'Some policy implications of the uses and gratifications paradigm', in Blumler, J. and Katz, E. (eds) *The Uses of Mass Communication*, London: Sage Publications.

Milligan, S. (1972) *The Goon Show Scripts*, London: Woburn Press.

—— (1974) *More Goon Show Scripts*, London: Sphere.

Montgomery, M. (1986) 'DJ talk', *Media, Culture and Society*, 8.

—— (1991) '*Our Tune*: a study of a discourse genre', in Scannell, P. (ed.) *Broadcast Talk*, London: Sage Publications.

Moss, P. and Higgins, C. (1984) 'Radio voices', *Media, Culture and Society*, 4.

Murdock, G. (1981) 'Organising the imagination: sociological perspectives on radio drama', in Lewis, P. (ed.) *Radio Drama*, London and New York: Longman.

Murdock, G. and Golding, P. (1977) 'Capitalism, communication and class relations', in Curran, J., Gurevitch, M. and Woollacott, J. (eds) *Mass Communication and Society*, London: Edward Arnold.

Nathan, D. (1971) *The Laughtermakers*, London: Peter Owen.

Nicholson-Lord, D. (1991) 'Radio growth is put in doubt', *The Independent*, 8 August.

O'Donnell, W. and Todd, L. (1980) *Variety in Contemporary English*, London: George Allen & Unwin.

Ong, W. (1982) *Orality and Literacy*, London and New York: Methuen.

Parker, D. (1977) *Radio: the Great Years*, Newton Abbot: David & Charles.

Paulu, B. (1956) *British Broadcasting: Radio and Television in the United Kingdom*, Minneapolis, Minn: University of Minnesota Press.

—— (1961) *British Broadcasting in Transition*, Minneapolis, Minn: University of Minnesota Press.

—— (1981) *Television and Radio in the United Kingdom*, London: Macmillan.

Pear, T.H. (1931) *Voice and Personality*, London: Chapman and Hall.

Pegg, M. (1983) *Broadcasting and Society, 1918–1939*, London and Canberra: Croom Helm.

Peirce, C. S. (1960) *Collected Papers*, vols I and II, Hartshorne, C. and Weiss, P. (eds), Cambridge, Mass: Harvard University Press.

Priessnitz, H. (1981) 'British radio drama: a survey', in Lewis, P. (ed.) *Radio Drama*, London and New York: Longman.

Quirk, R. (1982) *Style and Communication in the English Language*, London: Edward Arnold.

Raban, J. (1981) 'Icon or symbol: the writer and the "medium"', in Lewis, P. (ed.) *Radio Drama*, London and New York: Longman.

Raphael, F. (1980) 'The language of television', in Michaels, L. and Ricks, C. (eds) *The State of the Language*, London: University of California Press.

Roberts, D.F. (1971) 'The nature of communication effects', in Schramm, W. and Roberts, D. (eds) *The Process and Effects of Mass Communication*, Urbana, Ill: University of Illinois Press, revised edn.

Rodger, I. (1982) *Radio Drama*, London: Macmillan.

Rosengren, K.E. (1974) 'Uses and gratifications: a paradigm outlined', in Blumler, J. and Katz, E. (eds) *The Uses of Mass Communications*, London: Sage Publications.

Scannell, P. (1991) 'Introduction: the relevance of talk' in Scannell, P. (ed.) *Broadcast Talk*, London: Sage Publications.

Scannell, P. and Cardiff, D. (1982) 'Serving the nation: public service broadcasting before the war', in Waites, B., Bennett, T. and Martin, G. (eds) *Popular Culture: Past and Present*, London: Croom Helm.

—— (1991) *A Social History of British Broadcasting: Volume I 1922–1939 Serving the Nation*, Oxford: Basil Blackwell.

Scholes, R. (1982) *Semiotics and Interpretation*, New Haven, Conn and London: Yale University Press.

Schramm, W. (1971) 'The nature of communication between humans', in Schramm, W. and Roberts, D. (eds) *The Process and Effects of Mass Communication*, Urbana, Ill: University of Illinois Press, revised edn.

Schramm, W. and Roberts, D. (eds) (1971) *The Process and Effects of Mass Communication*, Urbana, Ill: University of Illinois Press, revised edn.

Seymour-Ure, C. (1991) *The British Press and Broadcasting since 1945*, Oxford: Basil Blackwell.

Sieveking, L. (1934) *The Stuff of Radio*, London: Cassell.

Silvey, R. (1970) 'Reflections on the impact of broadcasting', in Tunstall, J. (ed.) *Media Sociology*, London: Constable.

—— (1974) *Who's Listening?*, London: George Allen & Unwin.

Smith, A. (ed.) (1974) *British Broadcasting*, Newton Abbot: David & Charles.

—— (1976) *The Shadow in the Cave*, London: Quartet Books, revised edn.

—— (1990) *Broadcasting and Society in 1990s Britain*, London: W. H. Smith Contemporary Papers, no. 4.

Smythe, D.W. (1972) 'Some observations on communications theory', in McQuail, D. (ed.) *The Sociology of Mass Communications*, Harmondsworth: Penguin.

Snagge, J. and Barsley, M. (1972) *Those Vintage Years of Radio*, London: Pitman.

Took, B. (1976) *Laughter in the Air*, London: Robson Books/British Broadcasting Corporation.

Trethowan, I. (1970) *Radio in the Seventies*, BBC Lunch-time Lectures, eighth series, no. 4.

Wade, D. (1981a) 'Popular radio drama', in Lewis, P. (ed.) *Radio Drama*, London and New York: Longman.

—— (1981b) 'British radio drama since 1960' in Drakakis, J. (ed.) *British Radio Drama*, Cambridge: Cambridge University Press.

—— (1983a) 'Chat is going up the charts', *The Times*, 8 January.

—— (1983b) 'Topical sense', *The Times*, 8 October.

Waugh, P. (1984) *Metafiction*, London: Methuen.

Webster, P. (1984) 'Radio concessions to beat pirates', *The Times*, 9 August.

Whale, J. (1969) *The Half-Shut Eye*, London: Macmillan.

Williams, R. (1974) *Television: Technology and Cultural Form*, Glasgow: Fontana.

Wilmut, R. (1976) *The Goon Show Companion*, London: Robson Books.

—— (1980) *From Fringe to Flying Circus*, London: Book Club Associates.

Worsley, F. (1948) *ITMA*, London: Vox Mundi.

Wroe, M. (1988) 'A needling issue aired', *The Independent*, 13 July.

—— (1989) 'Coming soon to an FM dial near you', *The Independent*, 19 December.

—— (1992) 'Mixed messages over the airwaves', *The Independent*, 9 September.

—— (1993a) 'Sweet music to an adman's ears', *The Independent*, 20 January.

—— (1993b) 'Dublin sound is a hit with British listeners', *The Independent*, 30 January.

Index